CULTURE and CHANGE

An Introduction

LARRY L. NAYLOR

BERGIN & GARVEY
Westport, Connecticut • London

76521

Library of Congress Cataloging-in-Publication Data

Naylor, Larry L.
  Culture and change : an introduction / Larry L. Naylor.
    p.   cm.
  Includes bibliographical references and index.
  ISBN 0–89789–464–2 (hardcover : alk. paper).—ISBN 0–89789–465–0
  (pbk. : alk. paper)
    1. Anthropology. 2. Culture. 3. Social change. I. Title.
  GN27.N39   1996
  306—dc20   95–36904

British Library Cataloguing in Publication Data is available.

Library of Congress Catalog Card Number: 95–36904
ISBN: 0–89789–464–2
      0–89789–465–0 (pbk.)

First published in 1996

Bergin & Garvey, 88 Post Road West, Westport, CT 06881
An imprint of Greenwood Publishing Group, Inc.

Printed in the United States of America

The paper used in this book complies with the
Permanent Paper Standard issued by the National
Information Standards Organization (Z39.48–1984).

10 9 8 7 6 5 4 3 2 1

Copyright Acknowledgment

The author and publisher gratefully acknowledge permission for use of the
following material:

Figure 4.4 from Arthur Niehoff, *A Casebook of Social Change*. Chicago:
Aldine. 1966.

CONTENTS

Figures		vii
Preface		ix
Chapter 1	**Introduction**	1
	Anthropology	5
	Foundations for Culture Change	6
	Anthropology and Culture Change	7
	Applied (Practical) Anthropology	12
Chapter 2	**Culture Context**	14
	Culture	16
	Human Multiculturalism	28
	Culture Forms	29
Chapter 3	**Evolution and Change**	37
	Historical Background	38
	Evolution	43
	Interaction	47
	Innovation and Culture Change	49
	Acculturation and Change	53
	Diffusion and Change	55
	Model for Culture Change	56
Chapter 4	**Processes of Change**	61
	Voluntary Change	62
	Directed Change	67
	Interactional Model for Directed Change	77

Chapter 5	**Change Agents and Focal Groups**	88
	Culture Change Agents	89
	Focal Groups	106
Chapter 6	**Culture Change Strategies**	112
	Planning for Culture Change	113
	General Plan Strategies	118
	Implementation Strategies	125
	Focal Group Strategies	130
	Focal Group Response Strategies	135
Chapter 7	**Dynamics of Change**	138
	Cultural Forces of Change	140
	Specific Forces of Culture Change	142
	Interactional Forces of Change	152
	External Forces of Change	162
Chapter 8	**Accomplishing Change**	168
	Culture Change Model	170
	Chances of Success	173
	Changing Culture	179
	Changing Aspects of Culture	189
	Basic Principles for Changing Culture	196
Chapter 9	**Conclusions and Prospects**	199
	Evolutionary Trends	200
	Global Trends	201
	One World Culture	206
	Role of Anthropology	208
	Culture and Change	213
Bibliography		217
Index		223

FIGURES

2.1   Culture as Adaptation to Environment   15

2.2   Definition of Culture   19

2.3   Levels of Culture Groupings   22

2.4   Culture Forms   34

3.1   Culture Change as Ongoing Process   40

3.2   Adaptation   45

3.3   Pyramidal Effect of Problem Solutions   46

3.4   Environmental Adaptation/Interaction   49

3.5   Innovation and Internal Culture Change   52

3.6   Acculturation   54

3.7   Diffusion   56

3.8   Model of Culture Change   59

4.1   General Model of Directed Culture Change   69

4.2   George Foster Model for Directed Culture Change   71

4.3   Alexander Leighton Model for Directed Culture Change   73

4.4   Arensberg and Niehoff Model for Directed Culture Change   75

4.5   Niehoff's Influences on Directed Change Programs   76

4.6   Directed Culture Change   78

4.7   Component Characteristics   81

6.1   Strategies for Planned Change   119

8.1   Directed Culture Change   171

PREFACE

Few topics generate as much discussion among people as do culture and change. Today, one cannot open a newspaper or journal, watch a movie or television program, go to work or school without being confronted, directly or indirectly, with these topics. When not reading about a nation-state, regional, ethnic, minority, organizational, or special interest culture or conflict, people are reading about environmental, biological, demographic, technological, global, social, economic, or political change related to, or pressuring for still more change in, their cultures, communities, and lives. Socioeconomic and sociopolitical changes throughout the former USSR and other Eastern Bloc countries have focused the world's attention on culture, change, diversity, and multiculturalism in dramatic fashion. Suddenly, the United States is not the only nation-state to exhibit significant ethnic and racial diversity. There has been a consistent message that disappearing resources, overpopulation, waste, poverty, deforestation, global warming, ozone depletion, hunger, and other global problems threaten our continued existence unless some changes are made in our beliefs and practices. The small-scale or "primitive" cultures of our world continue to disappear at an alarming rate as they are assimilated into the various nation-states. Technology continues to change at a rate and volume perhaps unprecedented in human history. The development of a "world culture" seems assured as the money-dominated market-exchange economic system spreads throughout the world. The rate and scale of the changes now being experienced by people the world over is nearly overwhelming. In addition to the constant barrage of information on change occurring in our world, people everywhere are being asked to change some aspect of their lives or to bring about some change in the lives of others.

From its beginnings, the discipline of anthropology has been concerned with culture and change, focusing as it does on the origins, nature, and development of humans and their cultures. Culture is a central concept of anthropology, perhaps its cornerstone, and lies at the heart of questions about what it means to be human.

Despite the current tendency for scholars from many other disciplines to appropriate the term culture, if not the concept, in response to trends in their fields, in their concerns, or in their involvement with multiculturalism and cultural diversity, anthropologists continue to be in the best position to help people develop an understanding of culture as well as of the role it plays in their lives. Because of this, perhaps anthropology is also the best equipped to deal meaningfully with the problem of change, for change is ultimately a culture process, one that allows culture groups to respond to changing conditions that, left unattended, could threaten their continuing survival. Over the years, across changing circumstances, and under widely differing conditions, anthropologists have accumulated an impressive array of noteworthy, even seminal, ideas on both these things.

Given the increased attention to culture and change, it should come as no surprise that questions have arisen as to the usefulness, clarity, and order of some current thinking. It might be suggested that some of our thinking about culture and the change process has become stalled, locked into ideas cemented in the literature and ultimately in our perceptions of such things. This is not meant to minimize the contributions of the past or of those who have provided us with what we cumulatively know and understand about culture and change. But building on those contributions—the lessons, studies, and experience that have come with more involvement of anthropologists in change programs, it seems that the time has come to evaluate, rethink, and perhaps restructure this body of knowledge so that we can move ahead even further.

Culture and Change: An Introduction is designed to provoke thought and discussion about both culture and change. It will give students of change, change agents and agencies, and planners of change, as well as those being asked to change, some things to think about as they accomplish their task. It is designed to bring together what we have learned about change in slightly different yet useful ways. It surely will generate some new thoughts and needed discussions about things that so many people assume they understand, if not take for granted. In this sense, it is both theoretical and practical. It will not provide a prescription for successful directed/planned change, or propose a "textbook solution" to ensure success. Each context is unique and each solution will be tied to that uniqueness. It will provide a discussion of many things that must be kept in mind when one is involved in such a complex process. It will attempt to bridge and to apply what has been learned about culture and change from earlier studies to all culture change circumstances, but especially in the realm of planned or directed culture change.

Culture is the means by which individuals and groups of humans have adapted to both the natural environment and the sociocultural environment they have created through their cultures. It makes people everywhere the same yet different. Despite the many ways culture has been defined across the years and is defined at present, on one point there is agreement. Culture is a set of problem-solving solutions generated in response to the pressures of the environment. It represents the primary adaptation for humans, and it has given them considerable control over their world. The culture change process is an essential part of that control, providing humans with a response to the changing physical and sociocultural environments. The ability to change is directly related to the human ability to survive as conditions change. Spontaneous change, unplanned change, or the "accidents of history" play a significant role in culture change, as does planned and directed change. Although people continue to change from generation to generation without much considered thought or design, people have increasingly relied on designing, planning, and implementing change. In the modern nation-states, directed or planned change has become the primary way most people respond to changing conditions, regardless of the source of the pressure. When environmental changes cause (pressure for or make necessary a cultural change), the planned or directed process is now the predominant form of response, individually and in groups. In reacting to the many bioevolutionary, geological, climatic, demographic, and/or sociocultural change pressures, people now generate their responses, along with plans for implementing them.

The discussions of culture and change to be presented are grounded in both evolutionary theory and interactional models of change. The evolutionary model allows us to consider change on both the broad and the specific levels. It allows us to look at the change that has come along with humans per se, and on the other hand, it allows us to view change under particular circumstances of specific human populations. The interactional model focuses on human interactions that lie at the heart of the culture change process. Some ideas about culture and change to be presented will clearly go against the grain of popular thought. For example, the use of the concept of culture as it is usually applied in the nation-states will be questioned, as will the concepts of internal and external change in such contexts. The myth of homogeneity in such contexts has become obvious and raises the questions of when and how culture can be applied to such groupings ,and with what limitations. Both culture and change, as they are popularly applied to the artificially created nation-states, demand examination. The inability or unwillingness of so many professionals outside of anthropology to use the concepts requires that they be given a hard look, for the consequences to all directed or planned change contexts should be apparent. It will be suggested that within the modern nation-state, the change occurs within extremely diverse (multicultural) settings where individuals and groups representing different cultures come together. This is so, whether one is addressing a nation-state, a community, an organization, or any other culture or social grouping.

Given the consequences of the breakup of the former Soviet Union and Eastern Bloc nations, the world has come to realize the actual diversity of such human creations—cultural pluralism, as it were—and this has direct bearing on culture change, particularly planned or directed change. As complex nation-states have incorporated and/or created more and more identifiable cultural groups, direct or indirect culture contacts and interactions between people representing different cultures are involved in the change process. It is also the case that in the modern world change rarely occurs in isolation. It always occurs within a larger context as people are increasingly drawn into the network of an interdependent world. Whereas in the past, the internal change process may have dominated the course of events in societies and cultures with minimal outside contact; few cultural groups continue to live in isolation from the larger world context. Not infrequently, the outcomes of a planned change are determined by forces quite removed from the specific local context and specific efforts on the part of limited groups. The hows and whys of change—motivations and outcomes—are, more often than not, external to the group. The key to understanding the culture change process, its components and elements, issues and aspects, benefits and costs, is directly related to human interactions in such contexts. It will be suggested that it is within the interaction of the participants in the change process that the results of change programs, planned or unplanned, will be determined.

The volume is designed to appeal to several audiences. It is aimed at students of change in keeping with the need for some structuring of this body of knowledge. Although there may not always be agreement on what is presented or how it is presented, it should certainly act as a catalyst for further dialogue and the ongoing development of change theory. It is intended for the various participants in the change process. It should prove useful for change agencies and planners generating ideas. It should be helpful for change implementers, those individual agents of change asked to bring about changes in beliefs or behaviors of some person or group. It should help them keep things in perspective and context, to realize that what they do is part of a larger, integrated whole. Because the process of culture change so often involves cultural contacts, it also contributes to our understanding of the dynamics of that interaction that underlie so much of our current discussions on multicultural diversity.

Some historical, anthropological, and contextual foundation for the study of culture change, particularly directed culture change, is presented in Chapter 1. Culture change is not a new topic, nor is it something only anthropologists have thought about. An interest in culture change can be documented well before the establishment of anthropology as an academic discipline. But if the premise of evolution is valid, our current thinking about culture and change is grounded in the past, a product of history and the constant revisions of our ideas and theory. Chapter 2 focuses on culture, the context within which human responses to problems are generated. A model of culture change, proposed in Chapter 3, realigns, redefines, and restructures how we can look at it on both the general and the specific levels. Chapter 4 is concerned with the directed culture change process, and Chapters 5 and 6 address the various aspects or elements of this process. In these chapters, the components, and the participants in that process are examined. Chapter 7 is devoted to the dynamics of the process, or how the various contexts, components and participants come together in the interactional setting to produce some result. Chapter 8 addresses the question of actually introducing change and prospects for success, and Chapter 9 focuses on conclusions and prospects.

CULTURE and CHANGE

Chapter 1

INTRODUCTION

No culture is impervious to change. No culture today is as it has always been. All cultures change, and for a variety of reasons. Fundamental to what we have learned about culture change is that it goes on continually, is systematic, and in many ways can be viewed as inevitable. As the physical and sociocultural environments continually change, it is inevitable that people will adjust, or at least attempt to do so. With contacts between people of different cultures, it is inevitable that change will occur as they adjust and accommodate to each other. In situations of contacts between vastly different types of culture, new ideas and changing aspirations will insure that change will occur. Because people are always looking for something better, more efficient ways of doing the things they feel they must do, change is inevitable. It can result from existing activities or from the deliberate attempts of people to respond to perceived problems. It can occur as the result of simple contact between representatives of different cultures, and it can come by way of others who impose it. Change can come as unplanned or unexpected consequences of people's own activities, including their planned culture change efforts, and it can originate from a group's attempts to avoid it. Change also can be purely accidental, the result of unforeseen events, historical processes, or juxtaposition of events in time and place, as several unrelated things come together by chance, at the right moment in time.

Culture change can be so slight and gradual as to be almost imperceptible to the casual observer, as with any number of tribal groups, subsistence farmers, and pastoralist societies that seem to go on day after day just as they have always done. At other times, it can be massive and rapid, as with a newly discovered tribal group suddenly being brought into the mainstream of the modern world, a world conflict that changes nation-states' territories or relationships, or shifting political conditions such as those associated with the breakup of the former Soviet Union and Eastern Bloc nations. In a short period of time, the world seems to have been turned upside down. Anyhow, the simple fact remains that culture change has always been, and always will be, with us in one form or another. In the rapidly changing world of today, the reality of more and more culture change is a foregone conclusion. Much of the cultural change now being experienced, and perhaps a great deal more to be experienced in the future, will be a consequence of the steadily increasing contacts and interactions of people representing different cultures. While contact and interaction between culture groups have always characterized humans, right from their beginnings, now they come with the pressures for an emerging global culture organized around the money-dominated market-exchange system. It will come as part of the technological/informational revolution and the worldwide trend to adopt the products and practices of the Western industrial world. Somewhat isolated and self-contained culture groups and societies, once free of substantial outside influence, have now all but disappeared, incorporated into the modern nation-states. All manner and sizes of cultural groupings now must respond to the larger context, to increased cultural contacts, and to constantly changing social, economic, political, and military conditions throughout the world.

While in the past, events could be perceived as unrelated or unimportant to local concerns or conditions, they now determine or exert considerable influence on the activities. From the most complex nation-state to the smallest communities of the remotest areas, cultural groupings are being drawn together and made interdependent, unlike any other time in history. People everywhere face this reality, consciously or unconsciously, directly or indirectly. Nation-states have been brought together within the structure and operations of such international agencies as the United Nations, World Bank, International Red Cross, and others. What transpires in such places as the former Soviet Union, Bosnia, or South Africa can dramatically impact other nation-states, Serbs and Croats, African-Americans and Euro-Americans, Muslims and Christians, Republicans and Democrats. What happens with isolated Amazonian tribal groups has consequences for people far removed from them or their territories, perhaps even for the entire world. Because of this growing interdependence, the concepts of culture and culture change have been thrust upon the minds of social, political, and economic leaders—indeed, people throughout the world—as never before. The need to respond to and control the inevitable change that now must be faced, means that such concepts of culture and change can no longer be ignored or taken for granted.

Notable in the arena of culture change is the increasing importance of the change that occurs when people representing different cultures come together. Culture contact has nearly always meant competition and conflict, but now it also means a rise in importance, perhaps preeminence, of the "newest" form of culture change—directed or planned culture change—as groups attempt to control their own destiny or that of others. Interestingly, while this kind of change has been an aspect of human history for hundreds, even thousands, of years, its consequences and effects described in many cultural monographs, it is still largely ignored or presented almost as a footnote in traditional discussions of culture change in general anthropology textbooks, where deliberate acts, acculturation, or unforeseen outcomes of activities of people are still being emphasized. William Haviland (1994:651–652) includes it in a small discussion of applied anthropology and as part of a chapter devoted to change. Carol and Melvin Ember (1993:472) refer to planned change as part of a chapter focusing on explaining and solving social problems.

More amazing is the lack of even a reference to "directed change" in the many volumes on tribal peoples by James H. Bodley (1982, 1985, 1988, 1990, 1994), in which its consequences are well documented. Human societies, communities, organizations, and individuals continue to change through a variety of means, but directed or planned change has clearly become the primary means by which they face and attempt to solve their problems. This type of designed change is frequently not a matter of choice; it is a by-product of direct or indirect cultural contacts, actions, and interactions. While some current thought calls for more participation of those to be impacted, culture change remains the result of direct planning and implementation of changes in the lives of people by change agencies, groups, and individuals funded and staffed for the sole purpose of introducing some modification in a group's belief or behavior system. People in every corner of the world have turned to this process, and as a result face many of the same basic problems.

Even as culture groups continue to change as the result of someone in the group or society coming up with something new, more often than not the bulk of the change being experienced is the result of forces originating outside the immediate group. Tribal groups plan their responses to what they are being asked to do. Communities have their planning, development, and zoning departments. Nation-states have their development programs and agencies devoted to resolving social problems. Businesses have their planning and development departments. The United Nations and its cooperating agencies (e.g., the World Health Organization, UNESCO, the World Bank) focus on changing the lives, beliefs, and practices of people located all over the world. This has clearly become a dominant change force, if not the dominant process affecting humans and the world they increasingly design. In the process of gaining more and more control over the physical and cultural environments, the need to change and to control the process also has increased. For many culture groups, especially the world's complex societies already interacting in the money-dominated, worldwide market-exchange system, change is usually perceived as a matter of degree, a little more or less of something. But this may be changing as people everywhere are forced to interact and see beyond their immediate concerns and selves. For the developing world striving toward the Western industrialized model, and smaller groups only now being brought into the mainstream of the modern world, change is a matter of kind. The changes being experienced by these groups are usually away from traditional ways to a whole new set of beliefs and practices geared to a world of which they have had little awareness or understanding.

Historically, in the Western world, change has been viewed in largely positive terms, as a step in the "right" direction, as a move toward modernization or progress, or as evidence of the continuing development of civilization. This has quite understandably gone hand in hand with a strong belief that all change is essentially good because it separates us from our more "savage" or "primitive" past. Even the more negative aspects of change have been accepted as a necessary cost of advancing civilization. Because of this association, there is a very strong tendency in the West to use such terms as "modernization," "progress," and "development" as synonyms for "change," most people making few if any distinctions among them. From the American experience has come the idea that more is better, bigger is better. Linking the idea of change to good and better has been accompanied by a widespread belief and assumption that if a change has met a need as identified by someone, has met the highest standards as set or measured by someone, it will automatically be accepted. But innovations or changes are invariably accompanied by severe disruptions. Factionalism and divisiveness are common responses to changing circumstances as choices between the old and the new come into conflict. Antagonism between those who favor change and those who oppose it is inevitable, for choices introduced by change cannot always be made on traditional grounds. When change is introduced into culture contact situations, the antagonisms and disruptions are highlighted, and new dimensions are added. Some people readily accept any change, only to become disillusioned by its lack of fit with their beliefs or practices. Inevitably, movements generate a desire among the disillusioned to return to "the good old days." Such reactions representing loyalty to one's group and traditional beliefs and practices are fairly common. All of this leads us to recognize the cultural bias associated with change.

From the perspective of the anthropologist, if you want to develop an understanding of the change process, you must first understand its cultural context. Given the cultural relevance of any change to the integrated systems of beliefs and practices of people, there has never been a change, development, progress, or modernization that did not involve a cost. There has never been a change with only benefits. A benefit to someone or something invariably involves a cost to someone or something else. In American culture, where change is seemingly accepted by most people as positive and desirable, there is an overriding sense that it is usually approached on the basis of "rationality," as a good, better, and even necessary thing. The belief that people simply adjust to decisions of efficiency and pragmatism may not be as valid as it has been assumed, even in this context. In other cultures this "rationality" may not always be apparent—for example, in the peasant groups where adaptations are to land. Changes in such groups involve adjustments in social relationships that may be far more important than efficiency. The importance of the family may override any consideration of a desireable change in some other aspect of life. Members of all human culture groups have established ways to think, believe, and act. They already know the most appropriate or correct way to meet their needs, and they are secure and comfortable with such knowledge. Any proposed change in this learned pattern represents a potential threat to their survival; thus, it is nearly always resisted or altered to minimize such a possibility. As groups become players in the rapidly changing and developing world, the ability to resist or minimize change steadily decreases. The need to participate and compete in this system will dictate massive and rapid changes among every type of cultural group (complex nation-states, small-scale or more traditional prestate societies, agricultural or industrial state, and constituent cultural groups or culture scenes). Survival of the group and any part of its culture will depend on that change.

ANTHROPOLOGY

Anthropologists have always been concerned with the origins, development, and nature of humans and their cultures, not just in some general sense but in the total sense. Anthropologists are interested in everything about humans—all of them, regardless of where they are found, and throughout history and prehistory. To study humans is to be concerned with culture, to be concerned with the development of culture is to be concerned with culture change. Thus, the subjects of culture and change have always been important in anthropology. In fact, change has been a primary focus of the discipline since its inception, along with the concept of culture. Whereas the historian focuses on documenting and explaining events of the historical period after they have occurred, the anthropologist examines change over the entire course of human prehistory *and* history, up to and including that change now taking place (Smith & Fischer 1970).

But an interest in change has never been the sole property of anthropology, history, or any other academic discipline. Political science, economics, sociology, and other social and natural sciences also have focused on particular aspects of change and culture. Each takes the human experience apart, isolating one of its aspects for intensive study, based on the belief that a better understanding will result from such a delimited focus. Anthropology is different. Anthropologists study the human experience holistically, keeping it altogether, based on their belief that the physical and social aspects of humans are interrelated. They believe that all parts of cultures likewise are related, that they make up and define the whole. They subscribe to the idea that if one focuses on only one part of the human experience, separated or isolated from the other parts, that one part or aspect somehow will be skewed in the process. Although individual anthropologists do emphasize limited studies of what it means to be human, specific aspects of culture or society, they recognize that it is but one aspect or part of an integrated whole, and strive to keep it in the context of the whole. This sets anthropology apart from other disciplines, and makes the field eclectic and very difficult to categorize in the usual social science, natural science, or humanities groupings normally found in the academic environment. Anthropology would qualify for inclusion in all of these categorizations.

Tied closely to the concept of holism in distinguishing anthropology from other disciplines is the idea of cultural relativism (Downs 1975). Essentially, relativism holds that customs, beliefs, or practices of others can be judged only within their own culture context. To judge the beliefs or behaviors of another culture based on those of your own culture is fundamentally wrong. People do not biologically inherit their culture; it is something that must learned, generation after generation. The learned way will ultimately be the definitive characteristic distinguishing one culture group from another. Individuals have to learn the right ways to think and act in order to be accepted as members of the group. No culture teaches its young that someone else's culture is more correct. This naturally leads people to believe and judge their way as the more correct one, compared with another group's way. All culture groups are ethnocentric, judging others based on what they have learned.

Beyond violating the concept of cultural relativism, this tendency leads to faulty interpretations and misunderstandings of others.

Over its relatively brief history, at least in comparison with other fields of study, the anthropological focus on the concept of change has been fairly constant and conceptualized primarily on two levels. First, concerned with understanding human development, anthropologists have always been concerned with accounting for the change in humans and their cultures over time in the broadest sense, before the spread of Western culture. In this instance, the focus has been on how cultures have differentiated, progressed, or changed through time for all humanity, synonymous with evolutionary change. Second, they have been concerned with change occasioned by the massive intrusion of Western culture on the rest of the world. On this level, the focus has been on the impacts, effects, and changes such intrusions have had on specific groups of people. With change interests on these two levels, anthropologists have always had a kind of split vision: part concerned with the dynamics of change among primitive or savage groups before being "spoiled" or altered by excessive contact, and another part concerned with change as initiated because of contact and intrusion. Attention to planned or directed change, introduced by groups, agents, and agencies funded and established for this purpose, has added a new dimension to the anthropological study of change. It might be argued that this represents a third level of interest, or it might be argued that it simply represents another stage in the evolution of culture linked to a rapidly changing world.

FOUNDATIONS FOR CULTURE CHANGE

Popular thought on culture change within both the academic and the nonacademic communities obviously has historical antecedents. While it is beyond the scope of this volume to attempt a history of culture or thought on culture change, or even to list all the early thinkers, scholars, or philosophers who may have contributed to our present perceptions and understandings of change, it is interesting to note that some generally accepted ideas have a long history (Bohannan & Glazer 1988; de Waal Malefijt 1974; Harris 1968; Hogbin 1970; Honigmann 1976; Lowie 1937). Thoughts on the problem of change can be found as far back as Democritus (ca.460–ca.370 B.C.) and Aristotle (384–322 B.C.). Democritus proposed that cultural development was based on better adaptations to the environment, whereas Aristotle proposed a cyclical theory to account for human culture and change. Both of these ideas can be seen in our current thought about change. Michel de Montaigne (1533–1592) provided the concept of "savagery" to augment earlier Greek and Roman "barbarians'" ideas, obviously incorporated into the thinking of early evolutionists. Francis Bacon (1561–1626) contributed the idea of culture change as cumulative development. René Descartes (1596–1650) discussed culture change as the injection or grafting of new ideas over old ones. Perhaps the most lasting influence on culture change thought in the Western world came from a combination of Aristotle and Jean Jacques Rousseau (1712–1778). It is very tempting to suggest that together, they provided the framework and orienting base from which most people in the Western world tend to think about, perceive, and respond to change.

In his cyclical theory of culture change, Aristotle put forth the suggestion that all societies and cultures repeatedly go through the same basic stages of development. This idea of change, based on his perception of cultural regularity, dominated the intellectual thinking of the Western world for a great many years. In the eighteenth century, Rousseau added some structure to Aristotle's cultural regularity, holding that cultures and societies move from the simple to the complex. Rousseau believed that the people of Africa, America, and elsewhere represented a way of life that all people must have lived at one time. He viewed such societies as relics (artifacts) of the past. He did not perceive change as cyclical. Rousseau saw change as occurring in an orderly fashion from the simple to the complex. Even before the development of organic evolution in the 1850s, usually associated with Alfred Russel Wallace (1823–1913) and Charles Darwin (1809–1892), Herbert Spencer (1820–1903) and Gustav Klemm (1802–1867) proposed evolutionary models for the development of human culture with striking resemblances to the ideas of Aristotle and Rousseau. Klemm stated that all humans repeatedly go through three stages of development: savagery, tameness, and freedom (Lowie 1937:11–16). Spencer focused on change by equating evolution with progress (Harris 1968:108–141). These orienting concepts were clearly antecedents to the early development of the evolutionary theory of anthropology.

ANTHROPOLOGY AND CULTURE CHANGE

Throughout the developmental period of the discipline, anthropologists tended to view change only on the broad or grand evolutionary scale suggested in the writings of Lewis Henry Morgan, E. B. Tylor, and James Frazer. In *Ancient Society* (1964), Morgan proposed savagery, barbarism, and civilization as the principal states of history, and he concluded that social evolution moved toward an inevitable conclusion. Tylor presented much the same idea in *Primitive Culture* (1958), and James Frazer did likewise in *The Golden Bough* (1911). These early anthropologists subscribed to the idea that all cultures moved through the same sequence of development or progression toward some ultimate conclusion. The stages were more than a little similar to those suggested much earlier. Evolution to this group, and to those who followed their ideas, meant such things as origins, stages of progress, survivals, and a progression from the simple to the complex. Their interest in change as a process was minimal; their primary goal was to identify where on the unilineal continuum a group might fall. The development of any institution could be outlined by a survey of contemporary groups that then were placed on the simple-to-complex scale, lowest to highest forms. Cause and effect were simply not considered.

Several theoretical approaches developed in response to criticisms of this early evolutionary thought, but they did not fare much better on the topic of culture change. The historical particularists or Boazian School, developed in America and led by Franz Boas, shifted attention away from human culture per se, to specific cultures that they believed had to be studied by themselves. Their emphasis was placed on diversity, cultural relativity, cultural determinism, and the plasticity of humans: "culture made the man." These ideas did not provide for any real focus on change, but there were legacies of the school that would affect culture change study. Diversity and relativism are firmly entrenched in the thinking of modern scholars of culture change.

Another school of thought that developed in response to unilineal evolutionism was the diffusionism school. While there were variations of the school, all of them attempted to trace culture traits historically and geographically. The English or Manchester version, associated with G. Elliot Smith, William J. Perry and W. H. R. Rivers, suggested that all things originated in Egypt, and then spread to the rest of the world. The Kulturkreis or "culture circles" version, usually attributed to Fredrich Ratzel, Fritz Graebner, and Wilhelm Schmidt, maintained that things originated in one of nine core areas as combinations of elements or complexes. An American variation linked to Clark Wissler and Alfred Kroeber, focused on culture centers where traits developed and from which they then diffused. In all these versions, the emphasis was on the movement of techniques and material objects through migrations. For diffusionists, cultures were little more than accumulations of artifacts spread through borrowing, a view denying the inventiveness of people. Any concern with change at all came with the establishment of borrowing as a major means by which culture can and does change. Like those before them, the attention of these schools was centered on the broad levels and scales of culture change.

Functionalism and a new kind of evolutionary theory also developed in response to unilinear evolutionary thinking. While functionalism, like diffusionism, was represented in more than one variation, adherents to this general train of thought held the belief that all of the parts of culture are related and that together they establish and maintain the whole of it. In British functionalism, as represented by Bronislaw Malinowski (1922), various elements of culture functioned or played a part in the maintenance of society and the needs of individuals. Malinowski argued for the integrative nature of culture, based on what he saw as culture imperatives or needs. He also suggested that tracing any one element of culture would ultimately lead to the whole system.

The French sociology school, revolving around A. R. Radcliffe-Brown (1952), argued that all systems existed to maintain social institutions. Radcliffe-Brown saw the parts of culture functioning in the maintenance of the social institutions. Function was the contribution made by an institution to the maintenance of structural continuity— for example, the role of ceremony in maintaining the social structure. His version emphasized integration, morphology, and social physiology (functional laws). A newer version of this kind of thinking comes with systemic functionalism; looking at culture as a system composed of interrelated subsystems functionally related to each other and emphasizing process. Whatever the emphasis, all the variations of functionalism tend to see culture as static and involuted; the individual culture or culture system is examined in terms of itself. This thinking, combined with that of the historical particularists, and set within historical context, signaled a shift away from looking at culture change on only the broadest levels, to a consideration of culture change on the more limited scale. Anthropologists were increasingly going where others had already been. Cultures had to be reconstructed prior to contact with invaders, guns, and new diseases.

A new kind of evolutionary thinking also developed, usually referred to as neo-evolutionism to distinguish it from the earlier unilineal evolutionary theory. This newer thinking combined a concern for the trends of general evolution with allowance for the specific evolution of groups, given their own particular circumstances. The resurgence of evolutionary thinking grew out of a nagging belief among anthropologists that the entire human group was developing in a particular direction. The emphasis of this new evolutionary thought was on process, and evolution was seen as a consequence of something. For example, Leslie White (1949:368–369) proposed that culture evolves (changes) as its ability to capture energy increases. Julian Steward (1955) coined the term "multi-lineal evolution" to provide for obvious parallels in cultural evolution. Combining the ideas of Steward and White, Marshall Sahlins and Elman Service (1960) provided the distinction between general and specific evolution, in which the evolutionary process of culture continued through new means. The newer cultural ecology and political economy schools of thought are allied to this new evolutionism. Cultural ecology, linked Steward, looks at how culture traits may be adaptive to the physical or cultural environment. Political economy, as seen in the works of Eric Wolf, Sidney Mintz, and Eleanor Leacock, focuses on the impact of external political and economic processes on local events and cultures. This group stresses that all parts of the world are interconnected (Roseberry 1988). It is from the neo-evolutionary position, emphasizing culture as adaptation to environment in the general sense, and stressing the interconnectedness of the world, that most anthropologists now approach the subject of culture change.

While other paradigms have appeared more recently, patterned on one or another of the aforementioned schools of thought, but one is struck by the legacy to Western theory of the orienting concepts of earlier thinkers, all of which continue to influence how we view, react to, approach, study, and understand culture change. From the earliest intellectual thoughts came the orientation that there is a continuity, regularity, and cyclical quality to change. From these flow the idea that change is good and desirable, and the tendency to equate development, progress, and change. Out of the unilineal evolutionist position came a preoccupation with describing culture change after the fact, stressing change results, as opposed to seeing it as a process that required understanding. The equating of development, progress, and good was given added support. From the particularists, who became the observers of cultures in some state of change or as they had already been changed, we have the legacy of diversity and relativism, perhaps even the widespread tendency to lay all change failures on the culture or people asked to change. From diffusionism came borrowing, easily identified as a major means by which all cultures change. Functionalists provided the idea that culture is integrated: change any part of it, and there will be effects throughout the remainder of it. The neo-evolutionists brought us to the realization that culture change is a process on both general and specific levels, adaptation to particular environments. Elements of these schools of thought, theories, and suggestions have continually dominated anthropology's orientation to culture change, and can be seen in our present approach to, and understanding of, culture change.

Whereas studies of culture change based on any of the early theories focused on how foods, material items, and ideas spread across the world on the grand scale, it was not until the 1930s that anthropologists turned their attention to change on the smaller scale and became interested in the dynamics of culture change. There developed the recognition that change on the more limited scale could no longer be overlooked. Western influences had gone too far. Untouched peoples existed in only the most remote parts of the world: the Philippines, New Guinea, South America, and some Pacific islands. Throughout most of the world, there was a concentrated effort by colonial administrators, missionaries, and an odd assortment of other agents of change to spread ideas, objects, techniques, and financial assistance to the less-favored nations. This was coupled with an intense desire to offer much advice for purely humanitarian reasons. Change became any modification in a group's way of life, whether internally or externally motivated, through contact or any other means.

In 1929, Malinowski called for a new branch of anthropology, that of the changing native, which could not be divorced from what he called "practical anthropology" (Clifton 1970:12–25). Anthropologists were not to become social welfare workers, but they needed to feel themselves as people with moral obligations as to how their knowledge was to be used and applied. Anthropologists were deeply involved with people; thus they were in a position to help their friends, particularly with impact consequences. In Malinowski's view, this could be justified only if there was an analysis of recent change. Margaret Mead (1932) was one of the first to respond to this idea. Her effort was a reaction against the reconstruction of the Indian cultures from the memories of old men and in response to social issues raised by the Great Depression. I. Schapera (1934), Felix M. Keesing (1928) and Lucy Mair (1934) also responded to Malinowsi's suggestion. In a large measure, this set the stage for the more recent contributions in the study of change for many of the current issues were raised in these discussions.

A. R. Radcliffe-Brown raised the issue of interaction, not of cultures but of individuals and groups, within an established structure that was in process of change (1952). He suggested that the social structure, as described by the ethnologist, was a myth, no more than a conceptual tool that was not operational. In his view, members of societies were connected by the social structure, the network of social relations seen in kinship, neighborhood, sex, rank, and occupation. This assumes that in every social system the parts dovetail and work together with some degree of harmony. That harmony is social integration, functional unity, or consistency. When there is a lack of harmony (dysnomia), there is an attempt toward reintegration. Thus, for Radcliffe-Brown, change in culture was equal to the processes of integration and disintegration. George Homans (1951) challenged this model, suggesting that you cannot alter the characteristics of a society to see if it will survive. He used the example of fifteenth century Italy where the government fell but the society survived. He cited the problem of populations being equated with social structure. He suggested that some recurrent activity is organically interrelated with other activities, and therefore it makes a contribution to survival. This interrelatedness may be dysfunctional in one arena but functional in another.

Godfrey and Monica Wilson (1945), taking their cue from Radcliffe-Brown, developed a theory on the linkage between change and imperfect integration, an idea also espoused by Robert Redfield (1953). Based on what they saw as the unhappy consequences of change, they attacked the assumption of coherent social relations, and introduced the idea of oppositions: (1) ordinary, relating to who has power over whom, who is partner to whom, and the precise application of accepted ideas; and (2) radical opposition, the opposition of law and law, logic and logic, convention and convention. They proposed that where you have radical opposition, the society is necessarily in a state of social disequilibrium and change is inevitable. So long as it continues, there will be change. Margaret Mead (1956) then raised the issue of rapid versus slow change by calling attention to the difficulties and problems of piecemeal change.

Following a general negative view and reaction by many anthropologists to these suggestions, Edmond Leach (1954) suggested that change is not always as shattering as anthropologists generally believe. In his view, the anthropologist's description of a system is a model of how the system works, and only the model is in equilibrium. Social reality may not form such a coherent whole as suggested in such descriptions. It may, in fact, be full of inconsistencies. Attention to these inconsistencies will help us understand culture change. His point was that if we say society is stable, we do not necessarily mean that its institutions are static; rather, we are saying that stability implies the thing is firmly established and unlikely to suffer sudden change. Leach would have been skeptical about the suggestion that because of the massive intrusions of Western ideas on people throughout the world, natives are constantly in a state of flux and/or confusion. The Wilsons would likely back such a statement, for in their view, the process is inevitable.

Raymond Firth (1951) emphasized the need for techniques to investigate how individuals come to alter their regular behavior and relationships. For Firth, the process of change is best analyzed with reference to individual responses to particular situations. Choice, interpretation, interests, experiences, and temperamental disposition are involved in the change process. Structure and organization can be used to account for social continuity and social change, respectively. Expectations, which serve as guides to actions and give continuity and variance, come with decisions and choices that are made. The point and contribution of this to our current thinking is that any theoretical framework for the analysis of change must be concerned with what happens to the social structure and must allow for individual action. Ian Hogbin (1939, 1970) suggested that seeking a method for a systematic study creates a real problem. If social structure cannot be described in its entirety, the attempt to assess the extent of change is doomed to failure. Hogbin argued that Malinowski's institutions are transformations, units of organized activity with a purpose behind them. The agreement of values is implied, for practical, ethical, and legal norms are all involved. Inquiry into choice, responsibility for planning change and making decisions, coordination of manpower and resources, compensations, and rules of enforcement give clues to continuity and change factors.

From here we may be able to see how institutions are likely to develop or decay. Homer Barnett (1953) focused our attention on innovation, and Ralph Linton (1936), Melville Herskovits (1936) and Robert Redfield (1936) all contributed a refinement of the acculturation concept, along with providing a needed distinction between directed and nondirected change. Directed change was that which was generated from outside the group, and nondirected, that which came from within the group. Through the exchanges between many of these individuals, the issues and aspects of change were to surface. Arthur Niehoff (1966), Conrad Arensberg and Arthur Niehoff (1971), George Foster (1962), Margaret Mead (1955), Ivan Brady and Barry Isaac (1975), George A. Devos (1976), and many others have since proceeded to focus our attention on the various dynamics of change, issues and aspects of it, and strategies for it. But out of all of this development in our thoughts on change, we are left with a decided lack of order in the study of culture change, a tremendous vocabulary with which we attempt to speak of it, and the feeling that we lack predictive theory with regard to it. About the only unanimity found among all the scholars, thinkers, and students of change has been its existence, its context, and its negative legacy. among the people of the world. This is seen most clearly in our attempts to apply what has been learned.

APPLIED (PRACTICAL) ANTHROPOLOGY

The use of anthropological knowledge and techniques to help solve problems associated with people whom anthropologists have studied, has a long history in the discipline. While culture and change were part of anthropology almost from its inception, direct participation in change programs aimed at improving people's lives really got going during and after World War II with the development of applied or practical anthropology. The use of anthropology for a "practical" purpose was a characteristic of the British colonial government, which used it to maintain colonial rule. The American government used it to provide reliable data for establishing Indian policy, immigration policy, and its own colonial policy following World War II and the administration of U.S. trust territories. In the United States, applied or practical activity got a substantial boost during World War II when a great many anthropologists were hired as part of the war effort (Mead 1978:149). Following a resurgence of the basic research interests after the war, applied activities picked up again in the late 1970s.

In the 1990s, a large and increasing number of anthropologists can be found in virtually every sector of society, in all manner of government and international agencies, in medicine and other social services, development and planning departments, business and industry, and nearly everywhere else someone seeks to change people's lives. They work on specific projects in particular places, and they can be found monitoring the efforts of others attempting to bring about change (Van Willigen 1991). Applied or practical anthropology, until recently, had been viewed as no more than a role any anthropologist could assume and from any of the discipline's subfields (Naylor 1973a). Forensic anthropology and medical anthropology have come from the physical subfield. From archaeology have come the cultural resource managers who study, record, and preserve resources threatened by modern construction efforts. Archaeologists can also be found using their field techniques in various conservation efforts (Rathje & Ritenbaugh 1984). Education has benefited from the work of the anthropological linguist. Sociocultural anthropologists now roam the halls of corporations, government offices, international agencies, and anywhere else their skills and knowledge can help solve social problems. All of these activities in today's anthropology are concerned with change, not necessarily the sweeping change that once held the attention of anthropology, nor that associated simply with culture contacts. Now anthropologists themselves have become involved in planning and implementing changes in the lives of people and their cultures, or assessing the efforts of others, or they are being asked to help to ameliorate plans and projects already underway.

SUGGESTED READINGS

Taken together, the following books provide a good overview of anthropology, the development of its theory, and its interest in change.

Bohannan, Paul, & Mark Glazer (eds.). 1988. *High Points in Anthropology.* 2nd ed. Organized around what authors identify as "big ideas," which have significantly impacted the discipline, this book of readings presents the works of some twenty-nine significant figures in the history of anthropology and the development of its theory. Presents some materials not readily available in all university libraries.
de Waal Malefijt, Annemarie. 1974. *Images of Man: A History of Anthropological Thought.* Sets the historical and intellectual context within which anthropology was to develop. The author provides good discussions of evolutionist and functionalist thinking, and the development of American anthropology.
Garbarino, Merwyn S. 1977. *Sociocultural Theory in Anthropology: A Short History.* This volume is designed for those requiring an overview of the history of anthropology, with an emphasis on the development of sociocultural theory.
Harris, Marvin. 1968. *The Rise of Anthropological Theory: A History of Theories of Culture.* Although heavily biased to Harris's own particular theoretical position, this volume presents an in-depth historical overview of anthropology into the 1960s. This survey remains the best single source for gaining an understanding of the history and theory of anthropology.
Hogbin, Ian. 1970. *Social Change.* 2nd ed. Presents a good historical discussion of the study of change through 1958, along with a critical review of the issues and debates, among the scholars of change of the 1940s and 1950s, that combined to shape much of the current thinking about culture change.

Chapter 2

CULTURE CONTEXT

When one addresses the topic "human," one has to speak of culture, the unique characteristic that separates humans from the rest of the animal kingdom or world of living things. Whereas most animals learn and create, the human animal has taken such ability to a level achieved by none other. Culture is the basis for the vast majority of human thought and behavior, along with whatever is produced from these. Culture distinguishes and helps to define the human, just as the wings of the bird or the fins of the fish serve to separate and distinguish these animals. Whereas for other members of the animal world adaptations or adjustments to the physical environment are, for the most part, the result of biological adaptation and inherited physical characteristics, adaptation for humans goes well beyond their biological inheritance. Humans create, learn, and use culture to respond to environment, control it, even change it. Culture represents that unique ability of the species to gain significant control over aspects of the natural environment and even their own biology, within which the cultural capacity is grounded. Culture is used by people to create the sociocultural environment, to which they must also adjust or adapt. This sociocultural environment can overlie the natural environment. Culture exists in the natural environment, creates the sociocultural environment, and is also used to adapt to both those environments. It is used by humans as the mitigating factor between themselves and the environment, to respond to the limitations or problems imposed by the environment that directly affect their survival. No other animal has this capability, and no other animal has created culture. Regardless of where they may be located, all humans have culture. This means that at least on one level, all humans are basically the same—not necessarily equal but similar—in that they all create and use culture for the same basic purpose(s). At the same time that culture can be used to characterize humans as a group distinct from other animals, it is also used to differentiate between groups of humans.

Because culture represents the primary means by which people live and adjust to the problems and conditions of their environments, it also represents the end result

Figure 2.1
Culture as Adaptation to Environment

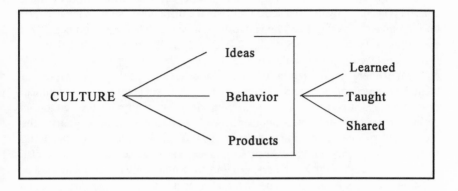

of choices made by them from among all the alternatives that are available to solve their problems, given the particular circumstances in which they find, or create for, themselves. In the context of adapting to particular environment(s), culture is inextricably tied to change. Within all cultures there must be some provision for coping with, or adjusting or adapting to, new conditions or problems that arise in the natural and sociocultural environments, both of which are always in a state of flux. The ability to change is an essential process if a culture and the people who share it are to survive. Human groups unable to meet the challenges, problems, or pressures of new circumstances are not likely to survive, nor will their cultures.

Change has always been an aspect of human culture, but now it means very different things than it did in the past: in the kinds of changes experienced, the circumstances by which change is made necessary, and its scale. In the earlier periods of human history and prehistory, change was not always as apparent as it may be today. In some periods, it appeared to come about very slowly, even imperceptibly in some cases. But as culture developed, and as humans increasingly affected the physical and sociocultural environments through their activities and accomplishments, change became much more extensive and occurred with greater frequency. As populations grew and as civilization made its appearance, things became even more complicated. With increased contacts among groups of people, the scale and speed of change has shifted even more dramatically. With the development of trade, improved transportation and communications, the world of humans became a dependent one. This emphasizes the relationship among change, culture, and contact as never before. Increased personal contacts and interactions, accompanied by a growing dependency and the development of a participatory world culture, have brought the topics of change and culture to the attention of people as never before. To speak of change is to recognize the culture context from which humans function, for although change can come from a great many different sources and address many things, humans deal with it, respond to it, and occasion it based on their cultures.

CULTURE

There are a number of major difficulties associated with the use of the culture concept. One has only to suggest the topic and the difficulties begin to appear. The term *culture* means different things to different people (Gamst & Norbeck 1976; Barrett 1984; Freilich 1972; Spradley & McCurdy 1972; Rosman & Rubel 1989). It is real, yet we speak of it in the abstract. It is something that applies to all humans and makes them similar, but at the same time it seems to differentiate groups of them. It is something that seems to apply to many different kinds or types of human groupings, and it comes in a many different of forms. On top of this, culture is defined in a seemingly endless number of ways. Even among anthropologists, the recognized specialists of culture, there seems to be little agreement on this thing called culture. They tend to take it for granted and assume that everyone else understands it as they do. For others, bringing up culture only raises the inevitable questions of why it is brought up or what relevance it has to what they are doing or talking about. They assume they know what culture is about and therefore see no justification for discussing or dealing with it.

For a great many people, *culture* means customs and traditions, while for others it means heritage, way of life, or material legacy. Still others see culture as a characteristic of only certain people and associated with only certain kinds of activities—for example, those who apply it to a knowledge and/or appreciation of "fine" literature, art, music, classical dance, or drama. In this long-standing popular usage, culture becomes the "refined lifestyle." Among anthropologists, the term has come to mean many different things. It is in the conceptualization of this unique characteristic and distinctive human ability that the problems arise. The label *culture* is applied to a wide variety of constructs, abstractions, or conceptualizations intended to provide some measure of understanding and to serve as the basis for actions. Culture is real in that people have created it out of the sum total of their problem solutions, but it is also an abstraction, created for the purposes of understanding. People create constructs of this thing called culture to enable them to make sense out of what they hear or see others doing that is somehow different from what they do. What they create is at best a representation or abstraction that allows them to talk about and understand those actual differences that exist from group to group.

Because it is conceptualized in so many different ways, culture is not always easy to work with, and as a result is frequently ignored, particularly when one is engaged with the consideration or implementation of culture change. The fact that so many people choose to ignore culture in their work is associated with the many definitions that abound, and perhaps with anthropologists' own diversity of conceptualizations and their tendency to take it for granted that everyone knows what they are talking about. The unwillingness of others to see or use culture in the change context may be the product of the seemingly esoteric conceptualizations or abstractions provided by anthropologists, as well as others, and their failure to transpose lessons learned from their concentration on traditional small-scale cultures and societies to larger, more complex ones. Using case studies of such groups to highlight differences between societies and cultures, as opposed to similarities, has produced a situation where culture is perceived as something only people in small-scale societies have.

A casual glance at the literature demonstrates that anthropologists have developed a wide variety of constructs for culture, all for the purposes of helping us to understand this thing that so characterizes the human animal (Kroeber & Kluckhohn 1952). Topical, historical, normative, behavioral, functional, mental, structural, and symbolic definitions have been proposed for the concept. Although such constructs make some sense to anthropologists, they may not be particularly useful for others who try to use or apply them. The devised conceptualizations of culture used by anthropologists influence the research problems they investigate and the methods they use. For one group of anthropologists, culture is nothing more than a set of rules guiding the actions of members of groups sharing that set of rules. For those subscribing to this conceptualization, culture amounts to a set of mental domains or categories of experience people carry around in their heads that are used to interpret their world and give it substance. As a mental construct, culture exists only in the minds of people. Behavior, material objects, or sociocultural results become little more than outward manifestations or reflections of the ideas, some good and some not so good. Determine the mental or cognitive sets, categories, or domains of experience, along with the parameters or rules by which they were created, and a culture is described. Stressing ideas or rules for behavior is to equate culture with only what people think. That they think about something in a particular way does not necessarily what they actually do.

Other anthropologists see culture as manifested behavior, its existence evidenced and definable only through that which can be observed, touched, felt, or tasted. Describe these things, and culture is described. Based on empirical reality, this group argues that ideas cannot be seen except through behavior. In this case, the focus on behavior restricts cultures to assemblages of idiosyncratic or individual behaviors produced through mindless actions. A focus on the material reduces culture to assemblages of artifacts.

Still other anthropologists suggest that culture is both of these things, the beliefs and the behaviors together. This group would argue that the reality of a belief or an idea can come only with its translation into behavior. The behavior represents proof for the existence of an idea. A fourth suggestion, one that will be proposed as basically the most useful for the culture change context, sees culture as belief, behavior, and products. This conceptualization proposes that products are the consequences or results of the interaction of belief and behavior; therefore they must be included in the definition of culture. Ideas, translated through or by behavior, produce material or sociocultural artifacts that become part of the culture. This view maintains culture as a collective reality dependent for its existence on all three of these components, which are closely related. This would appear to be the most useful definition for culture change, for change can come in any one or all of these areas. All three together produce the sociocultural environment or culture setting. A change in one can potentially mean a change in all three.

Of course it must be recognized that all conceptualizations of culture, provided by anthropologists or anyone else, are based in philosophy, on the premise of what reality is, and this determines the perspective taken to culture. This can be very confusing for people who attempt to use culture in their work. Depending on the definition of reality that is elected, they or may not be able to relate culture to what they do, or to perceive it as germane in what they do. As attention is narrowed to the consideration of change within the culture context, one's conceptualization of culture influences how change will be perceived and addressed. It will determine what will be considered and what will not be, and this, of course, will structure the result. For example, if one assumes a mentalist stance, change becomes simply a change of idea or one of the rules for culture. For the behavioralist, change assumes a modification or alteration in behavior. The first position would ignore the fact that few, if any, changes have ever occurred simply because someone had a new idea. Thinking about a change does not make it occur, some actions are necessary. Change may begin with an idea, but behavior has to occur to bring it about. On the other hand, a behavioralist is tempted to assume that if a behavior has changed, the culture has been changed. This ignores the fact that until the idea behind the behavior is adopted, there is no completed culture change. If a holistic or collective view of culture is taken, quite another perspective and approach to change are mandated, one requiring that culture change be dependent upon modifications in all three of these areas. Ideas make for behavior(s). They generate actions. Behaviors (actions) reflect the idea that lies behind them. The products, either material or sociocultural, are the result of ideas being translated by or through behavior, reflecting these two things necessary to produce them. These are related and together represent the integrated culture system.

Despite differences in how culture is conceptualized, anthropologists do agree on some things. Most of them agree that culture is a uniquely human characteristic that must be learned. Each new generation of humans has to learn it all over again, for although the capacity for culture is grounded in their biology and physical natures, it is not something inherited through one's genes. Individuals are not born with culture; they have to learn it. Being born in America gives people rights of citizenship, but he or she must learn the beliefs and behaviors that makes and identifies him or her as an American. An individual can be born in France but can become English by learning those beliefs and behaviors of English culture. The fact that culture must be learned also means that it must be taught, making it a group and shared phenomenon. Whether one prefers such a term as *education, socialization,* or *enculturation,* or even a generic term such as *culturation* for the process, culture transmission and acquisition represent the means by which cultures are reproduced. Anthropologists also agree that cultures are always changing, because environments are always changing. No culture today is the same as it has always been.

Cultures as Integrated Systems

Culture is a collective and integrated whole consisting of learned ideas, behaviors, and products, all related to the needs of human groups. It is a coherent system in which ideas are generated out of people's concerns, a set of behaviors is

Figure 2.2
Definition of Culture

CULTURE — The learned way or ways of human belief, and behavior, and the

products of these which are shared by members of human groups.

tied to those ideas, and products (physical or social) result from them. These general components of culture are dependent on each other and together produce the coherent whole of culture. Even as the ideas, behaviors, and products are further broken down in relation to the basic concerns of culture, its systematic and integrated nature remains. Culture is not a haphazard grouping of such things that somehow accumulated over time. The ideas, behaviors, and products of culture are associated with satisfying some concern of the people. What is done in one area will be related to what may have to be done in another. It can even necessitate what must be done in the specific components of the culture.

All cultures consist of specific elements; the individual ideas, behaviors, or products manifested by members of a human group. Together, they represent the culture of the group and its way of life. Most elements exist in combinations, complexes, or patterns of related behaviors, ideas, and products that go together for a purpose. Institutions are networks of complexes woven together in relation to the basic interests and needs of social living. Some things apply to everyone in the group, and some do not. Alternatives allow for the choices that are acceptable, and specialties apply only to certain categories of people within the culture group. Although these bits and pieces are all a part of culture, some of them are clearly more important than others. What is important as one moves from culture group to culture group can vary quite substantially, but some things are important to all of them. There are some specific ideas, behaviors, and products that are essential for social and cultural survival, sometimes referred to as the core systems of culture. Institutions often reflect these core areas because they are networks of complexes oriented to some aspect or need of social living. They also reflect the basic needs of the human being. These must be addressed by all human societies because people are living or sometimes merely working together in groups.

For cultures to survive, the people who share such things must survive. For example, food and shelter are essential concerns of all people. Food may be the most important of all, for if people do not have enough food to survive, they die and the rest of their concerns become moot points. Tied as they are to available natural resources, it is not surprising that food and shelter lie at the heart of what we called economic patterns and institutions found in all societies and cultures. Economic systems are designed around people's access to available natural resources, their transformation into those things people require to meet their needs, and ways of distributing the finished products to the people who need them. A social system or structure is also an essential core area of culture, because humans associate with other humans in structured groups. To establish and maintain human society, there must be social relationships whereby individuals know what to expect and what is expected of them, the social claims and obligations members of the group have to one another. Social structure stipulates the actual relationships and the means by which these are established. It can include marriage and family, social stratification, and a great many other things that focus on the rights and responsibilities of individuals to other members of their group. Because people attempt to live together in groups, sometimes large groups, the need for social order is essential. Political and legal systems exist to establish social order, maintain it, and deal with disorder should it arise. They set the minimum standards of behavior for the group and provide the means for their enforcement.

Some system of cultural transmission and acquisition is another core area of culture, for this represents how cultures are reproduced. If the culture is not taught or passed along to new generations, it ceases to exist. The central role of language in the process can be assumed without prolonged discussion, for without language, culture as we know it would be impossible. Within this systematic code for the symbolic communication of any kind of information, all the rules, behaviors, and products of the culture are encoded. A worldview or attitudinal system is also a core area of all cultures, albeit it a little more abstract and less tangible than some of the others. A worldview encompasses philosophy, beliefs, epistemology, and general attitudes about the world. It provides people with a means to make sense out of their world. It serves as the basis for their beliefs, and provides for answers as to what is, why it is, what it should be, and what the individual's personal relationship to that might be. It provides a basis for perception and evaluation of the world. This can come from religion, political, economic or social systems.

If a culture is surviving, it represents a viable system. The parts are working together, much as the parts of a car together make up what we identify as a car. When it ceases to function, it is because one of its essential pieces has stopped working as it should. This demonstrates that the parts make up the whole and that some parts are more important than others. Change any part, and the whole system is affected. Where the parts do not fit together to keep the system working, the survival of the whole is threatened. Cultures function in much the same way. Each part contributes to the definition of the whole. Like an automobile that does not operate efficiently all of the time, cultures may not either, especially when considering the core areas addressed by the ideas, behaviors, and products. Malfunctions of cultures appear as contradictions, paradoxes, or inconsistencies. Ideas do not relate to the behaviors, or the products become inconsistent with the ideas and behaviors. No culture exists in perfect harmony or balance all of the time. Contradictions exist because there are gaps between how people think about something and how it may actually exist. A belief may not be translated into behavior or the products may not conform to the ideas or behaviors. Ideally, people can believe that all people are equal, whereas in actual practice inequality is institutionalized, as in caste, class, and race groupings. A group may believe that they have adequately provided for social order but the system fails to maintain order or may actually foster increased disorder.

There are other areas of culture that come to mind or can be identified as part of culture as well, but these have little or no relationship to the continued survival of the group or its culture. Such systems are not found uniformly in all cultures. For example, there are a number of societies and cultures throughout the world that exhibit minimal concern with art or music. Their presence or relative absence seems little related to the continuation of the group. On the other hand, understanding the specific components of culture as they address the core concerns addressed by all people, in all types and sizes of groupings, is crucial in any consideration of culture change. Any suggested change in a core area represents a potential threat to the group. Political, economic, attitudinal, language, social, and culture transmission systems represent the core areas of human culture. They address the concerns that must be dealt with if the society and culture are to survive and remain viable. Not unexpectedly, a change in any one of these areas of culture will have great impact on the whole. It is also the case that change in these areas will be much more difficult to achieve than changes in areas not so important to survival. It can also be expected that a change in a core area will occasion consequences to other core areas, for core areas are closely interrelated. For example, what a group does to satisfy its basic food requirements will impact other aspects of its economic system, as well as its political, social, and its religious or worldview systems.

Cultural Groups

Humans are most assuredly social animals existing in collective groups. Humans seem to have a real need to associate with others of their kind. In so doing, they form societies wherein they share cultural traditions. When they do this within a locality, they form communities. Any community can become a cultural grouping when its members share the same ideas, behaviors, and things. A culture group is not simply a haphazard coming together of a number of people for a passing moment. The culture group has a relatively permanent existence that is evidenced in its social structure or recognized claims and obligations among its members, and in its social organization whereby the group gets things done. This produces the reason to exist. It may be that the group has a general or specific goal to pursue, such as survival in a particular environment, or it may be that a group comes together for the pursuit of a common interest. For example, a group of people may wish to carry forward a particular political or religious ideology.

Members of cultural groups are recruited through recognized rules and procedures. Membership is based on the teaching and learning of the things that distinguish the group. Members have common interests as well as incurred rights and obligations to one another. Through structure, the group can continue irrespective of the loss of individual members. There is also a clear sense of belonging associated with culture groups, for members gain elements of individual identity in the process and as a consequence. By extension, the group is identified

Figure 2.3
Levels of Culture Groupings

General Culture	The uniquely human adaptation to the environment, the panhuman characteristic.
Specific Cultures	Particular adaptations to particular natural or sociocultural environments.
Constituent Cultures	Adaptations to specific sociocultural environments, sometimes referred to as subcultures.
Cultural Scenes	Variations of specific culture patterns of belief and behavior unique to special-interest, specialty, and structural groupings.
World Culture Scenes	Variations of specific cultural patterns of belief and behavior unique to special-interest, specialty, and structural groupings that transcend national or state boundaries.

as such by other groups that do things differently. When people learn all of the rules, duties, or expectations required of members of a group, they have learned its culture. Once learned, culture becomes the measure of every other culture. People judge the actions of others based on what they have learned. In this sense, culture is a brand of "truth," for everyone learns the "right" things. It also means that culture can be attributed to all manner of human groups, of all kinds, sizes and makeup (Figure 2.3). This produces a great deal of confusion about culture, and accounts for the varied images and perceptions of culture that exist.

Every cultural group learns its own "truth," which then guides the beliefs and actions of all the members. Thus, it also means that as cultural groups come into contact, the contact is one of conflict or of truths in conflict. As humans interact with one another, the learned truths are in competition, each equally believed, followed, and defended as the "ultimate," "best," or "most correct" truth. There are many human groups who have culture, and thus there are many truths. Because humans learn their cultures as truth, they naturally tend to judge the cultures of others based on what they have learned and belief to be true or correct (Downs 1975). This means they are naturally ethnocentric. Cultures in contact always mean truths in conflict. In most culture change contexts, especially those involving representatives of different cultures, this can become a major element in deciding what should be done, how it will be done, and ultimately the success or failure of the whole effort. To understand the ramifications of this, and because culture can be attributed groupings of humans from the most generalized down to the specific, all specific, all at the same time, it is necessary to examine the various levels of human groupings to which the label *culture* can legitimately be applied. Culture is used with reference to the entire human group as a species, and it is used to characterize any human grouping whose beliefs or behaviors distinguish it from other groupings of humans.

General Human Culture. On the most generalized level, culture consists of the learned beliefs and behaviors used by humans to adapt to the environment. All humans do this; thus all humans have culture. On this level of usage, culture pinpoints the unique ability of humans to adapt to, even control, aspects of any natural environment. Whereas all other animals must respond to the dictates of the phenomenon. Whether one prefers such a term as *education, socialization,* or *enculturation,* or even a generic term such as *culturation* for the process, culture physical environment, humans can change the environment to suit their purposes. A dog cannot grow bananas in Alaska to meet its food requirements, but culture has given humans this ability. When used in reference to all humans on this panhuman level, culture represents that unique characteristic separating the human from all the other animals with whom they share the planet. Because all humans share this ability, which they exercise, all humans are essentially the same. Using culture, humans provide for all of their basic, and nearly all of their derived, needs. Such basic needs as food, shelter, human association, and whatever warmth seems to be required as part of that are common to all humans, regardless of where they are found. A person in the New Guinea highlands is just as concerned about sufficient food, shelter from the elements, and human association as is an individual in the United States, Japan, or anywhere else. Humans everywhere laugh when they are happy, cry when they are sad or hurt. In the satisfaction of basic needs, every human is the same as every other human, regardless of how they meet such need. It is only how they satisfy their similar needs that makes humans and the groups they form appear different from each other. It is because humans elect different means of satisfying their needs that culture can be applied to all manner of more specific groupings.

Specific Cultures. Although all humans have the characteristic of using culture to adapt to the environment and they also tend to develop local varieties or manifestations of this universal human characteristic. As particular groups of humans adjust to the specific problems and circumstances of the particular environments in which they find themselves, they create their own versions of this general human characteristic. First, human groups have to adapt to the particular natural environments in which they find themselves. For example, the Eskimo must adapt to a harsh Arctic environment, whereas the Bedouin adapts to a desert environment. In adapting to the particulars or limits of possibilities within such natural environments, they create particular or specific cultures, obviously tied to, and reflective of, those environments. Representing local adaptations, cultures are seen for what they really are, sets of problem-solving solutions in specific environments. As natural environments differ, so individual groups inhabiting and adapting to them take on different appearances. But groups within particular environments can also differ simply because choices are possible. In the same environment, choices made among alternatives can be dramatically different. The specific characteristics of the group are a function, in part, of the specific environment in which that group attempts to survive.

The problem of culture becomes a little more complicated at this point, because humans must also adapt to the very sociocultural environments they create in their efforts to deal with the natural ones. In adapting to different and varied natural environments, humans create versions of culture as they respond to the specific peculiarities or limits of those environments. In doing this, as they choose from among all the possible alternatives available to them, they create different sociocultural environments to which they then must adapt. There are natural environments in the natural order of things, and there are sociocultural environments created by humans to deal with them. In this sense, and in the process of doing this, it could be said that humans create elements of their own physical environments in responding to the natural environments. Although it is a common practice to distinguish cultures at this specific level in terms of some highly generalized natural environment, based on its physical geography (e.g., desert, Arctic, or tropical), on this level, *culture* also is used to refer to specific varieties of culture created along sociocultural lines associated with the nation-state.

Culture is used synonymously with modern sociopolitical units and nationality (e.g., American, German, Russian, and so on). This tendency frequently obscures more than it clarifies, for such national cultures are arbitrary and artificial creations. Because such groupings are created along arbitrary lines, their geographical settings frequently incorporate a number of distinct natural environments and culture groups adapted to them. Using the concept of culture with nations, states, and nation-states is a major source of difficulty and confusion. First, all three terms refer to political units with varying levels of sociopolitical integration. Second, that use presupposes that all people considered members of the group share the same set of cultural beliefs and behaviors. According to some current thinking, a nation is a society or community of people who see themselves as one people, based on common traditions, ancestry, institutions, ideology, language, and perhaps religion (Clay 1990:28). Unfortunately, this representation of nation rarely coincides with the actual cultural diversity present in all nations. The term *nation* is usually equated with the state, an integrated political unit within which the control (monopoly) of force to ensure member compliance with the rules of behavior (e.g. the United Nations, which is made up of such political states).

The definition being proposed for nation is actually little different from the traditional definitions of a *society* or a culture group. Few if any nations exist with the homogeneity implied in such a definition. This is not a particularly useful trend, for it overlaps the more traditional use of the term *society*.

States, on the other hand, are autonomous political units, encompassing many communities, that have a centralized government and the power to coerce (Carneiro 1970:733). The term *state* must be approached with caution because it actually refers to a level of sociopolitical integration that might characterize a society. The use of the term *nation-state* is an attempt to attribute culture to such sociopolitical units, but it fares no better. Rarely will the nation, the state, or the nation-state coincide with a specific culture, except on a most limited basis (e.g., on the basis of some level of shared values, behaviors, and the products of these). The term nation-state, well established in the literature, is used to refer to societies that have clearly defined borders separating them from others, have reached the state level of sociopolitical integration, and more often than not have monopolistic control over the use of force (laws and centralized government) to ensure that their members comply with the rules of the society. It is tied to industrial societies. It has been used synonymously with *culture* as well, for centralized governments have been concerned with creating a national culture (set of beliefs and practices that apply to everyone within its borders). Should they be successful, the definition of *nation* offered by Clay would be appropriate. Thus far, such attempts have achieved only limited success, for there is no such nation-state in existence with only a single culture shared by all of its people. Equally unfortunate has been the tendency to perceive nation-states as having a culture in the same sense that a small-scale society has a culture. Any differences that might be noted among the lifestyles of the various members incorporated into the arbitrarily established "culture grouping" are seen as simply subcultures or groups within the nation-state. Although people in these groups may share in some things, the plain fact of the matter is that they have their own sets of beliefs and behaviors that distinguish them as culture groups. Legislating something different does not necessarily make it so. Such groupings might be better referred to as *constituent cultures,* to avoid the more negative and misleading aspects of the term *subculture.*

Constituent Cultures. Along with the creation of the arbitrary and artificial sociocultural environment and/or sociopolitical nation-state comes the use of *culture* to refer to differences among the many human groups incorporated into any one of them. This means that culture can be used to identify the different ways of belief and behavior of the varied groups that were brought together, by one means or another, to make up a particular sociopolitical or national grouping. At this level, culture is usually associated with ethnicity, identifying groups on the basis of their common origins and common characteristics, as in the United States, where the cultures of Mexican-Americans, African-Americans, Anglo-Americans, and other groups are differentiated. It is interesting to note that the idea of ethnicity, developed to refer to culturally distinct groupings, is now resisted by scholars and ethnic groups alike. Generally, constituent groups appear to subscribe to many, if not all, of the ideas and behavior required of all people within the boundaries of a larger sociocultural unit. They may even adhere to many of the same behavioral expectations of the larger national group of which they have been made a part.

At the same time that such groups may share some of the beliefs and behaviors of the larger grouping, it is apparent that they also maintain their own distinct patterns of belief and behavior that distinguish them from other identifiable groups. For example, the Kurds in Iran, the Basques in Spain, or many Native-American groups refuse to recognize their relationship to the nation-state. Still others may see themselves as part of the nation-state but with unique beliefs and behaviors they should be allowed to continue. On the whole, these groups steadfastly refuse to become participants in the nation-states that claim them or have attempted to incorporate them are specific cultures in their own right. Those which choose to recognize their affiliation with the nation-state should be seen as constituent cultures, for they remain distinct cultures despite being included in the nation-state.

The term *constituent* means *to form, compose, or make up something*. Every nation-state is composed of people with distinct cultures who have been brought together. Constituent cultures collectively make up the modern nation-state.

The most popular tendency has been to refer to such constituent cultural groupings as subcultures, suggesting that they are simply micro-cultures within the macro-culture. This would be acceptable if the term subculture recognized the legitimacy of such groups as viable cultures in their own right. Unfortunately, this is not the case, for the term has come to mean that these cultures are somehow less viable than the nation-state culture. It has also come to mean they have been absorbed, when in fact, this is rarely the case. Examples are easy to find. Mexican-Americans have a distinct heritage and way of life. They are also Americans. African-Americans have a heritage different from Hispanic-Americans, but they, too, are Americans. The same can be said for the many Native-American culture groups incorporated into the American culture. *Constituent cultures* would seem to be a more appropriate way to identify groupings of this type. They help to constitute the national culture, each playing a part in the definition of the larger grouping, yet each is also identifiable as a culture group in its own right. People sharing a constituent culture follow their own distinct beliefs and behaviors while, at the same time, subscribing to some of the same ideas and following some of the same rules of behavior required of all those who have been incorporated, willingly or unwillingly, into the particular nation-state.

Cultural Scenes. Although large sociocultural groups such as the nation-state, nation, or state nearly always consist of a variety of culturally distinguishable constituent or specific cultures, they also include cultural groups created along different lines. These are the culture groups associated with the developing complexity and specialization of culture. This last level of human grouping to which the culture concept can be applied is perhaps the most difficult to deal with, for at this level, culture groupings are created by gathering members of various cultures of the sociocultural environment into new ones. Members can be drawn from specific, national, or even constituent culture groupings. Such cultures can even be made up of people drawn from all of these. They can even be created by incorporating members from throughout the world, in essence transcending physical geography, national boundaries, and/or nationality. On this level can be found adaptations or learned ways of belief and behavior in response to the whole world as a sociocultural environment. Spradley and McCurdy (1972) refer to these kinds of cultural groupings as cultural scenes, denoting their legitimacy as culture groups. According to these authors, the cultural scene is where one finds information and behavior being shared by a select group, perhaps as few as two. The scene is related to social situations, emphasizing its relationship to the complex sociocultural environment created by humans in adapting to the natural environments. In essence, cultural groupings are created in response to the social environment, to cope with that environment and the limited sharing of culture that is actually possible among people in an age of complexity and specialization. According to Spradley and

McCurdy, it is impossible that all the people of any culture share all the beliefs and behaviors that may be attributed to it.

Culture groups that are identified as cultural scenes draw their members from among the constituent groups within the nation-state for a variety of purposes and procedures. For example, some groups are created on a regional basis (e.g., Southwestern, Texan, Yankee, Southern). Other groups can be created on the basis of sex or gender (e.g., male, female, homosexual, heterosexual). Still others can be based on age (e.g., infant, teenager, young adult, mature adult, retired), occupation (e.g., business, academic, white collar, blue collar), religion (e.g., Muslim, Christian, Catholic, Baptist), politics (e.g., Democratic, Socialistic, Communistic, Republican), and according to special interests (e.g., environmentalism, pop culture, conservtion, etc.). The list can go on and on until all the full complement of cultural scenes for any complex culture is complete. According to Spradley and McCurdy, even within cultural scenes, additional breakdowns are possible. For example, the business scene can be further broken down into distinct types (e.g., restaurant, industrial, shipping, service, etc.), and even more specific breakdowns are possible. For example, in the restaurant business there are cooks, hostesses, waitresses, waiters, management, and customers. The education cultural scene is capable of further division into public and private, preschool, primary, secondary, and higher. Each of these has its own constituent groups: teachers, students, service staff, administration, history, mathematics, anthropology, and so on. The cultures of IBM and Texas Instruments are clearly distinguishable. The academic culture of Harvard is not the same as the culture of East Texas State College or Pomona Community College. Virtually any special interest group can be viewed as a cultural group at this level. The possibilities are almost endless when identifying culturally distinct groupings at this level. It simply depends on how specific one wishes to get. It also depends on whether the identified group learns specific beliefs and follows specific behaviors that distinguish it from other groups.

World Culture Scenes. The newest type of human grouping and level of culture has been created out of the spread of some beliefs and behaviors throughout the world, such as world economics and technology. For example, as information technology has spread into the various parts of the world, a computer culture has been created, its members drawn from throughout the world, all of them learning, sharing, and identifying with a distinct set of beliefs and behaviors. As the money-dominated market-exchange system has spread throughout the world, a culture of international business has been created. There are many more such examples and there will be more to come. Even world regional groupings can be identified on this level (e.g., Western, Eastern, Middle Eastern, and Latin American cultures). The significance in the creation of such culture groupings lies in the fact that they almost always transcend specific national, constituent, or cultural scenes groups.

In the final analysis, given that culture can be applied on all these different levels of human groupings, it is not surprising that the concept is a difficult one for many people to understand and apply. It perhaps makes some sense to anthropologists, whereas for others it is not so meaningful. Although culture can be credited to all kinds of human groups, making it something that can be used at successive levels of adaptation, from the most general to the most specific, the essential point is that culture characterizes any relatively permanent human group that learns a specific way of belief or behavior that serves to distinguish it from other groups. Viewed in this manner, a culture group becomes any distinguishable group of people who learn their own ways of thinking and behaving, and then pass these on from generation to generation. Understanding the complexity of culture as it applies to groups is essential in addressing the topic of culture change.

HUMAN MULTICULTURALISM

Culture is a set of shared beliefs, behaviors, and products transmitted and carried on generation after generation. All people, regardless of level of human grouping, must learn specific beliefs and practices in order to become accepted as members of groups with which they identify. Once the culture of the group is learned, it becomes part of their reality and the driving force in their lives. It determines how they will think and behave in particular circumstances. It determines the day-to-day activities of people in their total round of living, in all their work and play. Culture represents the primary guide or blueprint used by people to get through each day, as the prescription for doing all those things the other members of their group expect of them. It can be likened to the complete set of rules by which the individual is accepted and will function as part of a group. It is also the behavior that reflects those rules. How well the rules are followed by individuals in actual practice speaks to how good members of the group they are and how well they have learned their culture lessons. Last, it is the product of the ideas and behavior of people. We begin to acquire culture at birth and we continue to learn culture, or better cultures, throughout our lives as we acquire membership in many cultural groupings. Culture is something to be learned by every child, every immigrant, every initiate into any group.

Because people learn many cultures in their lifetime, that they will identify with a number of them simultaneously at any given point in time is also true. For example, a worker in an organization carries a great deal of cultural baggage into the workplace, itself a cultural context. This frequently produces great conflict for the individual, who must choose which culture set (beliefs or behaviors) to follow in particular circumstances. The different cultures to which we affiliate may actually be in direct contradiction or conflict with one another. For example, a conflict can easily develop between one's political, national, and/or religious cultures. The business culture frequently can conflict with the conservation culture, the religious culture, or even the national culture of which it is a part. The demands of occupational culture can easily conflict with religious, political, or even social culture. In such cases the individual is forced to choose which culture set will influence decisions.

Most people separate the parts and aspects of their lives into distinct categories, then use the culture set most appropriate in each. It may very well be that one of the cultures becomes the dominant force in someone's life, the sole determinant of the choices made in all circumstances. For example, some religious groups disavow any allegiance to nationality or national culture. This is in direct contradiction to the interests, goals, and beliefs of the nation-state. Unfortunately, the same culture group will not guide the choices of everyone else, except perhaps in the totalitarian state, where, at least superficially, everyone is guided by the same things. Some people are more influenced by politics and political groups, others by economics and economic groups. Still others are influenced more by their religious beliefs and religious group than anything else. Normally when we find such individuals, we judge them to be shortsighted, narrow in view, perhaps even fanatical in their steadfastness. Sometimes the choice of culture set will be determined entirely by the circumstances of the moment. Humans are not simply influenced or motivated by a culture; rather, humans are motivated by cultures, any one of which can exert the greatest influence on their actions at any given moment in time or under any particular circumstance. Unfortunately, anthropologists have not addressed this multicultural aspect of individuals.

CULTURE FORMS

Just saying that humans have culture is not enough, for, as we have seen, there are many different cultures, depending on the level of human adaptation one focuses upon. Saying that culture is *a* learned way of believing and behaving is not enough either, for people learn many cultures in their lifetime, each of them as truth. Although this goes a long way to erasing some of the confusion and difficulty with the culture concept, it does not eliminate all of it. Culture comes in a variety of forms, and this needs to be understood. There are at least three different forms we learn for each of our cultures. Ask people to tell you about their culture—explain some idea, belief or action—and he or she will tell you. All people are taught such things as they are brought into membership in their culture groups. These are the standards of the group, the expectations, the rules, the ideas and values the individual must learn in order to become part of the group. The answers provided in response to such questions about their culture represent ideal culture, but there is also a real culture that can be quite different from the ideal one, and there is a culture construct that attempts to bridge these two for specific purposes. These different forms of culture must be understood if one expects to understand the role of culture in the lives of humans and the basis for their responses to culture change. Ideal culture exists in the minds of people. Real culture exists in the adaptations people make to survive. Culture constructs provide for individual and group action.

Ideal Culture

Ideal cultures are learned, both formally and informally taught to aspiring members of culture groupings by those who already know them and are already members of the group. they are provided or transmitted as the required knowledge, beliefs, and behavioral expectations of the group. To become a member of a group, be identified, and accepted into full membership requires the individual's knowledge and acceptance of these. One is also expected to adhere to the group's rules. For example, Americans are generally taught to believe that lying, stealing, and cheating are unacceptable, that honesty is the best policy. Americans are generally taught about "fair play," that how one plays the game is as important as winning. Ask whether America is the land of freedom and equal opportunity, or whether Americans believe in the worth of the individual, free enterprise, honest competition, or providing an honest day's labor for an honest day's pay, and the answers will inevitably be yes. Americans are taught about the importance of the individual and that all people are created equal in the eyes of God and in the eyes of the law. Americans are taught to be responsible citizens, honest, truthful and law-abiding. No one in the system teaches Americans to be dishonest, to lie, cheat, and steal. When questioned about such things, Americans have the responses on the tips of their tongues, for they have learned these things from parents, teachers, religious leaders, peer groups, and television. All Americans know what their culture is *supposed* to be like, for they are taught such things at home, at school, in church, in the training or orientation programs where they work.

Ideal culture is the product of the culture group deciding what needs to be taught and learned by new members. This statement of culture, its required beliefs and expected behaviors, is presented to each new recruit in its most idealized form, as the beliefs and behaviors to which the group subscribes. It represents what the group believes itself to be all about, how they think of themselves or wish others to see them. It is designed to bend the individual to the group, to establish consistency and regularity in what is taught and learned. On the other hand, when people are asked about their culture, responses are frequently qualified. "Yes, we believe it should be that way, but it isn't in all cases," or "We haven't achieved it quite yet." Actually, it is rare that our real thoughts and actions live up to the ideals we have learned and stated for ourselves or our groups. It is also the case that ranges of behavior are acceptable in all societies, and these are learned along with the ideal ones. Individuals learn how far they may deviate from the stated norms and still be accepted by the group. The culture of any complex society is largely the result of compromise or coercion. It results from a group effort, but the individual is left to play it out. It may be impossible for the individual to live up to the ideals established by the group. This leads us to identify another form of culture, the real form.

Real Culture

In actual practice, American society is a stratified one, based on categorizations of people we understand as social classes. Because each class has a different access to the natural resources, prestige, or status positions of the society; inequality is structured in. The class system revolves around stored wealth, the bulk of which is increasingly monopolized by fewer and fewer members of the society. Thus, it would appear that America (the United States) could never be the land of equality or even of equal opportunity. It could mean that equal opportunity exists according to class, but no American wants to admit this. America is supposed to be the land of equal opportunity for all. The reality of differential opportunity is not lost on Americans in general. Various constituent cultural groups in America such as African-Americans, Mexican-Americans, Native-Americans, and women, certainly understand the lack of equal opportunity within the society and culture.

By the same token, although individuality is highly valued in American society, it is simply not possible within a large social group. Individuality has to be sacrificed for the common good, the stability and order of the group. In short, individuality threatens the unified and continued existence of the group and its culture. This is closely related to freedom. America is the land of the free, or, more precisely, a land where individual freedom is greater than elsewhere. No nation could actually exist where individuals were free to do anything they might like. America is the land of the free, but only up to the point where freedom does not threaten the continued survival of the group. Competition and fair play are desired qualities of Americans, but the competitive nature of the society and its members is obvious at a casual glance. Ask any football coach if how one plays the game is as important as winning. Do Americans really like a loser? In sports and leisure activities, in politics and business, competition translates into beating the opposition; winning is all-important. Winning by any means, fair or foul, is evidenced in the growing attention being placed on ethics in nearly all walks of life. Honesty being the best policy is contradicted by the success of those who choose otherwise. Law-abiding behavior goes only so far.

How many Americans really drive at the speed limit? How many Americans drive just a little faster than the law allows, ignore the stop sign, traffic light, passing zones, or other symbols and rules of the road adopted for safety and order on the nation's highways? Why do so many people live in fear of a federal tax audit each year? How many people really play fair in their private, religious, or business lives all of the time? How many really do give their employer an honest day's work for an honest day's pay? Again, a cursory glimpse of Americans in various aspects of their daily lives is revealing. What they may think or wish to think about themselves is rarely the actual case. This kind of discussion could go on for some time, but the point has surely been made that while Americans have all learned the rules, values, and behaviors of the group and believe these guide their actions, there is some question about how closely they may actually follow them. What Americans say they believe and do rarely correlates with what they actually think and do as individuals or as a group. The difference leads to the conclusion that real culture can be very different from ideal culture. There is a real culture that denotes what beliefs and practices are all about. One might suggest that real culture is the practical test of how well individuals actually live up to the stated ideals of the group. It might also be that real culture includes learning the limits of variation the group will accept.

As a general rule, most people do not go around with a list to remind themselves what their culture expects of them. They learn what the culture is supposed to be all about, learn the limits of acceptable variation, then simply go through the process of living on a day-to-day basis. They think as they have been taught and do what they know must be done insofar as what they interpret that to mean or may capable of doing. Ideal culture is a group phenomenon, whereas real culture is played out on an individual basis. Not many people consciously think about all those little things they have to do after getting out of bed in the morning, reminding themselves of every step and all the behaviors necessary to get themselves ready to go out and face another day, a job, a task.

Sometimes people do things with the conscious thought that they are not exactly following the rules. They know that they are not living up to the standards they were taught and had to learn. Formally and informally, people learn what their fellow group members expect, but they also learn what they will accept. Sometimes little deviation is acceptable, and at other times the latitude is great. People learn how far they can go in stretching, bending, or even violating the rules. For example, Americans apparently learn, through trial and error, where it might be acceptable to "cut corners just a little" or "cheat just a little." Maybe it is no more complicated than the fact that Americans also learn what they can get away with and remain an acceptable members of the group. How many times do people actually think about cultural values learned in school or from their parents as they move through a typical day? Do Americans really think about honesty being the best policy just before driving beyond the speed limit? Do Americans consciously consider that they will be cheating just a little bit, or do they know just how far they can push it before a police officer will issue them a speeding ticket?

Sometimes there is a small difference, and sometimes there is a substantial difference, between our *ideal* and our *real* cultures, between what we have been taught to think and do, and what we actually think and do. Recognizing this difference between culture forms is an essential step in understanding culture and its influence on the lives of people, their behavior and beliefs as individuals or as groups. Regardless of what kind of group we can credit with having culture, members may learn ideal culture, but they must function and live in the real culture. On the one hand, all members of every group learn the rules and the ideals, but they also learn just how far they can deviate from those rules and ideals. There are many other areas in which a substantial difference can be noted between the ideal and real cultures of American society. Although most Americans know what their culture is supposed to be, how they want it to be, they are usually very quick to note where the culture as yet to meet its lofty goals. The same can be said for any culture at any level of human grouping. Given the development of the modern nation-state, the difference between the cultures can be extreme, for the arbitrary basis of such societies frequently necessitates a great many compromises as to what they will be or how they wish the rest of the world to see them. The fact that most people in culture groups recognize the difference between their stated ideals and the realities of everyday living requires the understanding of yet another type of culture, the construct culture.

Construct Culture

The construct culture comes into being as people attempt to describe culture for someone else. Anthropologists have always operated on this level, describing cultures by way of the norms of belief and behavior of the group. But anthropologists are not the only ones to do this. All people do this for others as a way of trying to make sense out of what those others think and do. When members of one culture see others doing something differently than they do it, hear something different from what they think, they have to make sense out of it. To do this, they will refer to their own experiences, beliefs, and practices to interpret what they see or hear. Based on their learned way of belief and behavior, either ideally or using the culture construct with which they actually function, they will put the differences in perspective. They will draw conclusions, make judgments about the ideas or practices of others based on what they have learned as truth, as the most correct or best way to think and behave.

The ethnocentrism introduced by culture provides that such interpretations are quite likely to be incorrect. Misinterpretations and misconceptions abound when people interpret other cultural groups based on their own experiences. The conclusions drawn are then allowed to represent or stand as part of the description of that other culture. The interactions between the members of the different groups, based on often faulty conclusions, are thus made difficult. For example, members of Native American, Mexican, and a number of Middle Eastern culture groups do not value time as Americans do. The Americans' interpretation of this difference might be that they are unmotivated, waste a lot of valuable time, even they are lazy. In actual practice, the importance of time may not reflect any of these characterizations. The misconception will underlie the Americans' approach to the members of these groups, however. In parts of the world where only loose women or prostitutes display aggressive behavior, the attitudes and behaviors of liberated American women will surely be misunderstood.

Although most people create culture descriptions based on what they think they hear or see, others attempt to do this a little more systematically, limiting the ethnocentric bias as much as humanly possible, thereby reducing misinterpretations and misconceptions. Whereas people of one culture judge people of another based on what they believe is true and correct, the anthropologist attempts to avoid such judgments. The resulting description is, one hopes, more objective and closer to the real culture. It remains, nevertheless, a construct culture. It is a description that includes what people say they are all about and what in actual practice they really do. The ethnography or cultural description that is then provided is still only a representation that is allowed to stand for the real culture but is not a total replication of that reality. It represents the *norms* of belief or practice of a particular group, and describes the normal way that something is done. When anthropologists go to some remote part of the world to study the culture of a traditional group, attempt to describe a constituent culture or cultural scene, they are working with this type of culture. The resulting descriptions of cultures, whether based or the judgments made by one group about another, or based on the norms provided by

Figure 2.4
Culture Forms

IDEAL CULTURE – What people believe, think, and say they do.

REAL CULTURE – What people really think and do.

CONSTRUCT CULTURE – Combines what people think and say they do
with what they really do.

---

anthropologist, are in practice more than simple representations offered to make sense out of others. The descriptions, once created, also serve to guide the interactions between the people of the differing groups, for as we interpret the beliefs and actions of others, they do the same for us.

The culture construct is a creation that is allowed to stand for people, but all forms of culture are creations. Culture itself is a creation of people as they respond to the environments in which they find themselves. The response is a set of problem-solving solutions selected by human groups from all the alternatives that are available to them to solve the particular problems posed in those environments. They create their real cultures, pick and choose from the beliefs and behaviors that allow them to survive in those environments. Ideal culture is created by the group as the set of things that must be learned by each member of the group. It is the standard by which they wish to be identified, the standard by which they want to see themselves. Perhaps it is what they want to be. The construct culture is thus a creation by people that allows them to bridge the apparent gaps between group ideals and realities. It helps people recognize and account for the contradictions and paradoxes inherent in the culture.

Construct cultures are created for others for the same operational purposes, for actions. Creating cultural descriptions for others helps individuals make sense out of the differences they see, their conclusions then becoming the basis of interacting with others. The ideal sets the standards for the group, the real provides for the limits of variation as the individuals live their culture, and the construct culture provides the basis for action. As attention is shifted to the topic of culture change, the need to understand these different forms of culture concept is paramount. In one way or another, aspects of all of them become important to the process. It is important to identify which form of culture is being changed, the real or the ideal. On a more pragmatic level, agents of change are always going to operate from the level of the construct culture, but each can become *the* significant factor in the change context. What is important for now is to understand that the context of change for humans is culture, and culture is not a single or simple thing.

Every society, regardless of size, has a distinct culture all its own: an integrated, adaptive, and always changing complex of learned ideas, behaviors, and products suited to the particular environments in which its members find themselves. Culture is created in response to problems posed in environments. It is a set of problem-solving solutions learned as truth. In the minds of every people, their culture is the most correct. They will judge all others based on it. What they have learned is actually three forms of that culture, and each will play a role in the culture change process. Any one form of it can guide, determine, and impact the people's responses and actions to the suggestion of changing any part of their culture. The same form of culture ill also guide and direct the actions of those attempting to bring about change. In the situation of culture contact and change, all of these elements of culture can play a major role in the process, interaction, and outcomes.

Humans group for all kinds of reasons. They group in response to problems or interests that arise in the natural or sociocultural environments created by their actions in responding to the natural environment. But not everyone chooses the same solution to the same problem. When all the needs are satisfied, we end up with a system of solutions to problems that together we call culture. All of these solutions are related to one another and form a coherent whole. The system is an integrated one that is then passed down from generation to generation as *the* way of thinking, believing, and doing. It has been created by the groups, and it becomes their reality. Culture becomes life's blueprint for thinking, acting, and believing. It becomes the road map that gets the group from one day to the next. Putting together all the learned ways that individuals accumulate over a lifetime, culture in one form or another provides them with all they need to know, prescribes all they are supposed to think and do as members of the groups to which they belong. It represents truth, their truth as they have learned it. They operate as if it is the only truth, or at the very least the most correct one.

SUGGESTED READINGS

The following works provide discussions on the concept of culture, its meaning, the various approaches anthropologists have taken to it, and its role in the human experience.

Barrett, Richard. 1984. *Culture and Conduct.* 2nd ed. This concisely written introduction to the concept of culture presents some good discussion on the adaptiveness of culture, the symbolic meaning of culture, and its persistence over time.

Freilich, M. (ed.). 1972. *The Meaning of Culture.* Through selected readings, this volume presents several different views of culture that were developed by some of the most significant figures in the history of anthropology.

Gamst, F. C., & Edward Norbeck. 1976. *Ideas of Culture: Sources and Uses.* This book is a collection of readings on the culture concept, and is considered a basic reader for anyone desiring to gain an understanding of the development of the concept in the discipline.

Rosman, Abraham, & Paula B. Rubel. 1989. *The Tapestry of Culture: An Introduction to Cultural Anthropology.* 3rd ed. This introductory textbook provides a clear statement of the basic concepts of cultural anthropology and shows the interrelatedness of the various aspects of culture. It also contains good discussion of how anthropology has applied its concepts to help solve some world problems.

Spradley, J. P., & David McCurdy. 1972. *The Cultural Experience.* Although primarily an introduction to cultural fieldwork, this volume does provide some interesting discussion of culture in the complex society with its presentation of twelve ethnographies taken from the American culture.

Chapter 3

EVOLUTION AND CHANGE

Change is a necessary part of culture whereby groupings and individuals adjust or alter their beliefs, behaviors, and material and sociocultural productions. If humans and their cultures are to survive, they must adjust to the constantly changing environments. Understanding the cultural context of change for humans, in all of its ideal, real, and construct forms, and as it can be applied to the general, specific, constituent, and cultural scene groupings, is crucial to any practical understanding of the process. Change for humans is basically a culture process, and this means it is part of the truth that all individuals learn as members of culture groups. All the members of culture groups share ideas, behaviors, and material and sociocultural products that serve to distinguish them from others. But it is also important to keep in mind that people associate with a number of different, sometimes diverse, cultures in their lifetime. These cultures come in three forms. Culture is made real as groups of humans create it while solving problems of survival. The real culture exists as the sum of all the beliefs, behaviors, and productions of all those individuals making up the group. Because real culture is such a composite, the totality of it eludes most members of any culture group. Few people will ever know all of their culture(s). The more complex the system, the more likely that members of the group will know just bits and pieces of it. This is particularly true in the case of the arbitrary and artificial nation-state, which by its very nature is a composite of many specific, constituent, and scene cultures. Members of culture groups actually learn, and are guided by, different forms of their cultures.

Ideal culture is transmitted to aspiring members of cultural groups, who must acquire it for membership in the group. Although they are presented this ideal culture and learn it, ideal culture rarely translates into actual practice on a one-to-one basis. Members of any culture group learn its ideals, but they also learn how far one can deviate from the ideals and still be accepted as a member of the group. They learn the limits of variation allowed, and they learn their own individual limitations in living up to the ideals. This means that operationally, individual members of a culture group live on a day-to-day basis with an individual construct form of their culture.

What is presented to people, and what they learn about their world in both ideal and real forms, is a complex system of interrelated ideas, behaviors, and material and sociocultural products that together make up the whole of their culture as they will know it. It exists as a set of problem-solving solutions to ensure their individual and group survival in the natural and sociocultural environments. A change in either of the environments poses a problem that must be solved, and this can mean a change in any or all of their culture's specific component parts. All cultures are continually changing as the environments change, but not all of them do it at the same rate, nor do they necessarily go about it in the same way or under the same circumstances.

The purpose of this chapter is to begin the process of ordering and developing a theoretical and practical framework for the complex topic of culture change. Building on the lessons of the past, a model will be presented that is based on both evolution and interaction. Evolution points to the continuous nature of change or adaptation. It is interactional, for adaptation itself speaks to interaction: between environments and cultures, individuals and groups, and between cultures. Interaction between culture groups dictates, directly or indirectly, most of the culture changes in the modern world. This model is not being proposed as the final ordering of culture change material; rather, it is presented as a start in that direction. It accounts for change on the broad level of continuous cultural adaptation and allows for its understanding on the specific level. The model is the result of the evolution of our thinking about change. It is also an invention, the recombination of ideas produced by a great many scholars who have made contributions to our developing understanding of the process. The model depicts the processes by which change is accomplished in any of its forms. It identifies the major components and dynamic interactions of that process, and it allows for some level of predictability.

HISTORICAL BACKGROUND

Anthropologists have always been concerned with change on the grand scale or as it pertains to the entire human group (Spindler 1977; Woods 1975). As they began to realize that not all cultures develop at the same rate or through the same developmental stages, they became concerned with change on a more limited basis, as it occurs in specific cultural groupings. Still later, as the impact of the Western world reached proportions that could not be ignored, they became interested in the change occasioned by contact between culture groups. In the first instance, the concern was to account for culture change across human prehistory and history, and for how individual societies experienced that change. It was clear that human cultures were moving in a particular direction, but equally clear that the experiences of individual societies in that movement were based on responses to their own specific or peculiar circumstances. Some of the change experienced came about simply because groups were in contact with other groups, as evidenced by the spread of Western culture through exploration, conquest, colonialism, and trade. Change from cultures in contact has increased substantially and steadily.

Culture contact and change now emanate largely from the activities of focused agencies, staffed and funded for the sole purpose of introducing some modification or alteration in a group's beliefs, behaviors, or the things that result from these. Culture change has assumed new dimensions and proportions unequaled in human history and prehistory. Because the world and its human cultures now change faster than they can be studied, because anthropologists have had to focus on the study of cultures that have already undergone substantial change, and because more and more people have sought help in influencing this process, the study of culture change has gone well beyond the broad and specific levels. It now encompasses change at any level and in any kind of group. It is fast becoming an encompassing, if not a consuming, concern of a great number of anthropologists.

Over the years, the topic of change has always received intense consideration from anthropologists, and a great many case studies have been done. Through those efforts, much has been learned about this culture process. Many models have been generated to account for culture change, some directed at the sweeping course of human history and prehistory, others focused on more narrow or limited circumstances of change as they might apply to specific groups and circumstances. The grand models aim at explaining the broad sweeps of human existence and are oriented around the basic premise that when environments change or modify, people generate new cultural responses. Environments pressure people to alter some aspect of their learned way of believing and behaving, their social or material culture. People respond with some modification, alteration, or shift in the general components of their culture to meet the demands introduced by the new conditions. In this sense, culture change is part of a definite and continuous process of human adaptation. (See Figure 3.1.)

A host of valuable terms and concepts have been generated to address the topic of change, but each has serious limitations. Most of the terms generated have not changed since they were introduced, despite the addition of new information and advances in culture change thinking. Whereas on the one hand, they have helped us to delineate the different aspects of this problem, even helped us to organize the multitude of case studies that have become available, they also have limited our ability to establish order and structure in culture change. They have focused our attention and energies on the end results of the change process as opposed to the process itself. The overriding concern has been to describe or identify results. On the broadest level, most people continue to use such terms as *progress*, *modernization, urbanization, development*, and *civilization* to speak of broad-level change. On a more specific level, they continue to use the concepts of acculturation, innovation, diffusion, and voluntary, nonvoluntary, directed, and nondirected change to address more limited aspects of this change. The proliferation of terms has not made the understanding of change any easier. The limitations of the change vocabulary have only highlighted the difficulties, especially in the arena of broad or generalized change.

The first terms to appear regarding change focused on change at the broadest

Figure 3.1
Culture Change as Ongoing Process

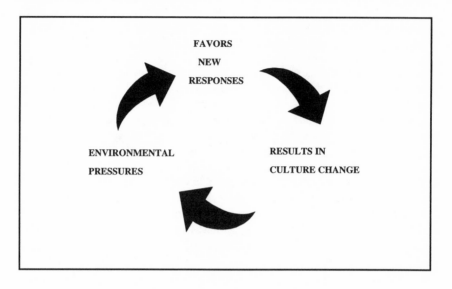

levels, as it impacted the entire human group. To identify movement by a group toward a better, more advanced, or more efficient way, the term *progress* emerged. Needless to say, progress depends on a perception of what constitutes a better way, and thus it is a highly biased, value-laden, and ethnocentric term. In popular usage, *modernization* has been used to speak of this same kind of change. *Modernization*, as it is most commonly used, distinguishes the new from the old. More often than not, the term is applied to technological changes, which are inevitably viewed as improvements (Magnarella 1974). Like *progress*, this term is value-laden for those who use it. Inherent in such terms as *progress* or *modernization* is the belief that new is always better than old. Both terms are readily applied to the once relatively isolated societies that now experience massive amounts of change moving them more and more toward the models of the highly complex societies. Use of these terms is also related to the tendency of people representing the complex societies to justify or rationalize the changes they have occasioned in small-scale societies. *Civilizing* and *civilization* are also used synonymously to speak of *progress* and *modernization*. These terms are used to speak of change on the broad level as well, but they are the most biased, ethnocentric, and value-laden, for they mean to cause or to emerge from a "savage," "barbarian," or (more often) "primitive" existence into the more polished and advanced state characterized by relative progress in the arts, science, and statecraft. These particular terms are used by those who tend to see themselves as having arrived at the pinnacle of civilization.

Referring to any progress, modernization or civilization is *development*, another highly ethnocentric term. Although development is nothing more than a simple act or process of unfolding, as applied to culture change it is most generally used by people who have assumed that change is for the better, or that it represents an improvement in the lives of the people. In practice, most people use it to refer to movement in the direction of the modern nation-state or civilization. Even *urbanization* is used for the broadest-level change and is equated with all of the other terms (Spindler 1977). Many models have been proposed to describe the relationships between various processes that produce these results. The tendency to focus on results probably originated with such terminology, as did the general failure to recognize the ethnocentric or biased assumptions associated with them.

Although most, if not all, human cultures appear to be moving in the general direction of more complex forms, not all societies and their cultures go through the same stages of development, do so at the same pace, or using the same processes to get there. Beyond the grand design for human culture, and to account for the specific sequence of change for particular culture groups, an interesting array of other models and terms has been generated. Louise Spindler (1977) refers to these as "mini-models."According to Spindler, such models can be viewed as "subprocesses" focusing on particular circumstances within the grand process. In nearly every one of the models proposed for change on the specific level, innovation, acculturation, and diffusion appeared as subprocesses of adaptation. Some have gone so far as to identify them as the sources of evolutionary change over the broad expanse of human existence. Most of these models represent attempts to account for aspects of general evolution, taking into consideration specific circumstances. Unfortunately, scholars and lay people alike continue to use them in almost the exact fashion they were originally proposed.

Innovation was generated to address how individual cultures internally went about changing to meet new needs. It provided that cultures changed through: *discovery* and *invention*, sometimes referred to as primary and secondary innovation. *Discovery* or *primary innovation* refers to the chance discovery of some new principle never perceived before. *Invention* or *secondary innovation* refers to the result of deliberate application of known principles. *Diffusion* was later added to account for the spread of a new trait. Innovation was viewed as a nondirected process that produced change within a particular group. The idea was to distinguish between change that originated within a group and change that came as a result of being in contact with others. In its simplest form, innovation pointed to change initiated through invention or discovery by someone within the group. Diffusion was offered up as the means by which it spreads throughout the group, basically copied or borrowed by the other members. *Acculturation* was generated to account for the change that comes with close and continuous contact with other cultures. According to this model, change that comes with contact is either voluntary—a trait was simply borrowed—or it is nonvoluntary, imposed by fiat or forced draft. People in the cultures in contact can simply borrow from each other, or the change can be forced by one of the groups onto the other.

Initially, the major thrust of acculturation thinking was to the result of contact, primarily the *assimilation* of one culture group to the beliefs and behaviors of the other. The idea that there is actually some assimilation of both cultures in contact was later added in recognition that in contact situations change is experienced by both dominant and subordinate groups, and dominant groups are also changed in the process. But this again reinforced the focus on the results of the contact as opposed to its dynamics. Diffusion became associated with the acculturation process by virtue of the voluntary borrowing observed in most contact situations. Voluntarily accepting a change from some other group accounted for the spread of many traits among cultures. Acculturation theorists recognized that in contact situations, borrowing is a major means by which cultures changed, and thus acculturation was deemed a process of changing cultures; and diffusion became synonymous with change through borrowing. It was also recognized that in contact circumstances, although change can come from voluntary borrowing or forced draft, some change is simply the result of historical accident. Still later, *planned* or *directed change* was identified as a variation of acculturation, not really diffusion (borrowing) or forced imposition but change through direct intervention, planned, directed, or implemented from one culture to another. Each of these subprocesses, as they became known, provided new information on circumstances of culture change. Putting them together into a coherent theory on change has not been easy, however.

A whole new change terminology emerged from a large number of acculturation studies, almost all of which pointed to the end results of cultures in contact. As one might expect, there were all manner of suggestions as to the kind of assimilation that results from contact. For example, assimilation can mean incorporative, partial, or complete assimilation, and it can also mean integration, fusion, or simply reorientation. All kinds of changes were then noted, which only added to the proliferation of terms. *Forced draft, fiat,* and *decree; voluntary* and *enforced; syncretism; surface* and *accidental change* were all, at one time or another, identified as among the possibilities. When acculturation studies were undertaken, the predisposition was to document the result, to identify which of these kinds of changes were experienced by the group under scrutiny. The emphasis on result naturally led to the assumption that the change was completed in one or another of these forms. That change is ongoing and dynamic was overlooked in the process. Reflecting on such studies, it is probably more appropriate to say that the kinds of changes noted for such cultures were only steps or stages of this ongoing process. Restudies would undoubtedly produce vastly different conclusions.

Although the creation of this vocabulary attests to the idea that a great deal has been done to add to our body of data and knowledge about culture change, the lack of theoretical and practical structure in our theory is apparent. Increasingly, people are asking for help in planning and coping with change, especially its more negative aspects. Scholars, on the other hand, continue to call for more case studies and to utilize concepts and ideas about change exactly as they were originally proposed. Cultures are changing, but the scholars of change perhaps are not. Louise Spindler noted that while all cultures are constantly changing, there is also universal persistence of culture forms. Her comments can easily be applied to the culture of anthropology: "Any culture will be made up partly of ways of doing things and thinking that are in the process of change, and partly made up of ways of doing and thinking that have persisted past the point where they are useful" (1977:4).

EVOLUTION

Change is nothing more than an alteration–perhaps an addition, subtraction, or modification—to something. In cultural terms, change is an addition, subtraction, alteration, or modification in belief, behavior, or sociocultural product. No culture today is the same as it has always been. Cultures have changed as the social and natural environments have changed. Another way to speak of the totality of the changes that have occurred in human culture from its origins to its current state(s) is to use the concepts of evolution and adaptation. Normally, when people hear the term *evolution*, they immediately begin to think about the physical development of humans. This is unfortunate, for the concept of evolution applies equally to the sociocultural aspects of humans. *Evolution* simply refers to a kind of change whereby what is now, is a product of what has preceded it. It bespeaks of how all things modify, grow, and develop over time. It can even be applied to our thoughts about culture change. Evolution speaks to change and, as applied to cultures, suggests that they have developed over a long time into what we now can see them to be, just as individuals have developed into what they are at any particular point in their lives. Neither humans nor cultures appeared miraculously out of nowhere, or in the forms in which they presently exist. From elemental beginnings, human cultures have taken a few million years to develop into the varied stages in which they now exist. Over those many years, cultures evolved as surely as they will continue to evolve, for evolution is an ongoing process. What culture is today is only the current stage of a process not yet complete.

At the heart of the evolutionary process is the concept of adaptation, which relates to the capacity for surviving and reproducing. An adaptation is a specific change in structure that allows for more efficient operation. In physical terms, this has meant the selection of physical traits in the continual adjustment of the physical organism to the natural environment. Adaptation focuses on the natural biological processes in the selection of genetic traits enhancing the chances of survival of the organism. For most living things, it is the process by which the organisms adjust to particular environments or changes in them. Physical organisms must adjust to the natural environment, or they cannot survive. It is in this sense that environment dictates to most of the animal world. In the case of the human animal, physical adaptation remains important, but culture has allowed humans to respond to, supplant, even overpower many of the dictates of the natural environment.

Whereas other animals must largely adapt physiologically for survival, humans use culture to respond the environments pressures and limitations. Learned culture, as opposed to biological inheritance, is the major adaptation process for humans. Although certainly grounded in a biologically inherited capacity, most of human adaptation is through culture, which must be learned. It has given the human animal the capacity to overcome many limitations of the natural environment. Humans cannot prevent such things as earthquakes or severe weather conditions, but they can adapt to them by using culture. They can adjust to the limits imposed upon them by the natural environment, control its impacts to a large degree, change it to suit their purposes, even supplant it with an artificially created sociocultural environment or culturally created substitutes. Culture has given humans the capacity to mitigate, even to override, much of the naturally occurring selection process that accounts for their physical nature and that of virtually all other living things. As humans adapt to their environment, as they change to meet new challenges posed by their constantly changing environments, their cultures change and evolve.

In the beginning, as humans first relied on more than their biological inheritance to respond to pressure from the natural environment, stepped beyond their physical limits to survive, the relationship between that natural environment and culture was a direct one. Humans simply adapted to the problems posed with something other than their innate physical capabilities. That culture is the human adaptation to environment is accepted at some level by nearly everyone. It remains so despite the fact that much in the natural environment remains outside of the abilities of humans to impact. Even in today's world, with all the technological advances made by humans, when the natural environment changes dramatically, humans must still respond to that change or at least cope with the limitations imposed by it. Since the beginnings, coping with environmental conditions or changes in them has always been a regular part of culture, but now this adaptation presupposes a great deal more than simply responding to the natural environment. Humans have learned things that have allowed them to survive despite the limitations of the natural environment. What they have learned has created the second environment to which they must now also adapt to survive, the sociocultural environment. Although humans must continually adapt to natural conditions, the major environmental pressure for change now comes from the created sociocultural environments.

Because of the relationship between natural environment and culture, the most popular model for explaining adaptation and evolution on the broadest scale has been the ecological one. Based upon the idea that humans use cultures to adapt to the natural environment, this model seems quite reasonable, at least in addressing cultural origins and early developments in human culture. The ecological model was developed in response to earlier unilineal models deemed insufficient to explain cultural evolution. Unilineal models depicted all human cultures as going through the same basic stages of development, from the simple to the complex. But these models had a hard time accounting for the cultural variations that existed. Cultural ecology accounted for the differences among the cultures by relating specific environments and specific cultures. The basic premise of cultural ecology was that only after a group has reacted to an environment do people devise strategies to cope with it, become innovate, make decisions, or devise personal strategies to respond to it. The core of the model rests on coping behavior, which translates as a natural environment being mediated by the sociocultural environment or culture. Not only does this point to the adaptation of humans to the natural environment, it also allows for the consideration of the sociocultural environment. Cultures evolved in response realization that the evolutionary model had to encompass both a general and a specific consideration. Unfortunately, most people could not relate the model directly to the change process, for it was directed at "after-the-fact" phenomena. It

Figure 3.2
Adaptation

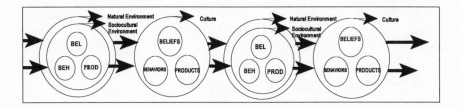

did suggest the dynamic interaction of environment with culture, however, and in this respect can be directly related to culture change.

To say that culture has evolved or continues to evolve is another way of saying that it has changed and is continuing to change overtime. Each new development or stage of its evolution is a modification or product of what has preceded it. Most of our present technology is primarily based on what has preceded it. New ideas and sociocultural productions are largely the result of earlier ones. In the general direction of change in human cultural components, a pattern has clearly emerged. Things have simply gotten more complex. Accounting for this complexity and directional movement has been a preoccupation of many scholars who have tried with measured effort to determine the prime mover in this directional development of culture. Energy capture, the control of water, irrigation, the development of food production, and even the control of fire have all been suggested as the ultimate source (or cause) of culture's development on the grand scale. All of these suggestions point to some increased control over environment that culture has provided for humans. Whatever the experts may ultimately identify as the prime mover in the evolution of culture, increases in population, specialization, fragmentation, and differentiation will all have to be taken into account, along with function.

If one accepts that culture is a set of solutions to the problems or limitations posed by the environment, the evolution of culture and its developing complexity can easily be visualized. For example, the first basic problem for humans, if not the most basic problem for all animals, is food. The natural environment initially set the limits of possibility in this regard. In determining how to resolve the subsistence (food) requirement, humans selected from among the alternatives available to them. But once a selection is made, additional problems are then created which also require solutions. For example, a group can elect to hunt whales for food, but then they face the problems posed by the choice: how to get to the whales, how to kill them, how to prepare then, and so on. As these secondary problems are addressed from among the alternative choices, their solutions pose even more problems that need to be addressed. In responding to a single and most basic need, sets of problem-solving actions are created (see Figure 3.3). Given the relationship of the first problem and its solution to the secondary problems and their solutions, the

Figure 3.3
Pyramidal Effect of Problem Solutions

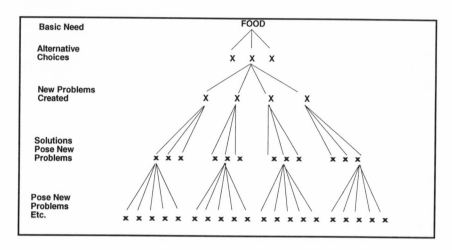

focusing on only this particular basic human need, one can see that culture takes on
integrated nature of culture is not only evidenced, it is assured. In many ways, by
a pyramidal appearance. One problem and its solution creates new problems for
solution, and these create still other problems requiring actions, until one reaches
the complete and complex set of problem-solving solutions used by the human
group to meet this most basic aspect of survival. Of course the developing
complexity associated with solving one basic need is only part of it, for that need
is directly related to other basic needs and their solutions.

When people address other basic survival issues, the same pyramidal effect is
created, but is made infinitely more complicated by the relationships between all of
these problems and their solutions. Each ultimately impacts the other, perhaps even
determines which of the alternative possibilities must be chosen. For example,
history has shown us that among the hunters and gatherers, certain social structures,
such as the extended family, are more efficient in adapting to the subsistence lifestyle. Without a regular surplus, the market-exchange alternative for distribution in
their economic system is not a viable one. In food production societies, where there
is a regular surplus and the market-exchange system develops, the nuclear family
is a better adaptation. As human groups moved from their simpler hunter and
gatherer existence, revolving around the family, to food production, other social
structures were more favored. In the modern industrialized nation-state, social
structure involves the most complicated and diversified social groupings of all. In
the hunter and gatherer systems, it is most often the case that the family becomes
for the society and its culture to survive. In the modern industrialized state, this is
not the case. In both circumstances, however, it is clear that the culture components
are closely related.

INTERACTION

Human evolution speaks directly to interaction between culture and the people who share it, and environment. Humans respond to the problems or limitations posed by the environment(s). In responding to the natural environment, as humans used learned ways to do so, they created the sociocultural environment. Culture is the primary means of adaptation for humans, the mechanism by which they adjust to their environments in order to survive. Once initiated, the process of culture evolution or change rests on continual interactions between the natural and sociocultural environments; between the integrated components of culture which are individuals and groups, groups and groups; and the broad and limited changes of general and specific evolution. The natural and sociocultural environments are the source of all change, for as environments change, cultures must change. Culture is the mechanism of adaptation for humans.

The model to be proposed for culture change incorporates this general idea and revolves around interactions between environments and the actions of people that allow for continual adaptation. Environment is the source of all change, keeping in mind that for humans the natural environment is augmented by the sociocultural environments. Cultures must adapt to changes in either one, or perhaps both, or they do not survive. The fact that cultures continue to survive is the best evidence that there exists in all cultures some means by which necessary change is accomplished. Change has occurred when the majority of the people have accepted an alteration or modification of their learned patterns. Either type of environment may pressure for a shift, but someone has to come up with the idea, behavior, or products to respond. If a response is already in existence somewhere else, the individual can simply borrow it and fit that response to his or her own circumstances. If it is not already available, the response must be generated. Before a borrowed or generated idea becomes a culture change, however, it must spread to the majority of a culture's membership. Until that time, it may simply exist as a "new" idea, "interesting" idea, or alternative to an existing pattern.

Adaptation is the result of humans accommodating to their environments by using culture. The major components of adaptation are environment(s), culture(s), and change process(es). The continuing adaptation of humans occurs via the change processes. In other words, the need or pressure for change comes from either of the environments, perhaps both, but then someone has to come up with a response and initiate a change in existing beliefs, behaviors, or products to meet the need. No culture change has ever occurred simply because someone came up with an idea, some action is required. Coming up with an idea is only the first step. For a culture change to actually occur, the idea must spread to the other members of the culture group and become part of their learned patterns. As with environment and culture, the process of spreading a new or altered belief, behavior, or sociocultural product can occur only through interaction, and this is the process of culture change. An individual or group of individuals must interact with other members of the culture group to spread the change. Interaction lies at the heart of the change process from its beginnings to completion. Natural and sociocultural environments interact, as individuals interact with individuals, and groups interact with groups.

Adaptation points to the interaction between environment and groups of people who have created and learned ways to deal with environment and its limitations. Culture change is initiated in one of two ways: (1) people come up with the response themselves or (2) they get it from someone else who has already satisfactorily solved the problem. The concepts of innovation and acculturation are used to differentiate between these ways. Innovation and acculturation are useful in identifying the specific circumstances or contexts of change, but are incorrectly identified as the processes of change. Although they indicate the context within which the response to environmental pressures will originate, they are not the processes by which the change will ultimately be accomplished. For this reason, the distinction generated with the terms remains useful in identifying the origins or context of change, not the process by which it is actually accomplished. A group of people can create their own response or they can take it from someone else, but then it must be integrated into their learned ways of belief, behavior, and productions that constitute their whole culture. For the response to become a culture change, it still must be accepted by the group and integrated into the learned system. How this is accomplished directs us to the real change process, the spread of the new trait from the individual to the majority of the group. This can be accomplished only through personal interaction.

Environments pressure human groups to devise new ways to cope with new conditions or limitations imposed by the environments (see Figure 3.4). People respond with culture belief, behavior, or products, which then impact the environments, producing additional pressures for cultures to change. The resulting pattern is a continuous one, as is shown in Figure 3.2. The natural environmental pressures can come from available resources, changing states of those resources, climate conditions or changes, catastrophic events, population pressures, even culturally introduced changes in the environment. For example, cultural activity can change the environment, change the air or natural landscape, even destroy parts of the natural environment, supplanting it with culturally created physical environments. Sociocultural environmental pressures can come from the area of human relations, changes in these and relations between cultural groups, material products and their consequences, technological changes and their consequences, or changes in political, economic, or religious ideas, beliefs, or products. In responding to such changes and pressures, people find ways to deal with the problems they pose. By themselves, they can discover a cure for the problem by using what they already have or know in some new or unique combination. They can also get a solution from somebody else either directly or indirectly. They can get it directly from others who may have successfully addressed a similar problem, or indirectly by borrowing something that they sense might work and adapting it to their particular problem. In this respect, they can simply borrow the solution, the solution can be imposed upon them, or it can be planned and directed from outside their own group. To understand the processes of change, one begins by identifying whether the idea for change originates internally (involving only one culture group) or externally (as a result of cultural contacts).

Figure 3.4
Environmental Adaptation/Interaction

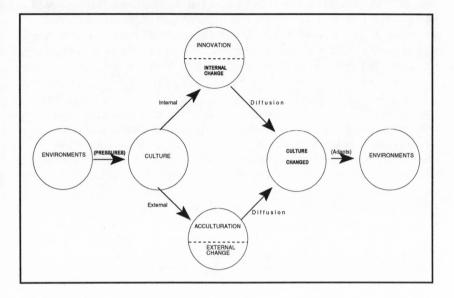

INNOVATION AND CULTURE CHANGE

Nearly everyone would agree that culture change is important to the survival of a culture. Culture groups unable to adjust to changing conditions litter the garbage heaps of history and prehistory. Innovation has always been important in understanding the change process (Barnett 1953). By themselves, and with no contacts or interference from other cultures, people always seem to come up with some new idea, behavior, or product to better adapt to changing conditions. Innovation is based on the notion that someone within a culture group perceives a need for a change and develops a new idea, behavior, or product to respond to it. Once the new idea, behavior, or product is generated and accepted by a majority of the group, as an addition, subtraction, substitution, or modification to any of the existing cultural components, it represents a culture change. Of course, this assumes that the new or modified trait becomes part of the learned ways of aspiring group members. Unfortunately, innovation is cemented to the notion of "internal process" of culture change, used only with reference to the way in which people within culture groups go about changing their established and learned ways. As such, innovation is limited to that context and viewed as a nondirected, self-generated, and voluntary process. In the sense that innovation was viewed as only an internal phenomenon, one not occasioned by outside contact, interference, or direction, it became synonymous with nondirected change. This clouds the actual circumstances.

To say that innovation is limited to change that results from just internal activities ignores other realities. Change associated with external forces and groups (e.g., borrowing, induced, enforced, directed, or planned change) is usually associated with acculturation. Innovation, acculturation and diffusion have long been held to be the "major processes" of culture change. As has been suggested, innovation and acculturation may be useful in identifying the contexts or parameters within which change occurs, but not as change processes. Neither one is a process of change. Going one step further, innovation is the first step and last step in all culture change, with or without culture contacts. Ideas must be generated internally somewhere, and they must be operationalized within a group somewhere, before one can speak of culture change. As for acculturation, or what has been identified as change resulting from culture contacts, contacts between different cultural groupings must assuredly be involved in nearly all culture change. This will be so because nearly every specific culture group consists of a number of subgroupings or constituent cultural groupings, at the very least, a number of cultural scenes. This is especially so in the case of complex nation-states, that are made up of a number of specific constituent cultural groupings and cultural scenes. Virtually all culture change will involve contacts between culture groups.

Innovation is constantly occurring in all cultures. Initially, all innovations represent variations that are made available to members of the group, perhaps as choice variations. Someone is always coming up with a unique twist in style and fashion, technology, or whatever. Most are individualist, fleeting, transitory, or idiosyncratic, and are quickly rejected or replaced by the newest fad. The reasons for their rejection are many and varied. In American culture and society, to change clothing styles, automobile design, or computer chips each year is a regular part of the culture. In such cultures, it is economically necessary that such changes be introduced, then made quickly obsolete. Sometimes, such fads are rejected almost immediately, as impractical or too far from basic values or established patterns. At other times, such transitory innovations become choice variations within the group. For example, in American fashion, only those in the highest economic strata may be able to participate in the system, and even temporary acceptance is limited to this minority group. As long as the change remains within the limits of variation allowed in the culture group collectively, it can continue to exist as an alternative choice. Over the short and institutionalized period of time for fashions, the new and the old exist side by side as acceptable choice variations. Whatever the case, innovations are constantly occurring, and only when they have been accepted by the majority of the group is it appropriate to refer to them as culture changes.

As the term *innovation* has been used, the people responsible for it have been called *innovators*, and the changes introduced have been perceived as nondirected in the sense that they were self-generated within the group, with no outside contacts or pressures. The internal change in any of culture's components was seen to come from either discovery or invention only. Invention represented alterations or syntheses of existing things into new forms of material, idea, or action (Barnett 1942). It could take on a concrete form, as with a material or action pattern, or it could come in abstract form, as with an idea. Discovery was to perceive something never perceived before. For example, physical elements in science all represent discoveries, but neutron separation would be seen as an invention. When science adds new elements to its inventory, each one of them represents a discovery. The first tools used by humans were discoveries, each representing something never considered or perceived before. Modern technology is probably more invention, for once energy capture was perceived, new tools were generated out of older ones, perhaps as recombinations or as the result of the synthesis of existing information and knowledge. Although both discovery and invention would seem to identify how changes originate and take form within culture groups, they do not identify all the ways change can be accomplished. Internal change or innovation can also be tied to change introduced through borrowing or through some form of coercion.

Innovation certainly represents the first step in any change process, regardless of circumstances. All change must be initiated by someone already within a culture context, the innovator. If this were not so, there would be no change anywhere or at any time. But innovation is related to culture contact situations as well, a significant part of acculturation. When something is obtained as a result of contact with others, the individual who borrows it from the other group will still be the innovator as far as generating culture change within his or her own group. All changes occur within specific contexts, regardless of their origins. When a trait is borrowed from another group, invention is quite likely to come into play once again. For example, when speaking of borrowed items, it has long been recognized that rarely are such things taken without some alteration or adjustment by the borrower so that it will fit into his or her particular culture system (Kroeber 1940). A trait can be borrowed with or without direct contact, but in nearly every case the borrowed trait is reworked. A borrowed trait taken directly or indirectly, with or without content (as in stimulus diffusion), is reworked in form, use, meaning, or function to fit the context into which it is introduced. How does this differ from invention? The borrower becomes inventive in adapting the item taken from somewhere else to the specific needs of his or her own group. Invention is not limited to innovation or internal change; it applies equally to changes originating outside the group. This suggests that innovation is not only associated with changes that come from within the group but also is relevant to change in any context.

Although innovators generate ideas for change, they may not be the agents who actually bring it about or who ultimately spread the change throughout a culture group. Because something is invented, discovered, or borrowed does not mean that it will automatically becomes a culture change. Someone has to assume the responsibility or task of getting others within the group to accept the trait until it spreads to all, or at least to a majority of its members. For any new idea, trait, behavior or product to become a culture change—whether the source be invention, discovery, or contact and borrowing—it must spread throughout the group and be adopted as part of its learned ways. When something is innovated or obtained through contacts with others, the individual(s) who borrow(s) it from another group is (are) still going to be the innovator(s) for the group. But borrowers may not be the actual change agents, just as innovators may not be. An individual can discover something, invent it, or borrow it from others. But that represents little more than "planting the seed" for change. The seed must still grow or, in the case of human

Figure 3.5
Innovation and Internal Culture Change

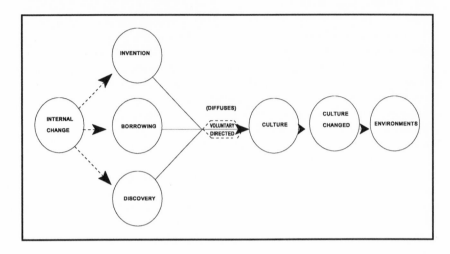

change, the new trait must spread to the majority of the group and be adopted into its learned patterns. This focuses our attention on the real processes of change, the dynamics through which an innovation actually becomes a culture change. The importance of innovation in the change process remains, but now it becomes the essential step in all change, with or without culture contact.

Addressing the innovator or change agent, and how an innovation spreads or is spread to the other members of the group, points to change process(es). This obviously involves interactions, individual and group, perhaps group to group. Because of this, the question of the role of the individual in culture change process arises. In essence, it is the role of the individual in human history that is questioned. Does man make history, or does history make the man? On one side of the question are those who suggest that culture takes precedence over individuals, who do not even choose their beliefs, which are provided by the culture. This position belies human inventiveness or innovativeness. On the other side of the argument are those who suggest that it is with the individual that culture is determined, for ultimately all culture groups consist of individuals. In reality, it should not be an either/or choice; both must be considered. There is little doubt that for most members of a group, the culture beliefs, behaviors, and products are already determined. This is what the culture group passes along in order for the culture to survive. In this sense, individual achievement is a product of the culture pattern applied to the individual. It is the group who will determine whether the individual achieves. If they recognize the individual as having met the criteria they have established, in that recognition of it, the person has achieved; if they do not, he or she has not. One achieves through recognition of the group; without the group there is no achievement. Most individual members of a culture group will go through life doing and thinking as they have been taught, albeit unconsciously for the most part.

On the other hand, cultures do change. This must start with an individual or group of individuals. Because cultures change, there cannot be a determinism of culture over all the individuals within the group. Someone will innovate a change in the culture's beliefs, behaviors, or products. But the new idea must spread to the remaining members of the group. In some cases, there are those who will involve themselves solely with that. In the natural sciences, one scientist may discover something, another may apply it, and still another may diffuse this throughout the group. Innovating in a culture is only the first step in the process, which remains incomplete until the change has been spread to the majority, at which point it represents a culture change. Obviously, the role of the individual is crucial in the innovation and spread of the modification, as well as in the acceptance of a new trait, for the collective of individuals constitutes the majority that must opt for the change. This suggests that there has to be some interaction between the individual and the group, a means whereby the idea spreads from one to the others. Innovations spread to the group through one of two ways: voluntarily accepted by others who choose to follow it, or directed. In this context,"directed" means there is an organized attempt on the part of someone, innovator or change agent to get others to accept the new idea, much as the advertiser attempts to sell the public a new product. To suggest that innovation simply occurs and then becomes internal change ignores the fact that any change may be adopted by the group. Other individuals within the group may simply copy the trait (no different from borrowing it), or they can be convinced through persuasion that they should accept it. In either case, it must be spread to the group, and this can be accomplished only through direct or indirect interactions of individuals and groups. Such terms as *directed*, *forced*, or *nonvoluntary change* are usually reserved for the acculturation process.

ACCULTURATION AND CHANGE

Although all change begins with innovation, there has always been a general recognition that the greater number of changes in any culture come by way of direct or indirect culture contacts and borrowing. *Acculturation* was generated to account for change that occurs with culture contact, such as the sometimes rapid and massive culture changes that accompanied the spread of Western culture across the world through the ages of discovery, exploration, and colonialism (Redfield et al. 1936). For the most part, it continues to be used for change that results from two or more cultures in close and continuous contact, the end product being the partial or complete assimilation of one culture into another. Acculturation occurs when a culture undergoes drastic alteration in the direction of conformity to another culture, through borrowing ideas, behaviors, or things from that other culture. As such, it can also mean the accommodation or adjustment, acceptance or assimilation of a subordinate group into the ways of a dominant one. It can even mean cultural loss by one of the cultures in contact.

As originally proposed, the idea of acculturation incorporated many ideas that

Figure 3.6
Acculturation

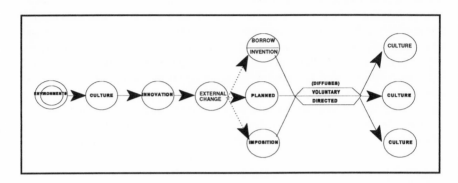

could be found in diffusion (e.g., borrowing, culture contact, voluntary and nonvoluntary change, nondirected and directed change). Most important, acculturation was identified as a culture change process. A great many studies were done on the properties of contact, the nature of contact, the coming together of cultures, and most important, the results of contact. As with traditional innovation, acculturation focused attention on context and result (see Figure 3.6). To take into account more specific circumstances in acculturation studies, modernization and urbanization models were generated as variations of the acculturation model. Simply stated, both were adaptive changes necessary because of the urban context. For example, change was necessary for rural individuals having to adapt to city conditions. Most cultural adaptations focused on scale, particularly in social relationships; and the urban environment, although variable, was based on rationality. People had to adjust to decisions of efficiency and pragmatism. Developing and modernizing societies involved such adjustments.

Nearly all of the acculturation studies were preoccupied with pinpointing the nature of the assimilation of one culture group to the ways of another. Integration, incorporative assimilation, fusion, or reorientation were some of the possibilities identified. Much of the present-day vocabulary of culture change and a multitude of different "kinds" of acculturation also were generated out of these studies. Planned change became solidified in the literature, as did voluntary change. The distinction between these two ideas rested on the presence or absence of forced draft, and on the kind of change that occurred simply because people were in contact. Much discussion on the prioritization of technical change, enforced change, syncretism, and superficial and accidental change was also a by-product of the acculturation studies. From such discussions, a number of change regularities were identified which demonstrated that change was patterned, not quixotic. This did not mean that it was predictable. There were similarities, but the process was independent of specific culture forms, an idea that has kept the element of predictability out of culture change.

At the heart of acculturation has always been the idea of nonvoluntary change. As with nondirected change in innovation discussions, the use of this term was unfortunate. It did speak to change that was not voluntarily accepted, in the sense that people or groups simply borrowed the idea, but it also suggested that directed change fell only within the parameters of acculturation. The usual arguments focused on the fact that without contact, the change might not have occurred. Quite possibly true, but the real point is that change resulted from contact between culture groups. As with innovation, the spread of the idea is the issue, and this can come only with interaction—which obviously had to occur first within a group, then between groups. The action patterns by which this is accomplished are the same with or without culture contacts. Changes are either voluntarily accepted or they are directed.

DIFFUSION AND CHANGE

Although most people recognize acculturation and innovation as the major processes of the adaptation of culture to environment, others viewed diffusion as important, perhaps second to innovation in the change process (Rogers 1983). The concept of diffusion was developed to refer to that change brought about through borrowing, with or without culture contact. This perception is tied to diffusionist theory about culture. Borrowing lies at the heart of that theory, which suggests that most cultures develop by borrowing from others. As originally conceived, *diffusion* also meant *syncretism* and *reinterpretation*, even *reciprocal borrowing* in contact situations. Such ideas were based on regularities that were noted in the case studies. Material items and technological processes were generally more readily borrowed than abstract things. In accepting these, people frequently reworked, altered in some fashion, what was borrowed to fit their context. In many cases, a trait or complex, but not its content, was borrowed. The reason for the borrowing was based on some perceived advantage in doing so. The idea of selectivity was central to this.

What happened after something was borrowed also received considerable attention. Diffusion actually did point to change processes, at least in the spread of ideas, behaviors, or productions. But its value became minimized as it came to mean change solely through borrowing and the spread of traits from one culture to another. Diffusion also has a role to play in internal change, because new traits must spread from the individual to the group (at least a majority of its members), and from culture group to culture group, as in the case of cultural scenes and constituent cultures of the nation-states.

Allied to past perceptions of diffusion were discussions on its mechanisms or circumstances. For example, diffusion could occur through direct contact, intermediate contact, or planned or directed conditions. This brought into play all manner of discussion on directed or planned change. As a form of diffusion, planned change engendered consideration of all manner of other things: change by fiat/draft, voluntary change, syncretism, superficial change, accidental change, barriers and stimulants, necessary components of change, and many other aspects.

Figure 3.7
Diffusion

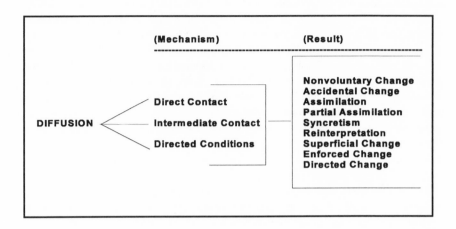

The tendency to see directed change as a limited form of diffusion is a natural by-product of continuing to see it primarily as borrowing. In reality, the former vision of diffusion as a primary process of change continues to inhibit its real value in understanding culture change. Diffusion is not a major process of culture change, but a part of that process accounting for how change moves from the individual or group innovating it to the rest of the culture. It is also part of the process by which a change moves from one group to another. Diffusion points to the interactional mechanism or action process whereby any change originated in any context is moved from person to person, group to group, until it is completed. It can be accomplished through an action process whereby people voluntarily accept the idea or change, or it can involve action processes that direct its acceptance. Either way, it still identifies the spread of an innovation throughout a culture or between cultures. Process implies a continuous change over time, as something proceeds, progresses, or advances. Diffusion is none of these and all of these, for it is the mechanism by which an idea spreads sufficiently to be classified as a culture change. Although diffusion can assume different forms (e.g., voluntary or directed), it is from defusion that change as an interactional process clearly emerges.

MODEL FOR CULTURE CHANGE

It would seem clear at this point that interactions lie at the heart of culture change, irrespective of its context. It begins with the interactions of environments, people, and their cultures as part of the adaptation of humans (see Figures 3.2– 3.4). Environment is the major source of change, and humans respond with their cultural beliefs and practices. When these prove to be insufficient for the problem, they devise new responses. Innovation, through invention or discovery, is the first step of the change process, regardless of whether change involves a single culture or a number of them (see Figure 3.5). A change starts with an idea, but thereafter some kind of interaction among people, within or between culture groups, is necessary to accomplish it. Internal change focuses on an individual or group of individuals coming up with an innovation for their particular group through discovery, invention, or borrowing from some other group (see Figure 3.6). External change bespeaks of someone borrowing an idea from another group, then making it an innovation for his or her group. In both cases, the innovation must then spread throughout the group to become part of its belief and action system. Spreading the innovation throughout the group can be accomplished only through the interactions of people. Neither innovation or acculturation is a change process: they only point to the context of the change. They are not, in and of themselves, the processes whereby a new or suggested modification in any of culture's components actually becomes a culture change. Both are dependent on the inherent idea of diffusion, the spread of new traits, and this depends on the interactions between individuals and groups (see Figure 3.7). Through such interaction, a new idea spreads to the majority necessary for it to be classified as a culture change.

The proliferation of terminology that accompanied traditional uses of *innovation, acculturation* and *diffusion* (voluntary, nonvoluntary, directed, nondirected, forced draft, fiat, etc.) pointed to the process of change, but the preoccupation with result clouded our ability to see it. All of these can be reduced to two basic processes of change: (1) a new trait can be voluntarily accepted or (2) its acceptance can be directed. Whether contacts between cultures are present or not, they represent the actual processes of change. Voluntary acceptance of change seems to be the easier to deal with, for people simply choose on their own to accept a new idea or trait, or they do not. An innovator comes up with the idea or trait, people become aware of it, and for any number of reasons begin to utilize, copy, or adopt it into their individual life patterns. When the majority of people in the group do so, as it becomes the accepted knowledge required for new members, a culture change has occurred. One of the major reasons anyone will voluntarily accept anything new is that it fulfills a need. In essence, people voluntarily adopt a new trait or idea when they are motivated to do so by virtue of a felt need. There are many reasons for people to accept a change, to be motivated to incorporate it into their lives. In terms of physical environment, the idea, object, or trait responds to a real problem. Motivation can also come from the sociocultural environment, in that a change may provide status or prestige to an individual, provide political or economic advantage, and so on. It may simply be tied to novelty, to status equalization ("keeping up with the Joneses"), or, in cases such as the United States, tied to the fact that it is new and all new things are judged to be better. Assuming that when a change meets any of the felt needs of individuals, it will be voluntarily accepted, is a false assumption. Some changes may not be accepted even if they meet such needs. There are other individual and group considerations that must be taken into account, and there are questions of fit, unplanned consequences, historical accidents, and outside forces that have to be considered as well.

The fit of a change to existing patterns is a significant element. Change will be measured against its perceived value in responding to a need, but its fit will also enter the equation. People can be motivated to accept a change, but that does not mean they will do so. A change may be acceptable in meeting a felt need, but actual acceptance will also depend on its fit into existing cultural patterns. For a change to fit, existing cultural values, social forms, economic and political realities, sufficiency of technology, and so forth must be considered. The question of whether the change is appropriate to existing things naturally comes up. Does it fit into the sequence, and is it timely for the individual and culture? A need can be met, but all manner of psychological, social, and cultural barriers can be put into its path. Its benefits are measured against its costs, and individuals decide whether to accept it. The barriers can be different from individual to individual.

The voluntary action process is the easier of the processes to understand or comprehend, because people accept change based on their perception of whether it satisfies a need they identify for themselves. Unfortunately, such rationalizations or excuses for accepting change are likely not to be cross-cultural, and it is probably rare that someone simply comes up with an innovation that then spreads through the culture group without specific efforts. Because of the nature of culture—the fact that ideas, behaviors, and sociocultural products are all oriented toward important tasks or problems—some specific actions are usually required to spread a new idea or trait throughout a group. Some individual interacting with others convinces them of its worth, directs its acceptance. Whether it is an explanation, a demonstration, or a designed campaign of implementation, the directed change process spreads the change throughout the group. Directed (intended) change represents the only other means by which culture change is accomplished, but in this process the problem gets far more complex. This process will be discussed in greater detail.

At this point, it seems clear that the essential considerations of culture change have been identified and a more useful change model has evolved (see Figure 3.8). Someone, the innovator, has an idea of how to respond to a pressure from either the sociocultural or the natural environment. If it is accepted by the majority of the group, the idea changing one or all of the components of culture becomes a culture change. This acceptance is made possible through the interactions of individuals and groups. Acceptance of change can be voluntary on the part of members of the group, or they can be convinced through the activities of someone that they should accept it. Either way, the fact that a new idea or behavior must spread to the majority of the group focuses our attention on the actual process of change. Innovation, the first step, occurs within a delineated group. In contact situations, new traits pass from one group to another. People representing different culture groups interact to accomplish this. Someone has to become the innovator who will borrow the idea, and probably rework it to fit his or her own context. Spreading a change from one culture to another, perhaps many others, can involve the simple (voluntary acceptance) of an idea, or it can involve planning, direction, and/or participatory interaction with the export of an idea from one culture to the other.

Another way of looking at change is that it results from internal process alone or from direct or indirect culture contacts. It happens without outside contacts, or it

Figure 3.8
Model of Culture Change

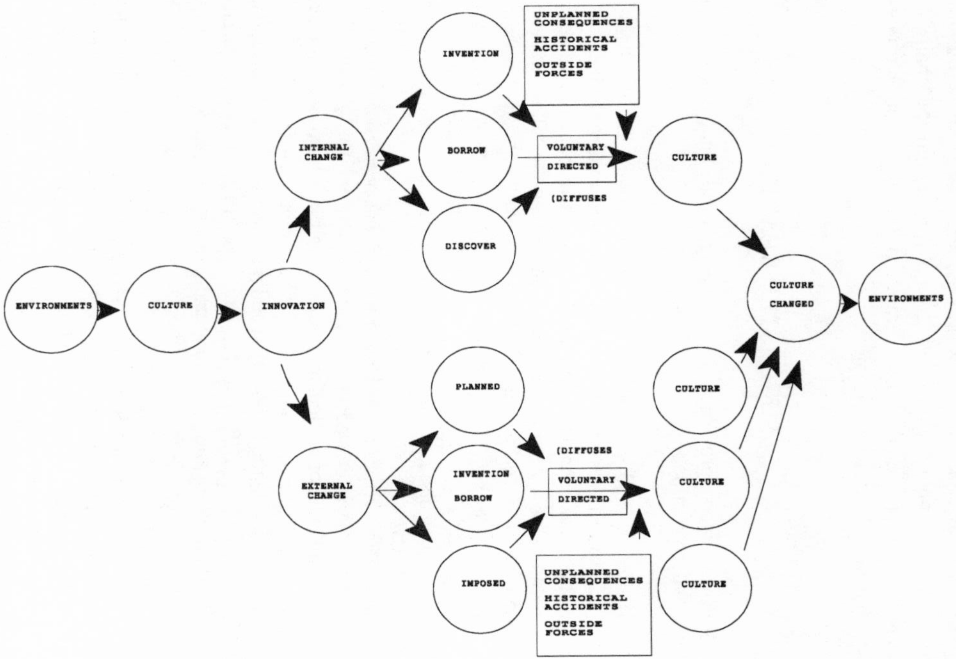

ENVIRONMENTS → CULTURE → INNOVATION → INTERNAL CHANGE / EXTERNAL CHANGE

INTERNAL CHANGE → INVENTION, BORROW, DISCOVER

UNPLANNED CONSEQUENCES
HISTORICAL ACCIDENTS
OUTSIDE FORCES

VOLUNTARY DIRECTED (DIFFUSES) → CULTURE → CULTURE CHANGED → ENVIRONMENTS

EXTERNAL CHANGE → PLANNED, INVENTION, BORROW, IMPOSED

(DIFFUSES) VOLUNTARY DIRECTED

UNPLANNED CONSEQUENCES
HISTORICAL ACCIDENTS
OUTSIDE FORCES

CULTURE, CULTURE, CULTURE → CULTURE CHANGED

occurs because of such contacts. Change is innovated through invention, discovery, or borrowing of a new idea, trait, or behavior from someone else. Change begins and ends with internal change. Internal change as the result of planning and implementation by representatives of one culture for another is the remaining possibility. This last possibility has now assumed the greatest role, involving every culture group in contact with other groups throughout the changing world. This brings us to the more detailed consideration of the major action processes of culture change that have been identified.

SUGGESTED READINGS

The following works provide in-depth coverage of the topic of culture change as it has developed within anthropology.

Barnett, Homer G. 1953. *Innovation: The Basis of Culture Change.* This is considered a standard work on the subject of innovation in culture change and has set the tone for how most scholars approach this topic. This book should be considered must reading for anyone who wishes to understand the culture change process.

Hogbin, Ian. 1970. *Social Change.* 2nd ed. This work contains a review of the various approaches to change, voluntary and forced acceptance of change, and the issues that dominated change study in the 1940s and 1950s. It also provides some interesting discussion of change in Melanesia and native efforts to achieve change themselves.

Linton, Ralph. 1936. *The Study of Man.* This work has been considered a standard reading for people interested in the study of humans. The sections on discovery and invention are of particular importance in the context of evolution and change.

Magnarella, Paul J. 1974. *Tradition and Change in a Turkish Town.* Good study of a community in the Middle East and introduction to modernization.

Rogers, Everett M. 1983. *Diffusion of Innovations.* 3rd ed. This work discusses the spread of innovations, how different categories of people adopt innovation, and how change agents affect this process. A large body of literature on the topic is reviewed.

Sahlins, Marshall D., & Elman R. Service. 1960. *Evolution and Culture.* This work provides a detailed discussion of neo-evolutionism in anthropology. This theory provides for a general evolution for the entire human group, and a specific evolution for particular groups based on their own specific sets of circumstances.

Spindler, Louise. 1977. *Culture Change and Modernization: Mini-Models and Case Studies.* This is a highly concise introduction to the study of culture change as it has evolved in anthropology. The volume contains some good discussions on the processes of culture change as they are currently understood in the discipline.

Woods, Clyde M. 1975. *Culture Change.* This volume serves as a good introduction to the topic of culture change, is short, and is very readable.

Chapter 4

PROCESSES OF CHANGE

In human terms, physical adaptation has been augmented by cultural adaptation. It is no longer the case that the biology of humans simply adjusts to changes in the environment, and thus they continue to survive. Humans, unlike other animals, use culture to respond to the pressures of changing environments, even to change or at least impact their own biological makeup. Change and environment are closely related, in the case of humans this means that change can come from the natural environment and the sociocultural environments they create through their cultures. Cultural adaptation means culture change, for human groups must constantly adjust to these constantly changing environments. In the Chapter 3, it was suggested that innovation represents the first step in the change process, regardless of context. In either singular (internal) or multicultural (external), the process of change originates with an idea. Someone perceives an opportunity or need for a change in existing beliefs or practices, and then comes up with the response. This person, identifiable only after the fact, is referred to as the innovator. An innovator invents, discovers, or borrows a new trait that alters, modifies, subtracts from, or adds to the existing ideas, behaviors, or products of a culture. The processes of change address how a new idea or trait actually becomes part of a culture's belief or action system. Change as process addresses how a new idea or trait diffuses throughout a culture group; spreads from the individual who originates it to the group, in order for it to become a culture change, and from one group to another.

The processes by which this is accomplished were identified as voluntary and directed change, and both revolved around human interactions. Culture change can occur through a voluntary process, or it can be accomplished through planning and directed change activities. In the case of voluntary change, the process is entirely informal and nondirected. Voluntary change means there are no direct efforts to bring it about through intervention or coercion. It simply occurs out of the association of people, and in particular out of the interaction of the innovator and others who accept or reject the innovation in their existing learned ways. In the case of directed or what is now being termed intended change, change is actively planned, directed, or sought by someone who assumes the role of a change agent and works toward the implementation or acceptance of change, with or without the willing participation of those to be affected. As already noted, an innovator may not be the same person who assumes the responsibility for actually bringing the change about. Change agents are those who attempt to convince other members of a cultural group to adopt change through coercion of one kind or another. This chapter will focus on these two processes of culture change and on identifying their significant aspects.

VOLUNTARY CHANGE

Voluntary change is based on a nondirected and basically informal interaction between individuals, those who generate new ideas and others who elect to adopt them. It is not limited to the single culture process but is tied to the multicultural and contact settings as well. In the single culture context, this informal and nondirected process leading to change occurs within the culture group, without culture contact or any direct interference by someone outside of the culture group. In the multicultural context, representatives of more than one culture are involved and cultural conflict plays a significant role. In this context, the process occurs without any direct intervention, interference, malice aforethought, coercion, or planning—just as it occurs within a single culture context. Traditionally, voluntary change has been portrayed as the internal process of culture change, the term *borrowing* being preferred for change when more than one culture has been involved, even if the change occurs simply because people of differing cultures come into contact.

It is very difficult to see the implied difference between a voluntary process of change within a culture group, and the voluntary process that occurs as representatives of different cultures come into contact. One involves borrowing between individuals within a culture grouping, and the other involves borrowing by individuals of one culture from those of another. In both instances, no specific actions are taken to introduce or implement change. The process of voluntary change is the same in either case. Both cases signify the same informal and nondirected elements, and associational interactions between individuals determine the course of events.

Going a step further, it has been suggested that culture change takes place in contact settings far more often than has been recognized. Many settings formerly assumed to be culturally singular are actually contact settings because they involve representatives of different cultures coming into contact. Perhaps many of the voluntary changes noted are actually multicultural, involving different culture groups. In societies where culture can be legitimately applied to various types of groupings, where their members learn different sets of beliefs and practices that then distinguish them from others, change settings will inevitably be multicultural, based on culture contacts, and external to any one particular group. It is relatively safe to assume that change aimed at an entire artificially and arbitrarily created nation-state, made up of numerous specific, constituent, and scene cultures, will nearly always be multicultural, involving direct or indirect cultural contacts and interactions between individuals representing a variety of culture groups. For example, in looking at change in the United States, it would be very difficult to imagine any culture change designed for the entire society as internal. Rather, just about any national change would have to be viewed as multicultural, external to most of the groups to be impacted by it. It would involve many culture contacts, for even career specializations may be characterized as legitimate culture groups in this context. It is tempting to suggest that all settings for change involve culture contacts, except for the fact that changes do occur within individual cultural groups, even those making up a nation-state.

Change also occurs in homogeneous and isolated small-scale societies without any contact with others. But the suggestion is even more tempting when one considers that it is extremely rare for a member of any culture group to know all of the culture. It has long been held that most people know only bits and pieces of the culture(s). They may know some cultural scenes very well, but it is not likely that they will know all of those that together make up their culture. Thus, even in the homogeneous or small-scale culture, cultural contacts can be supposed. Whichever the case, voluntary change remains the same, with or without culture contacts, it is a major change. It happens simply because individuals elect to accept a change initiated by an innovator through informal, unplanned and non-directed interactions and associations. The only necessary conditions for voluntary change are personal contacts or interactions, and motivation.

Motivation

People will alter their learned ways voluntarily if an opportunity to do so arise, and they are motivated to do so. Obviously, opportunity means they are exposed to an innovation, for if they are not, there is nothing to adopt. Motivation means that some desire to adopt a possible change is present. This desire can come from perceived problems or needs, either real or imaginary. If something new responds to a perceived problem or serves a perceived need, people will be motivated to adopt it. This may amount to copying what someone has come up with or borrowing it because of some perceived benefit. Once the majority of a culture group has accepted the new trait, and as it becomes integrated into the learned patterns required of aspiring members to the group, it represents a culture change. The felt need that serves to motivate people to adopt a new or altered way comes from the natural and/or the sociocultural environment. Because environments continually change, people and their cultures must continually change, or they will not survive. Both people problems and needs can be directly correlated to one or both of these environments.

As has been pointed out on many occasions, culture is the primary means of human adaptation to the natural environment, and as such it is directly tied to survival. An environmentally generated need to change something in order to survive is one of the strongest motivations for change. But it goes beyond simply adapting to the natural environment. In adapting to a natural environment and its limitations, humans have created a sociocultural environment with both physical and nonphysical components. In their quest to solve survival problems, they have created this sociocultural environment that has become equal to, and in some instances, even more important to, survival than, the natural environment. At the very heart of the need for change is the interaction between the environments. Change in either one can mean a change in the other. A change in the natural environment requires a change in culture. That response will change the sociocultural environment, which can then have an impact on the natural environment. A change in culture can mean a significant change in the natural environment.

The natural environment serves as a major source of change—produces constant pressure for change in a number of significant ways. Climatic shifts or alterations can necessitate a change in human culture. For example, during prehistoric periods associated with the advance or recession of glaciers, it was necessary for humans to adjust their cultural beliefs and practices to the changes in order to survive. Retreating glaciers changed natural environments, climate, and resources quite substantially. The shifts in climate associated with the greenhouse effect will certainly require some adjustments in human beliefs, behaviors, or sociocultural productions in the near future. Catastrophic events such as earthquakes, floods, tornadoes, or hurricanes pressure for more immediate human responses. Such dramatic events in the natural environment require that humans alter some of their learned ways if they and their cultures are to survive under the new or altered circumstances, regardless of whether the environmental change is of long or short duration. But change in the natural environment can also be produced by humans, as impacts or consequences of their cultural activities.

Human culture has produced significant changes in the natural environment by way of overpopulation, garbage, disease, pollution, depleted resources, and so on. In this sense, the very solutions that humans came up with to solve their problems or to cope with the natural environment, have caused changes in that environment. In response to the pressures of the natural environment, and in their creation of culture, humans have developed a substitute sociocultural environment with its own physical aspects, sometimes seen in steel, concrete, and asphalt. This created environment has been superimposed over the natural environment, in many cases replacing it in importance. This adds still another dimension to culture change: any change in the natural environment, including those introduced by humans with their cultural activities. Change necessitates additional change in the ideas, behaviors or products of culture for it to remain viable. Change in any part of the sociocultural environment (e.g., technological, material, or human relations) necessitates change in other of its parts because of the integration and interdependence of such parts of culture. This is particularly true when core systems are involved. Any environmental change can produce the basis for a voluntary acceptance of change by a culture's members. Continuing to adapt to the environment, as it is directly related to survival, must be listed as number one among the reasons for people to voluntarily accept change.

Surviving in the highly competitive national or international world of business is certainly sufficient cause for participants in that particular culture to change, but that does not mean they will. Peasant farmers moving into an urban environment certainly must alter their beliefs and behaviors in order to survive in that context, but that does not mean they will. Preferring older traditions, some businesses will simply continue to do business as they always have. Some peasants will simply go back home rather than change their traditional ways. In the perceptions of many people, surviving in their created cultural context is no less important than surviving in a natural environment. People will change, alter their belief and/or behavior, if their survival is threatened, but pure survival is not the only motivation for change. Not everything is seen as pertinent to survival. There are many others things in the sociocultural environment that can serve as motivations to generate changes as well. Satisfaction of basic needs certainly heads the list, but efficiency, comfort, security, prestige, and status, can also serve to motivate people to adopt a change in their learned patterns. In the sociocultural context, an interesting or novel alternative to some practice can serve as a motivation. In the modern industrial world, status, prestige, and economics have been identified as primary considerations. If recent events throughout the world are taken into account, political necessity may have to be added to this list of primary needs, although it is not often easy to separate it from economic or social needs.

Voluntary Interaction

The interaction associated with voluntary change, that between the innovator who comes up with a new idea, behavior, or product and those who accept it as part of their learned patterns, is not planned or nondirected, nor is it a formal process. Although there is some direct (face-to-face) or indirect contact between the innovator and those who voluntarily accept a change, the interaction is essentially an associational one. Innovators must associate with others, come into contact with others, if their ideas are to be copied or adopted. Such association is nondirected in that the innovator of a new idea or trait does not take any particular steps to convince others to accept the idea. Someone who innovates may simply be trying to maximize his or her own satisfactions or needs. Others who see the change or simply hear about it, copy it based on a perceived value or benefit in meeting their own satisfactions or needs. It might very well be that in the infant stages of cultural evolution, the change process was predominantly this informal and totally voluntary. In the dynamics of early cultural development, it is quite possible that individuals simply copied what seemed to work or helped them satisfy their most pressing need for food. Changes in their behaviors, ultimately creating complex culture, gave humans an edge in competing with other animals for limited food resources. Maintaining the competitive edge remains a primary motivation for change. Interactions were obviously involved, but changes were not planned or directed in any particular way. Perhaps people most closely associated with the innovator (e.g., the innovator's immediate family or relatives) were the first to copy the new or altered belief or practice. The interactional circle then enlarged as others began to accept it as well, until ultimately the circle extended to other cultural groups. Voluntary change usually begins among limited numbers of individuals within culture groups, but it also occurs when individuals representing cultural groupings come into any kind of contact. Borrowing between culture groups in contact with one another is based on the kinds of interactions between individuals that occur within a single culture grouping.

Borrowing between cultures was noted by diffusionists and those who concentrated on acculturation studies, both of whom recognized that a nondirected change can be easily documented in situations of contact. Diffusionists saw it in terms of syncretism and reinterpretation, noting that a voluntarily accepted new idea or trait is reworked to fit the group doing the borrowing. The acculturationists noted that some changes occur simply because of contact. They identified changes that fused the systems in contact or produced an overlaying of borrowed traits without impacting the core system. Some of these were identified as accidents emanating from the contact. In the main, it was generally recognized that some voluntary change has always been part of the change equation, with or without culture contact or outside interference. It is clear that the circumstances of externally generated change are not the same as those of internally generated change, but that may be a reflection of not being able to "see the forest for the trees"—in this context, the presence or absence of contact prohibiting our ability to see actual process, or how a change is brought about. It may be that the two situations are really are quite similar, only appearing more complicated because of the presence of contact between different cultures. Voluntary change has always focused on informal and non-directed interactions of innovators with other members of their group. Directed change has focused on what one group has occasioned with another by way of coercion and dominance of one of the groups. In contact situations, voluntary change had to be acknowledged, but it being tied to contact, and this presupposed some other process.

The voluntary change process always involves an innovator who generates an idea (through invention, discovery, borrowing) in response to a perceived need, followed by informal and nondirected interactions (associations) by which others, also responding to some felt need, simply copy a new belief, behavior, or product in a continually widening circle until the new trait is spread throughout the group. The trait may then spread to other groups based on their perceptions of its value as responding to their own needs, as keeping them competitive with others attempting to survive under similar conditions. This voluntary change process obviously accounts for significant amounts of culture change throughout history and prehistory, perhaps for the vast majority of cultural development or evolution during its early formative stages. The voluntary change process continues to be important today even with the shift in emphasis to directed culture change. There is little doubt that most change now occurs by virtue of directed intervention and within the context of cultural contacts. But the dynamics of voluntary and directed change are actually not all that different. In a very real sense, directed change centers on creating the same kind of conditions necessary for voluntary change—in essence, creating a felt need which can then serve as the motivation essential for any change.

DIRECTED CHANGE

Directed change based on planning and design is the second major process by which humans go about changing their cultures. Although the current tendency is to refer to this kind of change as intended or intentional, *directed change* is still the best term to use, because this kind of change involves specific actions aimed at bringing it about. In the past, such change generated visions of cultural contact and some level of coercion, particularly as the Western cultures spread throughout the rest of the world. Directed change became linked to such intrusions and to their impacts or consequences. It was also tied to the idea that it was solely an external process because it involved contacts with others. Direct or intermediate types of contact between cultures were recognized, along with the idea of planned change and directed implementation. During the time of the acculturation studies, some level of control was supposed in the changing of a cultural system. For most people, directed change became associated with the introduction, planning, implementation, or acceleration of change through coercion. The purposes, deadlines, and goals were established by one of the culture groups in contact. Change by fiat or forced draft became synonymous with directed change. In addition, unequal culture groups were seen to come together, and change occurred simply because of that contact. Because it was recognized that some changes under contact circumstances were not directed, the concept of nondirected change evolved. It meant that some changes occurred in the contact situations simply by virtue of the contact. Borrowing was used to account for much of this nondirected change, distinguishing it from directed change in the absence of control, planning, or direction in what was borrowed. Borrowing and voluntary change were unnecessarily distinguished or separated in the process.

Today, directed change and planned change have come to have other meanings as well, for organizational interventions through agencies created in response to "collective problems of society" have appeared nearly everywhere and on all levels of culture and society. These organizations are budgeted, staffed, and charged with bringing about changes in some group's beliefs or practices. With increased complexity of human societies and cultures, such agencies now appear on local, state, and international levels. Towns, cities, states, provinces, and nations have their planning and development offices. The world has the United Nations, World Health Organization, World Bank, and a host of other global organizations. Even within the recently recognized organizational culture of business, one finds design, planning, and development divisions or departments. It is interesting to note that directed change in this new context includes many of the elements of voluntary change. Need, motivation, and interaction among people are still integral to the process. Directed change can be seen in both singular and multicultural settings, with or without cultural contact. This kind of change is distinguished from voluntary change by the presence of the change agent(s), someone who actually attempts to implement change or get others to adopt or accept an innovation. It involves a idea or plan for change, a design for accomplishing it, and specific steps to bring it about. For example, science may be a major source of innovation in particular cultural contexts, and applied scientists serve as the change agents.

Change of any kind involves interactions, individual to group or group to group. The key to understanding the directed process lies in recognizing the difference between an innovator who comes up with an idea and the change agent who is dedicated or oriented to getting others to adopt that idea originated by an innovator. Sometimes they can be the same person, but the functions and activities of agents and innovators are quite different. An innovator comes up with a possible change through invention, discovery, or borrowing from someone else. A change agent comes up with a plan or strategy to get others to accept the innovation. When this is done internally, the agents are representatives of the same cultural grouping in which they work to spread a new idea. Being familiar with that culture, its needs, and what can serve as motivation, their task is not so difficult as it is for agents working across cultures. Changes being introduced by internal change agents are usually changes of degree, more or less of something with which the members of the culture group are already familiar. When representatives of different cultures are involved, cultures at any of the levels of human groups to which the term *culture* can be applied, the circumstances and elements become far more complicated because different sets of learned ways come into contact and conflict. The change can also be one of kind as opposed to one of degree. It can focus on something with which the members of the culture group are totally unfamiliar. The basic components of the directed change process include the innovator or source of the idea for change, perhaps an organization acting as an innovating agency, the change agent(s), the group toward which change activities are being directed, the setting wherein these will interact, and the results of that interaction (See Figure 4.1).

Someone has an idea to change something, returning us once again to the reality that all change originates with an innovator who comes up with a new, modified, or changed belief, behavior, or product. The innovator can be acting alone or as part of an organization or planning group. Any number of organizations, change agencies, individuals, or groups of individuals may actually initiate change, but they may not assume the role of change agent with respect to the grouping for which the change is proposed. The change agent or agency is the individual or group of individuals who assume the task of implementing the change, convincing or otherwise getting a group of people to accept and adopt the proposed change into their established belief, practices, or sociocultural product systems. The source of a proposed change is an important element of the process, but change agents are the major participants in the process, along with members of the focal group.

Focal group identifies the cultural grouping that is being asked to accept some change in their existing cultural patterns. This term is the much referred to either *target group* or *recipient group*, which were proposed in the past for those groups

Figure 4.1
General Model of Directed Culture Change

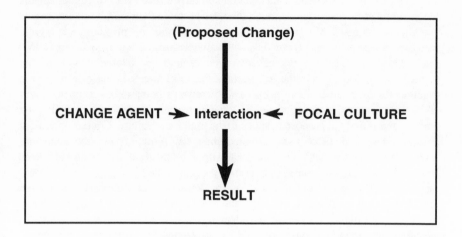

being asked to change. *Target group* obviously has many negative connotations. It suggests a one-way movement of change, similar to someone establishing a mark to shoot at, or an object of ridicule. *Recipient group* is a misleading term, for it suggests that the group members being asked to change are passive participants in the change process, simply receivers of new ideas, beliefs, or products. The terminology of the postmodern perspective fares no better. Using *collaborators* or *partners* suggests that people being asked to change always do so willingly. Although certainly desirable, this represents more wishful thinking than reality. *Focal group* appears to be a better term in referring to the object of change agent activities, for it identifies the group for whom change is being planned and to whom it is directed, but without subjective interpretation. It bespeaks the focus of the agent's efforts and leaves open the idea that focal groups are more than passive receptors of proposed change or are always collaborators.

The interactional context is created as the participants come together, and it, too, is a significant component of the directed change process. It is out of the interactions of the participants that a result is produced. In voluntary change, we noted that interactions are associational, informal, and nondirective. In directed change, they may be either formal or informal, but always with some form of direction or coercion. Participants in planned and directed change do interact, and thereby participate in the process of producing change. Individuals or groups can plan a change, just as individuals or groups can devise a strategy for implementing it, but change agents will be the ones responsible for introducing and implementing it. They attempt to direct its course. Focal groups respond to those efforts. What the participants bring into the interactional setting will significantly influence the result of their interaction. The presence or absence of culture contact becomes important in the interaction and outcomes, as do the unplanned consequences of planned culture change, the "accidents of history," and outside forces of the larger context within which all change is actually attempted.

Obviously, getting a better understanding of and control over directed change is the goal of a great many people, but it involves far more than simply identifying its essential components. Many scholars have struggled with this problem over a great many years, and each has provided us with valuable insights. George Foster (1962, 1969) proposed that the process revolved around the characteristics of the participants, the agent, and the focal group. For him, directed change was putting together the characteristics of agents and the groups being asked to change, and addressing barriers, stimulants, and fit. Change was equated with overcoming the barriers and fitting the proposed change to the traditional culture. Conrad Arensberg and Arthur Niehoff (1971) saw directed change in terms of coercion: ideas are formulated into plans, which are then acted upon by forces of action and reaction. Based on some minimal consideration(s) on the part of the agent, innovations would be adopted. Alexander Leighton (1945) saw directed change as an administrative handling of stress. Although scholars such as these, and others, did agree on many aspects of the planned and directed change process, each took a very different approach to directed change and tended to emphasize different components. Because of their particular contributions, a closer examination of these authors, their models, and their positions is quite useful.

George Foster on Directed Change

George Foster (1962, 1969, 1973) approached directed change in terms of barriers and stimulants, emphasizing the dynamics of the directed change process. In his model, Foster identified various "forces" that could serve to stimulate the acceptance of change and others that could serve as barriers to it (see Figure 4.2). Among those things that stimulate change, Foster identified motivation or the felt need as necessary for change, even proposed some specific desires that could serve as motivations. He identified fit as a necessary condition, arguing that in any attempt, the proposed change has to fit the existing patterns of the group in order to have chance for success. According to Foster, such things as values, social forms, and economic reality could play important roles in determining whether a change actually fits into the culture sequence of the recipient group. The idea of fit is also tied to the proper timing of the proposed change. If a change is not sequentially relevant, it will not be readily accepted.

Among the barriers to culture change, Foster listed all the forces that seek to maintain the status quo and preserve the equilibrium of the cultural system. This was based on the idea that any proposed change in an existing culture pattern represents a threat to that system. Potential barriers to change could be found in culture values and attitudes, social claims and obligations, or associated with perceptual differences between change agents and recipient groups. In discussing the barriers and stimulants to directed change, Foster provided us with significant insights into the cultural characteristics of change agents, as well as those of people

Figure 4.2
George Foster Model for Directed Culture Change

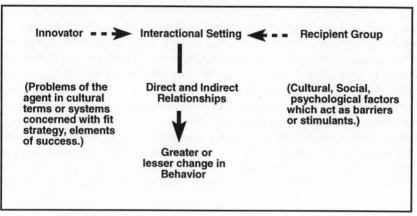

Source: Adapted from Foster (1969:44)

being asked to make the change. For change agents, Foster emphasized role characteristics that he saw as the elements of success and problems specific to change agents. For recipient groups, the focus was on traditional cultural characteristics. Unfortunately, his focus on the change agent, with all its insights, translated into the ideal proposition that if the elements of success were considered and certain problems are overcome, the change goal had the greatest chance of succeeding.

According to Foster, if the characteristics (elements of success and problems) of agents were put together with fit (not doing violence to existing cultural forms of the recipient group), if the innovations are timed properly, and if the innovations chosen do something without major dislocations to the culture of the recipient group, then favorable and basic considerations are created for success. Unfortunately, emphasizing these minimal conditions or considerations does not ensure success. In addition, the characteristics of the participants in the process were oriented to different things. For agents, the cultural characteristics were centered on those assumed by virtue of their role, whereas characteristics of members of the recipient group were centered on traditional culture. Barriers were laid almost solely on the recipient group. Foster apparently believed that not doing violence to existing cultural forms would minimize the barriers. For him, directed culture change can be equated with overcoming the barriers and fitting the change to the culture context of the recipients. Although almost certainly unintended, that assumption has led to the widespread belief that there is *a way* to accomplish culture change. It has produced the recipe approach and "school solution" mentality to planned and directed change which holds that if the agent does all the right things, the change will be adopted. All one has to do is find the "right" things. This has also come to mean that failures in change projects or programs have to be attributed either to a question of fit or to some characteristic of the recipient group that served as a barrier. Needless to say, failures were, more often than not, laid at the feet of the recipients.

In his approach to directed change, Foster provided us with valuable insights. There are social, cultural, and psychological barriers that have to be overcome in successful directed culture change. He gave us insights into the nature of change agents as participants in the directed change process. He reinforced the idea that for change to occur at all, there must be some motivation for it, a felt need on the part of people to accept change in any of their existing culture patterns. In this, Foster brought the idea of fit into clear focus, in terms of both cultural context and timing. Considering the integrated nature of culture, fit and timing are important considerations. He spoke to the interactional setting or context where the agents and focal group members come into direct or indirect contact. One of the real strengths of Foster's approach is with his identification of many of the dynamic aspects of this kind of change, the stimulants of and barriers to change. In doing this, Foster also provides us with a clearer picture of the agent of change and the specific role characteristics such individuals bring into the directed change circumstance and interaction setting that must be taken into account when trying to understand the dynamics of this change process. Although all this information has proven useful in our understanding of directed change, Foster left out the cultural characteristics that recipients bring into that interaction that are tied not to their culture; but to the situation of change in which they have been asked or forced to participate. People asked to change some aspect of their culture are not merely recipients, they are also participants in the process, and thus there are additional characteristics they assume, just as agents assume characteristics in the context of taking that role to introduce and implement change.

Alexander Leighton on Directed Change

Alexander Leighton (1945) although frequently overlooked in the literature, has much to contribute to our understanding of the directed culture change process. Because he never actually proposed a model for this process, he has not been seen as a major contributor to directed culture change. But through his work, he did provide some useful and valuable insights into the process that add significantly to what we have learned from Foster. The contributions of Leighton come mainly from his study of the Japanese relocation center at Poston, Arizona, where he served as administrator during World War II. Based upon this experience, Leighton wrote a monograph in which he presented a number of postulates and principles he considered important to administrators in situations of culture contact. Because he saw such administrators as agents of change, it is fairly easy to apply his material to directed change and the activities of change agents. From his administrative position, Leighton saw change in terms of stress. He recognized that all peoples are similar, yet different by virtue of their cultures. Stress is common to all people and inherent in the interactions where people representing different cultures come into

Figure 4.3
Alexander Leighton Model for Directed Culture Change

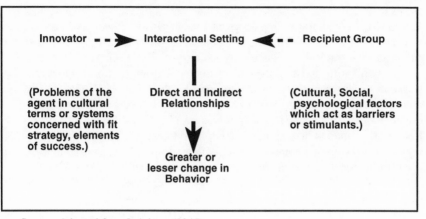

Source: Adapted from Leighton (1945).

contact. Any suggested change will evoke a response that, more often than not, will be based on sentiment. Like Foster, Leighton identified the need to select changes that are workable, that fit the social and cultural circumstances. On that note, he proposed that changes should be introduced in stage, and, in areas of social change, first tried on a small scale before being applied to the whole group. Communities under stress—and by inference, focal groups—are ripe for change, but in attempting it, people will be motivated more by emotions than by rationality. Leighton emphasized that administrators or change agents should think of basic cultural similarities and differences as matters to be understood and perceived in directed culture change contexts.

The legacy of Leighton comes with the additional considerations he provided on change agents and focal groups, and the need to understand directed change as occurring under stress situations. Based on his experiences, contact situations are always characterized by stress. The contact produces the stress as cultural beliefs and practices people have learned as truths and as the most "correct" ways come into direct conflict with other truths. Out of the obvious, Leighton helped to characterize the nature of the cultural contact and interactional settings of directed change. He reinforced the idea that focal groups are not passive recipients of change; but active in the interaction setting with agents. Cooperation, withdrawal, and aggressiveness are universal kinds of reactive behavior of people in situations of stress. These kinds of reactive behavior hold both advantages and disadvantages for the change agent. Because a contact situation is one of stress, responses are frequently based on sentiment and emotion, as opposed to rationality. Out of such interactions will come change, but not necessarily that envisioned by the agent. This suggests that change does not always occur because of what the agent does nor does not do. Rather, it tells us that from directed change interactions there will be a result, but not necessarily that which was intended by anybody involved with it—what I would call the "unplanned consequences of planned culture change."

Leighton provides us with some additional characteristics or problems of change agents to consider, and he pinpoints the cultural basis for focal group reactions and sentiments. He elaborates on participant characteristics, especially those of role, which produce the stress that seems to be inherent when interaction occurs, and that can produce a result that nobody intended or wanted. He reinforces the idea that change needs to fit existing patterns of the focal group (in his terms, it must be workable) and the need for agents to consider the basic social elements of the group. In producing change, he cites communication and education as the basic and essential tools of the agent, repeating what a number of others have also suggested. But he also cautions that communication from the people to the change agent or organization is no less important than communication from the organization or agent to the focal group. There is also value in some of his recommendations to administrators (change agents) based upon his experiences. For example, he suggests that change should be planned in stages over time, each evaluated before proceeding to the next, and that social change be tried on a small scale before being applied to the whole.

Conrad Arensberg and Arthur Niehoff on Directed Change

Conrad Arensberg and Arthur Niehoff published books aimed at technical advisers in an attempt to bring more social science into technical assistance programs (Arensberg & Niehoff 1971; Niehoff 1966). They present a model for directed culture change focused on the sociocultural component of such programs. In their model, directed change is portrayed in terms of coercion, the requirements of which are communication, motivation, a method of adapting the innovation to the cultural reality of the focal group, and the proper utilization of secondary strategies (Niehoff 1966). The many variables of the model are probably best described in the later volume (Arensberg & Niehoff 1971). In essence, these authors bring together many of the ideas found in Foster, Leighton, and perhaps others. For Arensberg and Niehoff, a change begins with an idea and ends with its integration to the culture of the recipient group. The model proposed is simple and clear. Change begins with an idea. A plan is then formulated to bring it about. Change agents act and recipients react. The change is integrated into the culture patterns of the recipient group.

In discussing their model, the authors suggest that ideas for change come from any number of different sources: a change agent or agency, an innovator, even the people themselves (Niehoff 1966). Once an idea has been generated, a plan is then formulated (planned) and is then acted upon by the forces of action and reaction. A number of influences are noted that could act as barriers or stimulants to proposed change associated with the role characteristics of change agents and generalized traditional cultural characteristics of recipient groups are also noted. According to Arensberg and Niehoff, the role characteristics of the agent, and the

Figure 4.4
Arensberg and Niehoff Model for Directed Culture Change

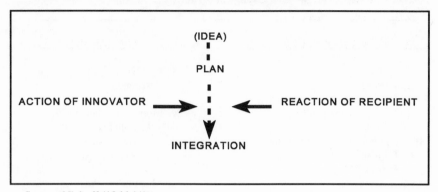

Source: Niehoff (1966:11)

recipient group perceptions of them, were much more important than the cultural characteristics of the recipient group in the change process. In essence, this shifts attention away from recipients and onto change agents. In doing so, the responsibility for the success or failure of directed culture change programs or projects falls squarely on the shoulders of the agent. Agents attempt to get people to change, not the other way around.

When a project or attempt at change fails, how can it be the fault of the people being asked to change? Niehoff lists seventeen different kinds of influences on planned or directed change (see Figure 4.5). Of these six are identified as primary variables: innovator communication, degree of participation the innovator obtains, innovator awareness and use of existing culture patterns, felt need, perceived benefit, and role of traditional leaders in planning and implementing a proposed change. When all six of these ingredients exist, Arensberg and Niehoff suggested, a proposed change will be adopted. In essence, these authors proposed a recipe approach for success, just as Foster did. Communication was the key element or consideration. For the change agent, communication with the recipient group could be formal, or personal, via demonstration or audiovisual aids. For the recipients communication is that which occurs only among themselves. The authors do not provide for communication by recipients with agents.

The legacy of Arensberg and Niehoff is not unlike that seen with Foster. Some additional and significant characteristics of the participants in the process that can influence potentially outcomes were identified. Both the characteristics of the focal group and those of the agents were considered, but the major influence was placed squarely on the sets and categories of the agent in terms of the ultimate direction a program of change will take. Relevant aspects of the primary culture of recipients which can also impact outcomes were also considered, but not the characteristics of recipients as the focus of change. Beliefs, traditional leadership, social structural, and organizational aspects of the recipient culture were also noted, but the primary culture(s) of the agents were not addressed. For agents, the emphasis was placed on

Figure 4.5
Niehoff's Influences on Directed Change Programs

INNOVATOR CHARACTERISTICS

I. Role Characteristics
  A. Personality
  B. Use of Local Language
  C. Technical Competence

II. Communication by Innovator
  A. Formal
  B. Personal
  C. Audiovisual
  D. Demonstration

III. Participation Obtained
  A. Labor and Time
  B. Material Contributions
  C. Organization
  D. Passive

IV. Utilization of Local
    Culture

V. Timing (utilization of)

VI. Flexibility (of
    implementation)

VII. Continuity (of
    implementation)

VIII. Maintenance
    (established)

RECIPIENT CHARACTERISTICS

IX. Communication Among the
    Recipients

X. Motivation - Felt Need
  A. Solicited
  B. Demonstrated
  C. Ascertained

XI. Motivation - Practical
    Benefit
  A. Economic
  B. Medical
  C. Educational
  D. Convenience

XII. Motivation - Other
  A. Competition
  B. Reward and Punishment
  C. Novelty

XIII. Leadership
  A. Administrators
  B. Educators
  C. Religious Leaders
  D. Other Organizations
  E. Noninstitutional

XIV. Social Structure
  A. Kinship
  B. Caste and Class
  C. Ethnic
  D. Political
  E. Central Authority

XV. Economic Pattern

XVI. Beliefs
  A. Supernatural
  B. Medical
  C. Attitudinal

XVII. Practices

Source: Niehoff (1966:12).

role, or how they appeared in that role by virtue of their personality, technical competence, and use of local language. Arensberg and Niehoff have provided us with a clearer understanding of the forces of action and reaction that inevitably accompany directed culture change, felt need, and practical benefit as motivations, along with competition, reward, punishment, and novelty. Although all of these things add significantly to our understanding of planned and directed culture change, the model represents another lockstep approach to directed change.

INTERACTIONAL MODEL FOR DIRECTED CHANGE

Building on the strengths of these contributions to planned and directed change, another model evolves that takes into account the multiple cultural characteristics of the participants in directed change contexts and notes the similarities and differences in these cultural characteristics that come together in the interactional setting. In this interactional setting where people come together, act and react to each other, success or failure of planned and directed change will largely be determined. The key in this interaction is communication, for what is transmitted, how it is transmitted and how it is perceived by the participants in their constant action and reactions will, in the end, determine the course of most directed change. Of course, other things can also impinge on the result that are totally outside the ability of either participant group to impact. The resulting interactional model, like those of Foster, Leighton, and Arensberg and Niehoff, contains many of the essential components upon which there seems to be widespread agreement (see Figure 4.6). There is an idea to change some belief, behavior, or product of a group. There are those who ask or otherwise become involved in getting others to accept an idea and integrate it into their learned cultural patterns, and there are those asked to change. In the asking, and in the response, individuals must interact. Based upon such interaction and the influence of any number of outside factors, there will be a result of some kind. Although these are the essential components of directed culture change, there are important differences between the interactional model being proposed here and those offered previously.

Ideas for change are always generated by innovators, for all change begins with innovation; but, as noted before, innovators are not always the agents of change. Thinking up a new or revised way of doing something is not the same as attempting to get others to adopt it. The distinction between the innovator and the change agent is an important one that must be kept clear. The culture group that a change agent or agency attempts to convince is not a group that merely accepts or rejects the attempt; they are not targets or mere recipients of change, but active participants in the process. They are the group being asked to change, the group upon which the agents focus their attention and activities. Although the previous models of directed change have spoken to the interaction of the participants, none has emphasized it to the extent suggested here. Foster speaks to interactions through direct or indirect relationships; Leighton to interactions characterized by stress; Arensberg and Niehoff, to actions by innovators (coercive) and reactions by recipients (based on

Figure 4.6
Directed Culture Change

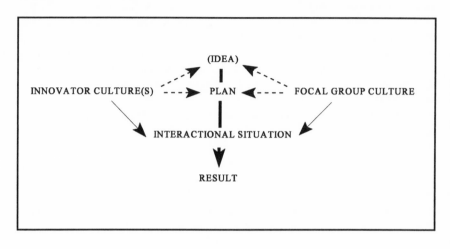

traditional culture, social or psychological patterns).

Everyone seems to agree that interaction is significant in the change process, but not on its specifics. It is in these specifics of interaction that the major differences appear. Foster emphasizes overcoming barriers to change. Niehoff emphasizes the character of the coercion. Leighton emphasizes emotion. This model takes into account all three of these ideas. All three tend to focus on what the agent should do or take into account in order to achieve the desired result. This model ties those questions to the individual context. All three characterize the focal group as recipients of the process somehow constrained by cultural characteristics. Although the agent is characterized primarily in terms of the cultural characteristics assumed in the change context, as problems to be overcome and particular skills that will produce the desired result, this model goes much further. This model considers all the cultural characteristics of the participants, all those brought into the change context by both participating groups, and those characteristics created by it. Foster, Leighton, and Arensberg and Niehoff all seem to agree that the important element is what the agent does or does not do, whereas the recipients simply respond. All seem to propose that if the agent takes the right things into account, does the right things to overcome their particular problems, uses proper strategies, a change program has the best chance of success. This model suggests that even with such things appropriately handled, the best one can expect is an outcome—that might not be what was intended by either group. The emphasis on one or another of the participants is misleading, for both participants are just that, both acting and reacting. The basis for such action and reaction is culture.

More often than not, the participants in planned and directed change represent different cultures at some level; thus the interaction will be one of conflict and stress. The interaction will be influenced by the cultural characteristics of the agent and the focal group, but both will assume additional cultural characteristics because of their interaction oriented to some proposed change in established cultural pattern(s). Change agents assume cultural characteristics associated with the culture change group with which they are affiliated (cultural scene), in addition to those they carry as members of other culture groupings (specific, constituent, even national). Portrayal of all members of a national or nation-state cultural group as sharing the same set of beliefs and practices is a faulty one. We have long accepted the idea that no one really knows all of his or her culture, rather, individuals know only bits and pieces of it. Cultural scenes exist in nearly all culture groupings, whether one is talking about hunter and gatherer societies, or addressing an organizational culture of some corporation or an academic or professional organization.

Why should it be assumed that all members of groups believe and act the same? This is certainly questionable in the context of the multicultural nation-state setting which is composed of numerous specific, constituent, and scene cultures. Each is a legitimate cultural grouping with its own learned beliefs, behaviors, and products that distinguish it from other groups. For example, when researchers go out into American society to gather data in relation to some problem they are researching, it is normally assumed that respondents share the researchers' beliefs in the value of, need for, and results of the research. It is easy to demonstrate that this is frequently not the case, a situation that results in faulty conclusions.

Based on such realities, to conclude that planned and directed change within any but the smallest scale societies is strictly an internal process within a single culture is suspect at best. Rather, directed change is nearly always an external process involving culture contacts on one level or another. About the only thing that can be assumed is that a change agent within something like the nation-state culture is in some way familiar with the group in which he or she attempts some change. The agent can indeed share something of that culture group. Although the agent can share orienting values, this does not mean that the agent shares all the beliefs and practices of the group. In reality, the agent could subscribe to the beliefs and practices of a particular group (e.g., business, religious or political) that are quite different from the group with which the agent works. Change agents may be misled by the notion that because the context is American, he or she and the group to experience the change share the same beliefs and practices. Assuming a shared American culture obscures the real cultural differences among all those who make it up.

In planned and directed change, each participant in the process will devise plans or strategies to cope with the other participant. The emphasis must be placed on this interaction, on the actions and reactions of people who may not share the same cultural beliefs and behaviors. This moves away from placing all the emphasis on the specific cultural characteristics of either participant group. The individual participants, singly or in groups, will act and react to each other. The interaction will nearly always mean that representatives of different cultures (at the very minimum scene or constituent cultures) will be in contact, acting and reacting to each other based on their cultural beliefs and behaviors. Cultures in contact mean truths in conflict, and conflict between truths means stress is automatic. The success or failure of a change project or program will be determined by what is transmitted and how it is transmitted between individuals and groups subjected to their own culture sets. Communication remains the single most important factor in the process, not only in what is transmitted but also in how that transmission is perceived. Actions and reactions on the part of the focal group and change agents will largely be guided by this. Because the results of the effort are going to be determined by the quality of that interaction, both the conscious and the unconscious actions of both participant groups, establishing a recipe for successful change is building a false hope, misleading and chancy at best.

In the interactional model, the action/reaction setting is influenced by all the cultural characteristics of the agent and the focal group. As seen in Figure 4.6, ideas may be generated from within or outside the group for which change is intended. The same can be said of the plan developed to bring it about. The dotted lines represent *possible* contributions in the generation of the idea for change or to the plan for implementing it. The plan itself becomes an element of interaction and, when combined with the unique characteristics of the agents and the focal group brought together in the interactional setting, yields the particular result (Figure 4.7). Although this portrays the theory in general terms, it is in the separate categories that the real significance of the model is found. Clearly, an idea must come from somewhere. It can be generated within a culture group or it can be generated by a change agency of another culture grouping. Nearly always, the change will involve culture contacts between cultural scenes, constituent or specific culture groups of the nation-states, or between nation-states themselves. Generally, given such culture contacts, the ideas will come from the group in the dominant position. This also means that in the majority of cases, the idea comes from outside the group being asked to change, as will the plan for implementing that change. In programs planned around interactional strategies, both groups can contribute to the origination of the idea and plan for implementing the change. In an interactional model, the participants, the plan of implementation, and the interactional situation become the prime components determining the outcomes, and understanding the factors associated with each of these is crucial.

At first glance, the component characteristics or factors (Figure 4.7), does not appear to be very different from those offered by Niehoff (Figure 4.5). On closer examination however, although many of the same characteristics are noted, some new ones have been added and their arrangement and categorization are quite different. On one level, the participants are similar, both characterized by primary culture and role characteristics. On another level, they are quite different. For example, both agents and focal groups are grounded in aspects of their primary culture(s). Role characteristics are products of their particular participation in the change process. Both the plan and the interactional setting have their own characteristics that can impact a change project. Together, all of these characteristics of agents, the focal group, the plan, and the interactional setting represent the factors of interaction that produce the consequence of the effort, whatever that may ultimately turn out to be.

Figure 4.7
Component Characteristics

AGENTS	PLAN	FOCAL GROUP

AGENTS

I. Primary Culture
    (Beliefs/Practices)
  A. Structural
    1. Family
    2. Associational
  B. Organizational
    1. Economic
    2. Political
    3. Culturative
    4. Religious
  C. Material

II. Role Characteristics
  A. Beliefs
    1. Values
    2. Motivation
  B. Practices
    1. Communication
    2. Specialization and
      Technical Ability
    3. Living Habits
    4. Participation
    5. Affiliation
    6. Strategy
  D. Personality

PLAN

I. Timing

II. Culture Fit

III. Strategy

FOCAL GROUP

I. Primary Culture
    (Beliefs/Practices)
  A. Structural
    1. Family
    2. Associational
  B. Organizational
    1. Economic
    2. Political
    3. Culturative
    4. Religious
  C. Material

II. Role Characteristics
  A. Beliefs
    1. Values
    2. Motivation
  B. Practices
    1. Verbal
    2. Strategy
  C. Personality

INTERACTIONAL SETTING

I. Idea Communication
II. Group Perceptions
III. Strategy
    A. Motivation
    B. Participation
    C. Utilization of
        Local Culture
    D. Timing
    E. Flexibility
    F. Continuity
    G. Maintenance
IV. Action/Reaction
    A. Change Agent
    B. Focal Group

Change Agent Characteristics

The characteristics of change agents fall into at least two distinct cultural categories, those that come from their home cultures and those associated with their role as agents of change. Together, they represent the characteristics or factors the agents bring into the interactional setting of planned and directed change (Foster 1962, 1969). When directed change is being attempted in a nation-state or between distinct nation-states, the primary cultural characteristics are the most important characteristics of the agent. Agents are usually representatives of cultures other than that of the focal groups for which change is being proposed. This is especially true when constituent or cultural scenes are involved. This means that the agent is guided by a different set of beliefs and practices than the group with whom he or she works. Agents are cultured individuals, just as members of a focal group are cultured individuals. The cultures to which the agents have been enculturated are probably quite different, however. Agents may have different political, economic, or religious beliefs than those with whom they will work. Agents may also be products of a different social system, familiar with different family forms, kinship systems with different expectations in claims and obligations, and nonkinship groupings. Agents can be grounded in different systems of cultural transmission and acquisition. Of course, agents from highly industrialized and technologically based societies will likely take their material culture for granted. Consciously or unconsciously this cultural heritage or baggage brought into the interactional setting will affect their actions. That their cultures come in multiple forms (ideal, real, and construct) only complicates the cultural baggage they carry.

The second category of characteristics consists of those attributes the agents bring into the change setting by virtue of being agents of change. Like primary culture characteristics, these also exist in three culture forms. Change agents are characterized by focused beliefs and practices, technical skills, expertise, communication abilities, and goals and objectives tied to culture change. Based on their belief in the value of change, their own personal and professional motivations, there are behavioral attributes created out of, and associated with, their role. For example, there are behavioral characteristics associated with the kind and level of participation with the focal group, characteristics tied to their living habits while among the group, and the affiliational relationships they establish. There are technical skills and technical expertise with regard to the change being proposed or implemented, as well as the ability to communicate with those asked to adopt the change. Being specialists skilled in a particular area can also mean that another set of cultural characteristics influences the agents, those associated with the professional group of which they are a part. There are also certain personal characteristics that correlate with the role and motivations of change agents. Personality, personal traits and behaviors, all represent important conduits for communication. Motivation is listed as a role characteristic of agents based on the idea that the agent must be motivated. Just as focal groups must be motivated. Naturally, the motivations of the change agent will be quite different from those of the focal groups.

Some of these characteristics in the role category point to actual practices and activities of the agent. The agent can assume or be assigned a particular role, and how that will be perceived can be tied to affiliations established in the effort. It can be altered or reinforced by the level of participation assumed by the agent, both in terms of the project or program and in relation to the group being asked to change. The agent's living habits while undertaking the task may serve to introduce contradictions into the situation, as can the personality traits exhibited. Naturally, the strategy of the agent is a primary characteristic of the role but is not directly related to other role characteristics. This can involve all of the elements of a plan that the agent might or might not include in program efforts to bring about a culture change. Strategy, in this category, refers to what the agent has in mind regarding how to bring about the change. As will be shown later, agent strategy is something quite different from strategy in other categories of the model.

Focal Group

As attention is turned to recipient characteristics, the categories are much the same as those established for the agents of change, although the content may be quite different. The characteristic categories of the focal group consist of those the recipients bring to the directed change setting from their primary culture(s) and as a result of their being the focus of change activities. Like change agents, members of focal groups have learned ways and behaviors which they bring into the change process. The primary culture(s) of members of the focal group take on added importance in the change process. In essence, these become highlighted, for it is some aspect of the focal group culture that agents are attempting to change. Whereas with agents the role characteristics focus mainly on technical abilities, for the focal group the role attributes focus on communication and motivations. The focal group role characteristics emphasize dealing with outsiders.

The actual beliefs and practices the members of the focal group assume in the context of culture change are substantially different from role characteristics associated with agents. Members of the focal group have expertise in their own ways of believing and acting. The correctness or truth of those ways is challenged as they are asked to change some aspect of them. They may appear to be receptive or they may not. Change may be valued within their culture or it may not. They may be willing yet unmotivated. Even to show motivation may be culturally frowned upon. To show interest and motivation may be required, whereas fulfilling action is not. They may demonstrate a willingness to talk but not to communicate. They may be able to talk in the language of the agent but choose to speak only in their own language. For the focal group practices do not stress living habits or participation, as is the case with the agent; rather, practice characteristics for this group point to their attempts to balance cultural expectations and actual cultural behavior under the stress of the change context.

The significance of the real and the ideal cultural beliefs and practices assumes critical importance in the role characteristics exhibited by members of the focal group. This category would also include strategy because the focal group frequently has a strategy of its own tied to the change setting that is similar to that of the change agent. In their case, the strategy revolves around how to deal with the agents and what they want. There may even be a highly stylized way of dealing with outsiders. Where there has been a long history of contact, the focal group may have learned which actions on their part tend to placate outsiders or enhance their own particular goals and objectives, perhaps even opportunities. The real point to remember about role characteristics of focal groups is that, apart from those of their primary culture, the remainder of their characteristics stem from being asked to change some aspect of their lives. The basic desire is to respond to new circumstances or conditions in proven and traditional ways. Given a choice, they probably would not change. The continued survival of the group and its ways will probably not be perceived from the traditional point of view. After all, they may be facing change of considerable magnitude or within a time frame greatly limited by the change agency or plan.

Plan Characteristics

The plan represents an important element of the directed change process that must be dealt with quite apart from either of the participant groups. Planning a change and the attempts to implement it are very different. Most would immediately assume that this is the product of the agent, but experience has demonstrated that this is not always so. Although the characteristics of the plan center on timing, fit, and strategy, and point to some well-established lessons for change agents, these frequently are entirely out of the agent's hands. Such things may be under the control of others—for example, a governmental agency that has determined that a change will have to take place. Timing may or may not have figured into their decision to implement a change. Politically or economically, a particular change may be pursued regardless of whether the timing is appropriate. The same can hold true for its fit into the cultural pattern of the focal group. The agent in such cases merely responds to the dictates of the government or employing change agency to undertake the project. Sometimes an idea to change is simply generated and then left up to the agent to implement. Under these circumstances, the agent given the responsibility assumes the task of fitting the change to the focal group culture, in terms of both its appropriateness and its timing. In other cases, both the agent and the focal group can be involved in the development of a change plan, each contributing something to it.

The strategy characteristic looms large in the plan for change. Like timing and fit, this, too, can be out of the hands of either the focal group or the change agent. The same government or change agency that has generated the idea for a change will directly impact the strategy incorporated into the plan to bring it about. Resources, technology, and expertise may be tied directly to the willingness and ability of the agency to provide them. The financial backing provided may determine the strategy to be utilized. Timing may impact the strategy, as well the kind of change being implemented. The wrong strategy can directly affect the results and consequences just as primary and role cultures can impact them. Given that both participant groups are characterized as having strategies of their own in the change context, the plan strategy can result from the contributions of both, but it may not reflect the working strategies of either one. Plan strategy dictated by the circumstances can be distinct and different from those of the actual participants.

Interaction in Directed Change Settings

It has been suggested that most change is determined in the interactional setting; thus the characteristics of this element of change are important. It is in this setting that cultural characteristics of both agents and focal groups can serve to stimulate change or act as barriers to it. But in their combination in this setting, new characteristics are created. The characteristics of change agents, focal groups, and plans will influence situations and outcomes in the interaction setting based on action/reaction, communication, perception, and strategy. In contact settings, it is in the quality and nature of the contact that the success or failure of change programs is largely determined. It is individuals who come together in any planned and directed culture change setting. From individuals, representing both primary and role cultures, new forces are created that exert considerable influence on the whole process. Both consciously and unconsciously, the success or failure of the change process is determined by what is transmitted and how it is transmitted. Communication is thus the single most important aspect of interactional settings. Seen another way, the interaction of people involved with culture change is structured by what is transmitted between the participants.

Change agents convey the ideas for change. An idea may have been generated by them or by an agency for whom they work. This will impact how the idea is conveyed, perhaps even determine how it will be perceived. The focal group will perceive the idea based on what they already believe, plus their perception of the idea as conveyed by the agent. In other words, focal group members will react to the conveyance of an idea by an agent. It will be filtered through both their current cultural beliefs and their perceptions of agent motivation. If the agent is enthusiastic and convincing, this will impact their response to the idea. If an agent is perceived as simply resigned to the idea, the focal group may respond with little motivation, based on their belief that it really is not important. Agents respond to their perceptions of the focal group response. The communication from the focal group may be less than enthusiastic, perhaps even a nonresponse. But the agent reacting to this can compound the problem of group reaction. Both participants in the process communicate their feelings and ideas. Both perceive such communications in their own way. In the combination, a communication characteristic is created that is different from that envisioned by the agent and/or the focal group. Communication involves aspects of cultural transmission, and which is always culturally patterned.

In the attempted implementation of a change idea, mitigated by perceptions and communication, strategy takes on significant interactional characteristics. The agent may be motivated to bring about a change; the focal group, to resist it. The resulting motivational characteristic is something neither envisioned. This can be augmented by participational aspects on the part of both agents and members of the focal group. For example, agents may not interact directly with members of the group being asked to change. Those asked to change may interpret this in negative terms, and the resulting participation characteristic is not directly tied to either group but to the interactional setting. Utilization of local culture by agents can be directly offset by the focal group as they respond with efforts to avoid the change. Timing may become more a response in the interactional setting than an element of the plan or the appropriateness of a particular change, given existing culture circumstances. Flexibility of either agents or focal groups may be a function out of the hands of either group. Continuity and maintenance may be more a function of forces outside the particular change program or project. Personnel changes in government or agencies responsible for the changes are natural occurrences. They impact the change process.

All of these interactional characteristics are the direct result of action and reaction on the part of agents and members of focal groups. Focal groups do not simply react to an idea of change or an individual change agent. Agents react to the actions of focal groups. Action and reaction are a constant throughout the process. In action and reaction, the characteristics brought by both into the setting are changed in the process. The characteristics of interactional settings that are created assume a power of their own over the direction and result of change efforts. Planned or directed culture change focuses upon cultures in contact, those of the agent and that or those of the focal group (emphasis on neither one in particular). Both participants in the process have their own interactional strategies (how to deal with the contact), and both will have their own perceptions of the interaction, along with well-established belief/behavior patterns. In directed or planned culture change, changes in the behavior and beliefs of interacting people will inevitably be combined and changed. This fact leads to the conclusion that in all planned and directed change, the possibility exists that the consequence and/or result may be something neither group intended. Naturally, it is at this point that outside influences can impact the project as well. Sometimes totally unrelated to the proposed change, the interactions of agents and focal groups can impinge on the project to bring about a particular result. The resulting planned and directed culture change process becomes infinitely more complex as all of these characteristics come together and extraneous factors come into play.

SUGGESTED READINGS

This group of readings provides some in-depth discussion of voluntary and directed change processes as they have evolved within anthropology.

Arensberg, Conrad, & Arthur Niehoff. 1971. *Introducing Social Change: A Manual for*

Community Development, 2nd ed. This excellent work shows how different cultural beliefs and behaviors have purpose and meaning in the context of particular cultures, and that a failure to understand the significance of such differences can lead to disasters in the context of directed culture change. This volume also contains some good discussion on the change process, American values, and motivations and strategies for change.

Barth, Frederick. 1981. *Process and Form in Social Life.* Collection of essays on human decision theory and choice models. Makes the point that people are like actors pursuing their own interests conventionally and often thoughtlessly. Judgments are based on values that organize choices to maximize benefits and avoid losses.

Brady, Ivan A., & Barry L. Isaac. 1975. *A Reader in Culture Change.* 2 vols. These two volumes serve as an introduction to the topic of culture change, providing a review of the various theories of change and an emphasis on the role of the individual in the process.

Foster, George. 1962. *Traditional Culture: And the Impact of Technological Change.* This is considered one of the classic presentations of how technological development and change can impact traditional cultures in ways that far exceed material things. It also provides insights into many aspects of directed culture change.

———. 1969. *Applied Anthropology.* This remains one of the classic presentations of and introductions to applied anthropology, built around the vague distinction between applied and basic research. It contains some valuable discussions about various participants, issues, and aspects of the change process.

Leighton, Alexander. 1945. *The Governing of Men.* Although frequently overlooked in the literature on culture change, this account of an anthropologist serving as an administrator in a Japanese relocation center during World War II provides valuable insights into the stress and emotion that characterize all change settings, and provides some guidelines for people working in the cross-cultural context.

Niehoff, Arthur H. (ed.). 1966. *A Casebook of Social Change.* This is a critical evaluation of various attempts to introduce change around the world, and provides valuable discussion on various aspects of the induced innovation process. Case studies are used to exemplify techniques of innovators, motivations of recipients, and their culturally based reactions.

Chapter 5

CHANGE AGENTS AND FOCAL GROUPS

In Chapter 4, it was established that for any culture change, there must be some contact between people. In the voluntary change process, interactions center on the innovators and other members of their group who choose to accept a change in their learned patterns. There is no functional role of a change agent taking specific actions aimed at spreading the new trait across the group. In the sense that innovators may be at the heart of the change, they can be considered agents of change, but no more. In the directed culture change process there also must be interaction, but in that case the interaction will be oriented around specific actions designed to spread an innovation throughout a cultural group. The role of change agent is created as someone assumes the task of introducing or implementing change through some form of coercion. Voluntary and directed change processes can be found in both types of change settings. Identifying the type of setting is an important first step in understanding the process of change because of the cultural aspects of interaction. Whenever the interactions involve contacts between representatives of different cultures, the setting of the change process will be a multicultural and external one. When there are no contacts at all between people representing differing cultures, or when the process occurs among members of a single culture group and involves no direct or indirect contact with people from outside the group, the setting will be singular and internal. Because most culture groups include specific, constituent, and/or scene cultures, most settings for change will be multicultural. Contacts between groups with different beliefs and behaviors will make it so.

To understand the culture change process is to understand the type and quality of the interaction that occurs within it. For any change to occur, there must be some direct or indirect interaction between individuals. In the voluntary process, it was suggested that only an associational interaction between the members of a group is required. People associating with those who will be ultimately identified as innovators simply elect to adopt a change for whatever reasons they may have. In the directed change context, there also must be interaction between change agents and members of a focal group. This can be their own cultural group, or it can involve members of other culture groups. Voluntary change in the multicultural settings means that individuals representing different cultures come into contact and some voluntary borrowing occurs simply because of that contact. In the case of directed culture change in multicultural settings, the complexity of the process is substantially increased because of the conflicting goals, objectives, and cultural characteristics of the participants (see Figure 4.7). In both internal and multicultural settings, the change agents attempt to motivate the members of the focal group (their own or some other) to accept a change in their traditional beliefs or practices. In essence, their role is to engage in activities which ultimately diffuse a change throughout a single group or from one group to another. In this chapter, the focus will be directed at developing some understanding or control of these change processes by examining the characteristics of participants and the interactional settings where these individuals with these characteristics come together. It is in the interactional settings of participants in the change process that outcomes of change efforts and activities are largely determined, particularly in the case of directed change.

CULTURE CHANGE AGENTS

Change agents, in both the internal and multicultural settings, are those individuals who through their actions, and using some form of coercion, attempt to induce people to change some aspect of their culture. Coercion is a good way to characterize what the change agent does, for left alone, a cultural grouping would probably choose not to change any of their learned ways. In internal change settings, change agents attempt to convince other members of their own cultural group to accept an alteration, modification, addition, or substitution in some aspect of their way of life. The agent and innovator may be one and the same person if the one who generates a new trait also becomes the one who attempts to spread it to other members of the group, but this is not a given. Someone can originate a new idea, behavior, or product, and another may seek or assume the responsibility of spreading it to the other members of the group until it is accepted by the majority of the group's members. In the multicultural setting, the change agent represents one culture and the members of the focal group being asked to change, represent another. In multicultural settings, change agents are more than simply agents of change; they are representatives of other cultures. They may also be specialists or technical experts, uprooted from their own cultural contexts and placed in an alien or exotic environment to practice their specialty (Foster 1969, 1973). The task and goal of the change agents in both types of settings will be the same, to get a group to change some aspect of their culture. Their attention will be focused on the same basic elements of opportunity, association, need and motivation noted for any kind of change. The fit of the proposed change to the existing cultural pattern will also play an important role in whether it will be adopted. In the directed culture change setting, the conscious and unconscious actions of the change agent will assume a crucial role, and central to this will be communication.

Internal Change Agents

When individuals within groups attempt to introduce, implement, or spread a change throughout their own culture, they assume the role of change agents. To a certain degree, they are already familiar with the beliefs and practices of the group. They had to learn such things right along with all the other members of the group. But it is important to remember that it is quite rare for individuals to know all of their culture. In point of fact, most people do not know all of their cultures, nor do they recognize all the interrelationships and interconnections of its parts. Even in the smallest groups, all individuals are not privy to everything. They may not be familiar with the specialized knowledge of the medicine people, the shamans, the religious or political leadership. For example, among Pueblo Indians of the American Southwest, religious life is separated into distinct kiva groups, each with its own special beliefs and practices. Individuals may be quite familiar with the beliefs and practices of their own kiva group, but they may not be knowledgeable about those of the other kiva groups. In the typical pueblo, the *cacique* reigns supreme, reinforced by a large body of tradition that enhances his position in the omnipresent religious life of the group, but most members of the pueblo will lack detailed knowledge about him and his activities (Lange 1968:236–237). In other societies, certain members, especially women members of the group may be institutionally restricted in their knowledge of some beliefs and practices of the culture because of their gender (e.g., among the Mae Enga of New Guinea and the Mehinaku of Brazil). In these societies, men's and women's worlds are institutionally kept separate. Women are prohibited from knowing certain aspects of their own culture.

Although the tendency would be to characterize all change within such groups as internal, the presence of different sets of beliefs and practices suggests something else. Because of this, the task of a change agent will be similar to that of the agent in the multicultural settings. It has to be considered and approached in that light. Cultural scenes bespeak of multiculturalism and contact, just as would the presence of special or constituent culture groups. Failure to perceive them as such has led to the assumption that many change settings are internal when in fact they are multicultural, at least on the pragmatic level. Be that as it may, although it does seem reasonable to assume or conclude that directed change in an internal setting would be easier to understand or deal with than directed change in the multicultural setting, that conclusion could prove faulty. The role characteristics of the change agents and the interaction of the agent with members of their own culture group suggest something else. Under the best of circumstances, the internal change agents work under severe limitations and handicaps, any one of which can subvert or otherwise seriously impact the process.

The major difference between voluntary change and intentional (planned and directed) change within a culture group comes with the specific actions that the change agent takes to spread or diffuse a new idea. As with voluntary change, change agents must associate or interact with the people they are trying to change. They must relate the change to a need, problem, or other motivation that can serve as the catalyst for its acceptance. For an internal change agent, the change process revolves around communication. Success or failure will reflect the agent's ability to communicate the new trait clearly enough that the change will not fail simply because it is not understood. If a proposed change corresponds to a real or perceived need, or if it resolves a problem that is recognized by the other members of the group, the task of the agent is made infinitely easier. The motivational feature of needs or problems, especially if they are directly related to survival, has already been pointed out. The agent's efforts will revolve around bringing the problem or need to the attention of other members of the group and convincing them to adopt the proposed change. If the members of the group are already aware of the need or problem, they may require little or no convincing of the merits of the proposal. They can then become willing collaborators in the effort. However, they may need some convincing that the proposed change addresses the need or problem better than anything else, or is better than doing nothing at all. The agent's main effort can then turn to the dissemination of information, as opposed to coercion. The agent's chief concern is to communicate the new trait clearly enough that everyone understands it. The greatest obstacle to success lies in the possibility the people may not really understand the change or how to implement it in their lives.

Failure to understand a change can produce negative feelings that serve to subvert the effort. To decrease this possibility, more direct communication and interaction between the agent and individual members of the group are likely to produce better results than indirect communication and interaction. Demonstration of the change and its immediate benefits will also increase the chances of its being accepted by the group. Changes with long-term or future benefits are much harder to accomplish, given the priority of day-to-day survival needs of any culture group. Changing ideas, as opposed to behaviors or products, does not lend itself very easily to demonstration. If the change being introduced is not tied directly to a real or imaginary need or problem, and if it is new or totally different from traditional beliefs or practices, the task will be much harder. Changes that address survival needs that everyone is aware of present the least difficulty. Changes that add to traditional ways with some kind of obvious benefit are also easy to accomplish. Changes that modify existing behaviors or ideas will be more difficult, as will those that attempt to replace existing traits that have served the people for many years. Changes that address core systems of the culture will be the most difficult because of the interrelatedness of core systems.

Like other members of the cultural group, change agents have already learned the beliefs and behaviors of their culture. They know the way things are supposed to be (ideal culture), and they probably have some control over things as they really are (real culture) or as they have constructed it for their personal lives. They already have status and role within the group. In attempting to introduce a change into their group, these things are called into question. The internal change agents set themselves apart from the group in both beliefs and practices. By suggesting changes in existing cultural beliefs, behaviors, or products, they are going outside the accepted system—in essence, becoming marginal members of their own group. Potentially, they may no longer be seen as members in good standing of the group. Quite likely, they will be perceived as disruptive and a threat to the harmony of the group. Their actions and motives will be questioned and judged on the basis of traditional beliefs and practices. These things will change the way people interact with them.

In all cultures there are individuals who are quite willing to entertain any suggestion of change, such as the young and those who by traditional standards are already marginal to the group. There are other members of the group who are always resistant to any change, perhaps because it threatens their current status and position, or they may view any change as a threat to their personal survival or that of the culture as they know it (e.g., traditional political and religious leaders, older group members, or members of the group who have been particularly successful under the existing system). Because there are those who will accept change and those who will not, what change agents ask openly divides the group into those two factions. The agents will be perceived as the cause of the fractionalization. As they become associated with the revisionist faction, their ability to proceed will be hampered even further, for their ability to communicate with the other group will be reduced or cut off altogether. In the final analysis, and given some of these limitations under which agents work, culture change in the internal settings involves many of the considerations as change in the multicultural settings.

Change Agents in the Multicultural Settings

In the multicultural or cross-cultural settings, change is much more complicated, for the interactions of change agents with members of the focal group revolve around conflicting characteristics, beliefs, and practices. People working in cross-cultural or multicultural settings is not a new phenomenon, for the same kind of thing can be documented well back in human history. Change agents representing organizations staffed and budgeted for the sole purpose of bringing about change can be found as far back as the beginning of the nineteenth century, when the profit motive serves to generate such activities. Although much directed change on the part of agencies and individuals is still oriented around the profit motive, by and for companies and shareholders, what is new or recent is the specialist who participates without the rationale of economic profit. In today's world, a great deal of the directed culture change is tied to the participation in a developing world-market-exchange system; meeting business goals or objectives as part of international foreign policies or particular political or religious ideologies, and, of course, taking civilization to the "less fortunate." Other motives generate directed change efforts as well.

On the worldwide level, a primary motive to direct change in a people's beliefs and practices is tied to the ethnocentrism of the developed and "civilized" world. In a very real sense, representatives of the developed and complex world feel moral obligations to take their world to the less developed, "small-scale," or "primitive" world. This is based on their conviction that their way represents the "most correct," "better," "more efficient," or "advanced" way that separates civilized society from states of savagery or barbarism. The value position that underlines such thinking is that all change is for the betterment of people. That "naturally" motivates the promotion of change among others in an effort to move them toward the more polished behavior of the "modern" culture and "civilized" society. Most of the time, this position assumes that change means to turn from the old to the new and is synonymous with technological improvements, the development of a scientifically based society, and complex social and organizational structures. In the final analysis, the entire position is based on the ethnocentrism of members of all cultures, on the belief in the validity and truth of one's own culture. What this also means is that members of some culture groups are in a better position to push their ideas onto the world than are other groups, whether what they push is appropriate or not.

On the nation-state level, governments push their artificial and arbitrary systems onto all the specific, constituent, or scene groups they have incorporated through one form of coercion or another. More often than not, this is referred to as the development of a national consciousness, justified on the basis of unity or conformity for national survival. Virtually every nation-state of the world is a multicultural one made up of a number of groups, each believing its way is the most correct or true one. This can readily seen in the current struggles for power by ethnic groups in the former Soviet Union, Yugoslavia, South Africa, New Guinea, and elsewhere. The group in the dominant position attempts to coerce all others to its patterns or in some rare cases, the groups come together and agree on a compromise consensus. It is exceedingly difficult to find any nation-state that is not made up of diverse cultural groups and is not motivated to bring such diversity together in some national cultural grouping.

This is certainly true in the United States. Ideally, the people of the United States take great pride in their diversity, but the push for conformity dominates their history. Over the brief period of their cultural existence, the people and government of the United States have made every effort to coerce all groups, be they Native-Americans, Asian-Americans, Hispanic-Americans or any other, into the dominant Euro-American patterns. (The hyphen is used with such ethnic groups to indicate they are not a combination of two cultures, but unique ones that evolved in context.) Throughout the modern history of Nigeria, the government has been occupied with bringing about a national consciousness among the many traditional and diverse culture groups within the boundaries of that nation. The same can be said of Indonesia, where the national motto is "Unity Through Diversity." Despite this ideal pronouncement, the government has never ceased its efforts to create a national culture by pressuring the many constituent groups within its territory to give up their former ways and conform to the new national identity. In the changing world of the Middle East, Eastern Europe, Oceania, Africa, the Far East, South

Asia, and Latin America, the thrust of the national governments has been and is the same: conformity to the artificially and arbitrarily created state culture.

The motives of people representing constituent and scene cultures are not unlike those of national governments. For both kinds of cultural groupings, motives are tied to the correctness or righteousness of their own particular sets of beliefs and practices, which they attempt to impose on everyone else. For example, in the American culture of the 1990s, there has been a perceptual shift away from the rule of the majority to the dictatorship of the majority, away from individual freedoms to more group conformity as determined by the majority group. The majority more often than not translates into those possessing power or influence by virtue of involvement in the decision-making process, financial resources, and organization. The "moral majority" represents a case in point. This group has established positions on a number of significant social issues that they constantly attempt to impose on everyone else. The anti-this and for-that groups push their opposition or support for any number of causes. In nearly every case, the various "pushes" are nothing more than attempts to change someone else's beliefs and practices toward those of the "pushing" group, to get others to conform to the ideas and practices the group holds are more correct.

This same kind of thing can be seen even within cultural scene groupings where factions attempt to push their own particular agendas onto others. In the church and religious arenas, the fundamentalists push their views on the moderates, one form of Christianity or Islam attempts to dominate the others, and so on. In the political arena, the conservatives fight with liberals for dominance, and in higher education, administration believes it has the monopoly on truth and the faculties believe that they do. In the business world, management, finance, marketing, engineering, and other divisions all compete for the dominant position within the company culture. In all, where do we not find some group pushing their beliefs and practices on some other culturally distinct group?

Another motive for planned and directed change comes from people asking for assistance with a problem they have identified, perhaps related to the developing world economic system, a "global issue," or simply a by-product of contact with others. It might be a consequence of not being able to deal with a natural, environmental, or cultural catastrophe (e.g., flood, hurricane, drought, earthquake, nuclear accident, or oil spill). Unfortunately, groups seeking assistance rarely recognize that what they get is far more than they bargain for. As most of the developing world well knows, there are always strings attached and the inevitable unplanned consequences of planned change are ever present. In any case, the change agent has a multitude of motives for engaging in the task of changing some group's beliefs and practices. Naturally, each and every one of these individuals is capable of becoming the inevitable do-gooder who is out to help the "less fortunate" or is moving some group toward an objective the agent identifies as worth pursuing. Regardless of circumstances, people who do this subscribe to the idea that what they do is "right" for their own or someone else's "good."

Cultural Characteristics

As individuals, agents are bearers of a number of distinct cultures, belief systems, and behavioral premises they carry into the culture change context (Foster 1969, 1973; Niehoff 1966). Each of these can potentially impact the individual's involvement in the project or activity (see Figure 4.7). Each can produce significant consequences for the change goal or objective. As bearers of a nation-state culture through being born or adopted into one or more of these, change agents subscribe to the major set of values, tenets, and practices of their national culture, at least to some degree. They may also represent particular constituent culture groupings found within these, and thus are bearers of learned sets of beliefs and practices that serve to distinguish such groups within the complex and larger nation-state groupings. They are certainly members of any number of cultural scenes that also serve to distinguish them from others and motivate them to particular action. All the learned beliefs and practices of multiple cultural affiliations characterize the change agent. They represent the "cultural baggage" the agent brings into the change context. They influence and impact the agent's motivations, roles, and actions.

Nation-State Culture

Agents represent their nation-state culture to a certain degree, share in its values, assumptions, premises, and agenda. They are first cultured beings, enculturated to a particular set of beliefs and practices associated with the nation-state level of culture. This means that although they may be experts or specialists of some kind, or another, they are basically equipped to live and work in their own society. They have learned the required beliefs and practices of their group, and they know what is expected of them in that particular context. They are familiar with those material things available to them from their cultures with which they play out their beliefs and practices. Although on the surface this would seem to be evident enough, given the diversity of the nation-states, it becomes far more complex than simply recognizing that agents operate from their particular nation-state patterns. First, there is a significant difference between how members of a group tend to see themselves and how others see them. Second, depending upon their constituent or scene group affiliations, they represent these culture groups existing within the nation-state culture. This suggests that change agents are not simply members of a particular culture; they are members of various specific, constituent, and/or scene culture groups that have been incorporated into the nation-state grouping. The American change agent is a good case in point. It is not sufficient to say the agent is just an American, for the agent may also be an African-American, Hispanic-American, a Christian, a Republican, and many other things as well. He or she can be a member of any one of the many culture groups that make up the national culture. The agent is an American, but that only suggests many other possibilities.

Jules Henry (1965, 1966) provided an insightful analysis of American culture and Americans focused on ideal and real behavior, which has relevance to the American change agent. Although his presentation is somewhat time-bound, he did make some significant statements about Americans and American culture, particularly with regard to motivations, values, and elements of the "national character," that remain valid today. He pointed out that American culture is a complex and diverse one. In such cultures, Henry suggested paradoxes or contradictions will always stand out. Americans tend to see themselves as peace-loving, yet their world is filled with violence, hate, and war. Killing is an abhorrent idea, yet millions of Americans are put into uniform and charged with that sole responsibility. Henry also pointed out that Americans believe in equality and equal opportunities, yet in practice they seem to believe in something else. The American culture is characterized by a social class system in which equality is relative to only members of particular classes. Americans subscribe to the tenet that all people are created equal, but everyone knows that mentally, physically, in the eyes of God or the law, they are not equal. Americans subscribe to mass education, yet funding for and valuation of education and the educated is exceptionally low compared with other complex nations. They see themselves as humanitarians and charitable, but limit this humanitarianism and charity to specifically bounded areas of their lives. This usually means "as it may be convenient." Beyond such obvious contradictions between their ideal and real cultures, other observations of Americans are possible.

Although Americans heap plaudits on their diversity and individuality, conformity is stressed at all levels of the society. On the national level and the local level, in education, law, appearance, and even their personal behaviors, Americans push conformity. Even with regard to the much-publicized "counterculture" groups, conformity is still the rule. In American culture, the common or average person has been codified, quantified, and made into a mystical reality. This is tied to the American preoccupation with quantifying everything. Americans must measure in order to know "exact things" (e.g., time, value, worth, size, gain, loss, self, and others). They are preoccupied with punctuality in their work, play, and even their sleep. They are one of the few peoples to have objectified time to the extent that it can be saved, spent, wasted, squandered, and lost. They have even equated time with money which has assumed a central place in their lives. The people of this culture are highly mobile, female-dominated, know no clear-cut divisions of labor, and represent one of the few irreligious nations of the world. Americans are irreligious in the sense that there is no national religion; rather, there is supposed to be complete separation of church and state. Most apparently believe that religion is what you do on Sundays, and must not be confused with what you do in your business, economic, or political life. Another observation that has been made about Americans, especially germane to involvements in culture change, is the absolute belief in, and orientation, to change. Americans believe all change is good and desirable. They change simply for the sake of saying that they have changed.

As pointed out by Francis Hsu (1972), there are a number of orienting core values that appear to be shared by nearly all Americans, including the members of constituent, minority, counterculture, and culture scene groups. The value of the individual permeates everything in American culture. Individuality and freedom are so tightly woven together that Americans are forced to recognize diversity and difference, although they are rarely acceptable. Equality for all, which actually translates into plenty for all, has been a constant value over the history of the culture and is related to a basic "Puritan morality" and work ethic. Equal opportunity and material success are tightly woven together in the achievement orientation. The pursuit of status symbols, material wealth, the worry over how others may view them (including world opinion), and competition extend even into leisure activities. Winning is everything. To lose is to be shamed and humiliated, and must be avoided at all costs.

To the world, Americans are skilled merchants who are willing to buy and sell everything. Virtually all things can be bought and sold in their marketplace. Their political system is inefficient and cumbersome; one of social contracts and compromises whereby everyone in the process "wins" and "loses" simultaneously. Costs are frequently excessive but justified as "the price one has to pay." They export their ideology as they export their armaments and everything else. Economic pressure supplants logic and reason in their international affairs—they have made their problems the world's problems. Even American wars have been exercises in supply and production. They sell their education in units and hours but with minimal fiscal inputs. Ethics have been replaced by rules and systems. There are "school solutions" for every problem. Americans are the worst example of the coming world, wherein technology, automation, and the marketplace will dominate. They are loud, bold, full of themselves, socially inept in international affairs, yet good-hearted and charitable to a fault. They are preoccupied with success measured in dollars, material possessions, fun and leisure activities, and most important, they want everybody else to be just like them.

Constituent Culture

At the same time that agents are representatives of their nation-state cultures, they are also representatives of constituent cultures. Their learned ways, specific to the constituent type of cultural groupings, distinguish them from other individuals and constituent groups within their nation-states. A member of a minority constituent group, having learned the set of beliefs and practices of that particular culture group, will not fit the nation-state patterns exactly. Although Americans subscribe to many of the same basic core values of the society at large, in practice, constituent groups can believe and act quite differently. African-Americans or Mexican-Americans may well subscribe to the general conceptions of what is valuable or desirable that are held by most other Americans, but in practice may believe and behave as if they subscribe to something else. For example, Americans tend to share in the belief of the importance of the individual in society; to believe in equality for all, equal opportunity and achievement, free competition, the democratic process (as defined by the American culture), the pursuit of material success; and to follow a basic Puritan morality and work ethic. In day-to-day living, however, the minority individual or group experience with such American ideals will be quite different from that of someone from the dominant constituent group. Inequality, favored employment opportunities, and reverse discrimination may characterize their beliefs as the only means of really attaining equality and equal employment opportunity, and eliminating discrimination within the society. Even among the dominant constituent group of American society, most individuals decry equality. No individual really wants to be equal to all others in any way. It is also easy to demonstrate that the majority will sacrifice the individual or the few for the "good of the many."

The discrepancies between ideal culture and real culture beliefs and practices are frequently greatest when constituent culture groups are taken into consideration. They are certainly instrumental in culture change contexts when trying to identify the cultural characteristics of a representative of a nation-state. This is a significant part of the "cultural baggage" that change agents bring into a culture change context. The discrepancies between stated ideals and real values, ideal behavior, and actual practice can frustrate those who would change people in their own cultural groupings, let alone people in other cultural groupings (e.g., those in the underdeveloped areas of the world). Although the beliefs and practices of a constituent group can differ from those of other constituent groups and the nation-state grouping, the implications of such difference come with the social, cultural, and psychological systems and practices with which each particular group is familiar. For example, social interactions among African-Americans are significantly different from those overgeneralized as Euro-American, Asian-American, Native-American, Latin-American and so on. Social interactions between members of these constituent groups also differ quite substantially, depending upon their positions in the social hierarchy of the society. For example, African-Americans tend to deal with Asian-American groups differently than they deal with Hispanic-American groups, and so on. People striving for equality within the larger culture grouping respond differently than those attempting to hold on to their favored position. These differences are reflected in the perceptions that members of constituent groups have of themselves.

How people tend to see themselves will be reflected in how they behave in interactions with members of other constituent groupings. They may be apathetic, submissive, or confrontational in dealing with groups in a more favored position than themselves. Constituent groups will also vary on the importance of social groupings. For example, the nuclear family is important to some constituent groups, the extended family is more important to others. Even the importance and role of the individual can vary from group to group. American Indian groups, as a whole, do not rely on nuclear families, whereas members of the Euro-American culture groups do. Other constituent groups follow the Native-American pattern (e.g., the Mexican-American, Asian-American and/or other Spanish-Speaking groups). Native-American groups generally do not stress the individual; rather, they stress the harmony of the group. Euro-Americans stress the individual above all else. Relations between kin-based and nonkinship-associational groupings can vary dramatically. Role expectations for and between males and females, young and old, may vary widely as well.

There is surprising conformity in most constituent cultures, but that can differ from constituent group to constituent group. Americans are taught to work and live in their own culture and society, but what is taught and learned differs from group to group. The enculturation system of the American nation-state relies on education, but this particular cultural learning also comes from other sources (e.g., family, friends, religion, and the media). Public schools are directed toward a national conformity in content, process, and outcomes. Up to the recent innovations in America's schools, brought on by multiculturalism and cultural pluralism, the educational system was almost wholly oriented around the "average" white middle-class American. The curriculum, methods, materials, outcomes, and even physical facilities are all based on this model, a heritage that reaches far back to the Euro-American origins of the American public school system. Prospective teachers are enculturated to this model and resulting system of education. Even teachers whose origins are ethnically diverse are molded into conveyers of white middle-class American beliefs, values, and practices.

Needless to say, such a system fails to meet the needs of other constituent groups, usually identified as minority groups, within the state as the enculturated teachers continue to convey the system they are taught as part of their enculturation to the education culture. The educational experiences of students in the American system are quite different as one moves from group to group. The same kind of variation in experience can be found in constituent groups' participation in the economic, political, and even religious systems of belief and practice. The point is a simple one. Even though a change agent comes from a culture group such as that of the American nation-state, one cannot assume that he or she will fit some stereotype of an American. What was learned as part of that nation-state culture, what was experienced as a member of a constituent group, and how this may have affected the change agent's worldview, will differ from what members of other groups have learned and experienced. The agent's particular experience can have a greater impact on the cultural behavior than will the lofty or ideal beliefs and behaviors they seem to share with members of all the other constituent groups as Americans.

Culture Scenes

The greatest cultural diversity is in cultural scenes, which represent the complexity and specialization of the specific and constituent cultural groups. Culture scenes are made even more diverse by the added breakdowns, for in essence, they are also characterized by constituent groups. Specialization brings cultural ethnocentrism that is equal to any associated with specific, national, or constituent cultures. For example, professional culture is one of the most pervasive in producing cultural characteristics for the culture change agent. Every change agent is aware of the symbols of their particular field that point to success, competence, and good role performance. In the discipline-oriented American educational system, these symbols, which also serve as competence markers, are made as much a part of the preparation program as the subject matter itself. These symbols act as motivations for many of the role behaviors that characterize a change agent at any given point in time and circumstance he or she applies their relevant expertise and skills. They are likely to become a major orienting element in the goals and objectives of the agent, as well as the goals and objectives of the project with which they are associated. They will certainly be instrumental in the initial activities of the agent who, because of that expertise, is involved in the change project or program. Discipline symbols will always be a significant part of the agent's approach to the change project. They may also lie behind the individual motivations of change agents in the sense that they want to be successful in their field. In any case, such discipline symbols of competence, sought by the specialists, are inextricably tied to the people with whom they work.   Competence and individual gratification are in the hands of the focal group, to provide or not to provide. Thus, agents are tied to the focal group, but in a personally threatening way, and their behavior is likely to be affected.

Change agents are also members of any number of other cultural scenes that distinguish them from others. They are members of religious, educational, political, special interest, and economic culture groups. Southern Baptists differ substantially from Methodists or Episcopalians, and these from Roman Catholics, Jews, or Muslims. Republicans believe differently than Democrats, the Klu Klux Klan, John Birch Society, or Libertarians. Conservatives and liberals, socialists, capitalists, and Communists all believe and behave differently, as do members of the upper and lower economic classes. Despite all characterizations and pronouncements to the contrary, male and female cultures are quite different, as are those of the young and the old. Change agents are also members of the cultures of innovating organizations for whom they work. All of these agent cultures will help in defining their role(s) and performance. Agents are also individual entities with individual psychological traits and needs that will be expressed in behavior, and these will have a great deal to do with their effectiveness as change agents.

Identifying which of the cultures (nation-state, constituent, scene) will have the greatest impact on the change agents, impact their beliefs and practices more than others, is not always possible because people tend to move in and out of their various culture groupings in response to motivation, direction, and goals. Some individuals are always guided by one cultural set (e.g., those subscribing to the learned ways of their specialty, discipline, sex, or religious culture). Such individuals may continue to steadfastly hold to this set of beliefs and practices even when they conflict with national, constituent, or other scene cultures. Others may move in and out of their cultures, depending on the circumstances or context. They may turn to their nation-state culture for questions of social order, to their social class culture on questions of economic well-being, and to their religious culture on matters of right and wrong. In the complex and pluralistic societies of the modern world, conflicts continually rage in each individual as to which of their many culture affiliations is more important.

Role Characteristics

Another set of characteristics that agents bring into the change context and process is tied directly to their role as change agents; some of them are assigned and some of them are assumed (Foster 1969, 1973; Arensberg & Niehoff 1971). Here again, there is not really one set, but potentially a number of differing sets that accompany the role of change agent, in terms of both real and ideal beliefs or practices. It has been established that agents represent their national cultures, but they also represent particular versions, as indicated by their constituent group affiliations. They are specialists or technical culture bearers, recognized members of specific professional or career cultural scenes. They may also be recognized members of other significant cultural scenes, such as female, Christian Baptist, Republican, upper socioeconomic class, highly educated, and environmentalist. On quite another level, as people assume the role of change agent, there are characteristics derived from that role. Curiously, this may not have as great an impact on the process, for all of these cultures provide the agent with role characteristics in the change context (see Figure 4.7).

American change agents are usually technical experts, trained and professionally equipped to work in their own society. As specialists, agents obviously subscribe to different ideas relative to the importance of their specialties. This is followed by different motivations. Like all societies, the American society can be, and usually is, characterized through reference to its problems, and in this sense, American problems are a function of American culture. Put another way, professional specialists in the American culture are prepared and trained in response to American definitions and problems. The American system of education is highly compartmentalized. It is a system that emphasizes specialization and one in which training is accomplished by way of programs. Specialists trained in a discipline-oriented educational system are thus discipline-, and program-oriented as opposed to problem-oriented. For every problem there is a "book" or "program" solution.

Such training rarely prepares specialists to live and work in or with cultures other than their own, nor does it provide the problem orientation essential to culture change activity outside of American contexts. Even within the American context, such an approach does not prepare specialists to function in concert with constituent cultures or scenes other than those with which they are familiar. The ethnocentrism that accompanies all culture acquisition leads specialists to assume that their own discipline-style program can be transplanted anywhere, can be equally fitted to other cultures, societies, and nation-states. Discipline specialists assume that their own field can either solve the problem better than any other discipline or at least can contribute the most to the solution of the problem. The "best" solution is the program proposed by the discipline. Because of this preparation, American specialists normally cannot distinguish between technical expertise and cultural values. Their philosophy and conceptualization of what must be done may not fit the circumstances in which they must work. Even with this complex topic of culture change, most Americans, whether they be scholars, business leaders, or educational leaders, look for the right program, the "recipe" or "canned" solution.

The role characteristics most impacted by field or discipline symbols, success markers, and all the beliefs that accompany these things are associated with personality, perceptions, and behavior. As a result of their culturally specific training, the agents will believe that they know what must be done and how to go about doing it. As change agents they will immediately begin doing what their discipline has provided them. Having learned how to go about it in their culturally familiar context, they believe they can simply do it in that same way, in virtually any context or regardless of where they find themselves. That it may be totally inappropriate in other contexts is generally not considered. Believing that what they do is the "right" and "correct" thing, they naturally assume that the people of the focal group with whom they are to work share that belief. This may or may not be the case. Whether one is addressing a change project in a totally alien environment, or in one involving constituent groups or cultural scenes, assuming that the focal group and change agents share the goals, objectives, or approaches to the project is faulty. The agents perceive themselves as the key to the effort, obviously guided by the tenets of their professional associations, whereas the members of focal groups perceive that they are the key to the project because it is specifically aimed at them. They may perceive the problem, how to go about it, and even the goal or objectives in significantly different terms. Behaviorally, such a situation can produce reactions on the part of agents that can have serious consequences for the project.

When members of a focal group fail to respond as expected or a change agent's activities do not produce the predicted results, "culture shock" can surface. The agent's competence, effectiveness and potential for "success" become threatened. Although measures of success and competence are set within specialty areas, such things are entirely in the hands of the focal group to give or to withhold. Faced with "failure" in this sense, the agent responds to what is seen as focal group obstruction or rejection. He or she may become more forceful in approach or may respond negatively to the people who have responded negatively to him or her. In either of these circumstances, the behavior of the agent is likely to compound the existing problem(s). Any accomplishments in the project become personal achievements for the agent or evidence of the competence markers the agent seeks. Failures are attributed to some flaw in/among members of the focal group for whom the project is intended.

Culture shock is a common condition for change agents living or working in a cultural environment different from their own. When faced with the circumstances described above, wherein their normal experiences no longer apply or their expectations are not met within the change context, the agents react. When others fail to share their belief in the value of change or in the value of their discipline, or to subscribe to their particular methods or practices, they become very unsure of themselves. They begin to question their reasons for being there, their own sanity or that of the people with whom they are trying to work. When learned beliefs and behaviors do not elicit the expected response, people have no experiences upon which they can draw. The reactions of people in culture shock can vary from total rejection of the people or project, to withdrawal from the project or area, or even a stronger commitment to traditional beliefs and practices. Behaviors while in "culture shock" may actually be counter to desired goals and objectives. But beliefs and allied behaviors associated with the agent role are only half of the role characteristics. Practices represent the other half of this category of characteristics.

Practices

Although an agent may assume or be assigned a particular role, his or her affiliations established within the local culture, participation in that culture, living habits, communication practices, and strategy will also become part of the role. All of these things can introduce contradictions into the agent role and the agent may be completely unaware of them. Agents do not simply go somewhere, do their specialty, and that is all. Their sponsorship establishes affiliations that can directly impact practices. On-site, agents establish affiliations with people based on what they are asked to do, many times with specific instructions as to whom they must work. Those with whom they affiliate may not be the people who are being asked to change some aspect of their lives. The agent's own personal living habits while engaged in the change project may be in direct contradiction to the goals of the project. Personal practices along these lines can be quite different from those espoused in the project.

The settings in which people work have a great deal to do with affiliation roles assumed by the agents and focal groups. If the agent is sponsored by a particular agency or government, that will be the basis for affiliations that will impact the agent's particular role in the context of the change program. For example, an agent sponsored by local government will be viewed as part of that structure. The particular relations of the focal group and government will then determine a great deal of what transpires between agent and focal group. The perceptions of the agent by the focal group will be a function of their perception of government representatives. An agent sponsored by management will be perceived by members of the focal group as part of management. An agent appointed by a school administration will be viewed as part of that unit, and so on. Of course, the question of motive and loyalty is also related to such affiliations. What the agent attempts to do may very well be interpreted by the focal group as furthering the aims of the government or particular agency, as opposed to changing something for the betterment of the group. In their eyes, government involvement in local areas usually means more regulation or, perhaps, taxes. Missionaries are trying to get people to convert. Management personnel do things for personal motives and gain. Change agents on local community levels (e.g., local development or planning offices) usually mean somebody must lose. This kind of affiliational role characteristic is meaningful in all change contexts.

Agent affiliation as part of role characteristics also extends to relationships established by the agents as they work with specific members of focal groups. For example, in development programs undertaken in traditional culture areas, change goes against learned and established ways of believing and behaving. Change is viewed as a threat to the stability of the group. The change agent must deal with members of the group willing or required to participate in the program or project. Relationships established will be either direct or indirect. Historically, in these kinds of circumstances, agents have been relegated to working with marginal people, those standing on the edge of their own culture. Their willingness to participate and become affiliated with the outsider is a function of their desire to improve their own lot. This can further alienate them from the focal group to which the agents are directing their attention. The consequence of such affiliations for the agents is twofold. First, the agents may not, in fact, be working with those directly concerned with any proposed change. Second, by the agents affiliating with marginal individuals, the majority of the focal group identifies the change with the marginal and may choose to ignore the proposal because of that. As most change circumstances fragment or produce divisiveness within the focal group, so they also produce aggressive and forceful resistance to the change being suggested or attempted. In any case, the status and roles of those willing to work with change agents will impact the agents' affiliational role characteristics in that change context.

Affiliational roles are also a function of the kind of relationship established by the agent in a change program. The real point to be made is that change agents can work only through some form of contact with those they are asking to change. These contacts can be direct or indirect. Agents can elect, if allowed, to interact with the focal group face to face. Or they may be relegated to indirect contacts (e.g., the professional, through another individual or some other channel). In such cases, the agents may never directly interact with those for whom some change is intended. This is the kind of relationship that characterizes engineers, architects, city planners, community development specialists, and planning specialists of industry, local governments, and the many special interest groups involved with change. In either direct or indirect interactions, the relationship established will have role characteristics and consequences for the ultimate result of the effort. Without the personal contacts, those asked to change may simply view it as one more example of management from above, government interference by those not really familiar with the local circumstances, or unnecessary interference in their lives by people who know nothing about their lives. Without direct contacts, the very minimum that can be expected is a situation where the members of the focal group will not have much of a commitment to the program or project.

The level of participation of the agent is another area of role characteristics that can impact change programs both favorably and unfavorably. For example, in situations where the culture difference is extreme, the agent who fails to participate at any level in the local culture of the focal group will be perceived in a negative way. Failure to utilize local language can be perceived as evidence of the agent's lack of concern for the focal group. The agent who comes around only to convince members of the focal group to change some belief or behavior is automatically suspect, an individual whose motives are questionable. How an agent participates with those being asked to change establishes role characteristics that ultimately impact the result of the change effort.

Living habits of agents are significant to the outcome of change programs. High-paid government development planners, change agents from middle and upper management in business, and others who may not be particularly affected by a change they propose have some difficulty convincing members of the focal group who have much less. For example, in the American community of the 1990s, *development* has become the buzzword. For the average community individual, the cost of development has become exceedingly high. Although all developmental projects are touted as being beneficial for everyone, those actually impacted by development know better. Every time someone speaks of community development, the community residents know they will face increased taxes, and decreased ability to meet their own goals and objectives because of that. Their perception of those seeking such development is that they will not be the ones to suffer—in fact, they will be the only ones to benefit from it. The impact of increased taxes for someone making $150,000 is negligible compared the impact on someone making $17,000 per year. Faced with increases across the board, from every level of government, the ordinary citizen has become quite resistant to any suggestion of development. The agent working in underdeveloped areas, but living in "Little America" or "Little England," or any special compound area that exhibits a much higher standard of living than that of a focal group living under very different conditions, will have difficulty working with members of that focal group. The standard comment in such circumstances is: "Sure, easy for you to say."

Another component of the living habits role characteristic is that associated with cultural discontinuity. American specialists living and working in other cultures may exhibit living habits that are quite objectionable in the culture context. An American female attempting to work in another culture may find that certain of the activities and behaviors quite acceptable in her culture are not acceptable in the focal group culture. This represents a direct contradiction of acceptable norms within the culture context, and thus the agent will be rejected. Male specialists who attempt to work in areas traditionally seen as female-specific, will not be able to do their work. Because every culture has its own set of beliefs and practices, continuing to do these in contexts where they are inappropriate will negatively impact the efforts of the agent. Missionaries have found that living habits frequently contradict their work objective. Everybody being equal in the eyes of God can be totally undermined by habits that show that everyone is not actually equal.

Communication practices and strategy are additional areas where role characteristics are created. The particular strategy selected by the agent or dictated by the circumstances produces role characteristics for the practicing agent. Some strategies, by their very nature, can minimize interactions between agents and those for whom the change is designed or to whom it is directed, and they can impact the perceptions members of the focal group will have regarding the agents. A paternalistic change strategy will cause the agent to operate with paternalistic attitudes and role characteristics. This can have a direct bearing on the kind and quality of communication flow that will be utilized in the change program, over and above any agent's use of local language while on the change site. A physical infrastructural approach limits communication to the essentials surrounding the construction effort and generally ignores communication in other than limited and formal educational settings. Even in a more traditional community development approach, the communication flow is determined. Through such things as communication and strategy, affiliations, participation, and living habits, all of which have accompanying role characteristics, focal groups come to "know" change agents.

FOCAL GROUPS

Focal groups consist of people being asked to change some aspect of their life. Like change agents, they are characterized by sets of beliefs, practices, and products associated with membership in their culture or cultures. The focal group beliefs and practices may or may not be compatible with those of the change agent or agency. All cultures have core systems that are essential to their continued survival. This is true whether one is addressing a specific culture, an artificially created nation-state culture, a constituent culture, or any one of numerous cultural scenes. It is also the case that in nearly every change project, program, or context, the goal or objective is to change something in one or another of these areas. Given the integrated nature of culture itself, change in one aspect means some alteration in its other parts. A change never impacts just one aspect or part of culture. No matter how limited or focused a change may initially appear to be, it can potentially impact all of the culture's social structure and organization, and will nearly always involve economic, political, social, and worldview systems. In their culture sets, the members of focal groups will always differ from change agents. They will respond to the proposed change and the agent based on their cultural learned behaviors and practices, and they will respond to those characteristics they perceived in the culture change agent.

Cultural Characteristics

Although it seems obvious that individual members of a focal group subscribe to and follow their "culture," there are some additional things to be considered. It was earlier suggested that culture is transmitted and acquired as group "truth." Year after year, perhaps generation after generation, people are taught and learn the "right" and "most correct" way to think and do. Following that acquired way, they have survived, met their goals, succeeded in their lives or their careers. Any proposed change in that learned way represents a threat to their continued success, the accomplishment of their goals, or the continuance of their survival as individuals and groups. A proposed change in the beliefs and practices of a culture group also suggests to focal group members that they have been wrong for however long they have practiced such beliefs and behaviors. Their "truth" is being assaulted, and this involves more than the area of belief or practice being directly addressed by change agents or projects. In any case, these things are perceived as threats to what they have always known and become important cultural considerations in the culture change context for both agents and members of focal groups.

When a change is directed at some aspect of a specific nation-state, constituent, or culture scenes, the proposed change will always represent a threat to those being asked to change. Change represents a shift away from the acquired learned way. It represents a shift away from the traditional or how it has always been done.

Whether members of a focal group recognize that there is a better way of doing something, more efficient way of accomplishing a particular task that may be important in their daily lives, or simply an alternative, actually changing established beliefs or practices does not necessarily follow. All people learn the right way to do things according to the practices of their culture group; the way things are to be done, as they have always been done. The specialist associated with a cultural scene has learned the ways members of that specialty are to do things. Representatives of American constituent groups have learned their ways, just as university administrators and faculty, people associated with the various levels of organization and business cultures, Christians, and Germans have learned their ways. Conflicts are inevitable as representatives of any or all of these culture groups come together in some kind of interaction. Cultures represent sets of problem-solving solutions. All cultures have provisions for change within their set of beliefs and practices. There may even be established ways of responding to proposed changes in their cultural beliefs or behaviors. This must be so because cultures are always changing. With survival at the heart of what cultures do, as long as the particular problems are being successfully resolved with traditional beliefs and practices of the cultural sets, members of cultural groups remain fairly comfortable and confident that they will survive or succeed. Why change what appears to work, or has worked over long periods of time, perhaps generations? Proposed change upsets that confidence for the members are being asked to gamble with their survival. The more closely any proposed change is related to core areas of culture, the greater the reluctance to entertain it.

The situation is made more difficult when it is perceived that the agent asking the change is not recognized as a member of the focal group and therefore does not know the right way to do things. Management is not finance, administration is not faculty, production is not sales, development specialists are not local residents, Americans are not Germans, and so on. The agent may not share in either scene or constituent cultures of the focal group. In the case of widely differing cultures (e.g., a developing society being changed by members of a complex industrialized society), the agent may not share either the constituent or the nation-state culture of the focal group. The agent, perceived as a member of another constituent, scene, or nation-state culture, is suggesting no less than that the culture of the focal group is faulty, lacking in some way, or incorrect, and thus needs changing. Whether a change represents a significant shift away from traditional ways or merely a difference in degree, it still presupposes that the traditional way was wrong, the truth learned and lived by members of the focal group was not the real truth. The agent of the change is the individual suggesting the inadequacies of the culture, and that person is an outsider. When agents and focal groups differ in their cultural sets, the context is not one of culture contact; rather, it represents cultures in conflict. One brand of truth comes headlong into conflict with another brand of truth.

There are certain areas of traditional cultures especially germane to culture change circumstances. For example, both formal and informal leadership patterns can have tremendous impacts on the culture change context. This has long been recognized as a very important area of local culture when culture change is contemplated or anticipated. Leaders have vested interests and positions to maintain. These are threatened when an outsider arrives to introduce change. Recognizing whether the leader is appointed, elected, or chosen by using some traditional process is important in the kind of response that can be expected. In business culture and developing-world culture, Leaders are frequently appointed. They may not even be recognized by the members of the group as the "real" leaders of their culture. Depending on the role of religion in the focal group, religious leadership may be of considerable importance. This can also apply to other cultural groupings within the focal group society. In complex society, it is not uncommon to have civic groups, numerous social club groupings, and special interest groups. Leadership comes from these areas of the culture, just as it comes from formally appointed or elected officials. Of course, there are leaders and there are leaders. Noninstitutional leadership is a part of all cultures. Perhaps because of family, ability, skill, knowledge, wealth, status, or other culturally significant role or position, individuals may assume leadership roles within their cultural groupings. Leadership assumes an important role in the cultural characteristics of any focal group.

All societies divide into smaller groupings. Each of these smaller groups within a culture involves rights and obligations, responsibilities to the society at large and interests of their own. In the small-scale society or developing world, the basis of the social structure frequently is family or other kinship groupings. In the complex world, such groupings come with special interests or purposes. Because social structure represents one of the core areas of culture, its potential impact on a change program or project is second only to leadership. Within constituent or scene cultures, structure is no less important although it is less obvious. When these smaller groupings also represent significant class, ethnic, political, or religious groupings, also tied to core areas, the impacts can be even greater. How these relate to central authority is another important consideration, for together they shape the positive and negative attitudes of the members of the group toward the world and proposed changes in it.

Another aspect of the cultural characteristics of focal groups is tied to the integrated nature of all these things that together add up to culture. It is never the case that a proposed change is simply something new, perhaps a shift, alteration, or modification in some part or aspect of culture. The parts of culture are integrated, the parts are related and integrated one with another. Members of focal groups are aware of this, although it is an unconscious awareness, and change agents should know this. History has demonstrated over and over again that change in one part of culture is followed by change in other parts. Sometimes the change to other parts is slight, and sometimes it is massive. For example, case study after case study has shown that economic change, like the shift to a money-dominated market-exchange system, cash crops, and so on, has produced significant changes in the social structure of small-scale or peasant societies. Whereas such societies have traditionally based their activities on an extended family structure, in the market system an immediate disintegration of that structure begins. In the world of business or corporate culture, a change in production will lead to corresponding changes in sales and all other aspects of the operation, just as a shift in a university system will ultimately impact students, faculty, and administration alike. In more recent times, the experience of Eastern Europe, as many former Communist countries have changed their political structures, has shown that shifts in social and economic structures soon follow. The magnitude of additional changes to the societies and cultures is painfully obvious to those who brought the first changes about.

The focal group members faced with changing some part of their culture are not always conscious of its relationship to other parts of their culture except in a limited way. As it begins to unfold, however, its relationship to that part of culture with which the individual may be concerned or involved becomes more apparent. Sometimes it does not begin to appear until the project or program is completed. In either case, the members of the culture respond to the "unplanned consequences of the planned change," and again this comes from the traditional culture base. In nearly all change contexts, the cultural characteristics are important, for they will come out in the responses or role characteristics of the focal group.

Role Characteristics

Whereas change agents are mainly concerned with technical abilities and expertise, the role characteristics for focal groups will center on communication and motivations. Just as agents assume roles in change contexts centering on actions or doing something, so members of focal groups assume roles with regard to the outsiders because of what they are asked to do. The first area in which such responses are noted is motivation. The second area focuses on communication. The role characteristics of both these areas are consequences of focal group members being primarily "responders" as opposed to doers. Focal group responses to the proposed change and the person or agency proposing it will come in both traditional and contextual terms. Group members, individually and in groups, will first respond as they have been taught to respond. Eskimos operate on a cultural norm that requires group members to respond to outsiders based on their perception of what the outsider wants to hear. Employees of a company normally will respond as they think their supervisor or the boss wants. Constituent groups of the nation-state systems respond as they have learned the government expects them to, or as they have learned is effective in dealing with that government.

Such responses can take many forms. For example, the Eskimo requirement is at best a perfunctory one, giving outsiders every indication that they have been accepted, that what they propose is acceptable, and that the people are agreeable. In fact, the response may in no way indicate any of these things. It is simply required, given the circumstances in which the members of this particular group find themselves. In other cases, when agents are older than individuals to whom he or she speaks, the reactions of the latter may be a function of the necessity of politeness with people older then themselves. Although this can appear to the outsiders as motivation or acceptance of the change, quite the reverse may be true. The group members may appear to be motivated, for to do otherwise might violate behavioral norms of the group. The major point is that cultural groups have established ways of dealing with outsiders, and they have standards of etiquette that are firmly entrenched in traditional culture.

Another aspect of these characteristics focuses on the way the group views those who associate with outsiders. Proposed change tends to fractionalize every group. Associating too closely with the outsider, appearing to be cooperative or willing to participate in the change, may be taken as disloyalty by the group or it may violate the security (formal or informal) of the group. As pointed out earlier, people who are willing to deal with change agents, perhaps even eager to do so, are those who are disenchanted with their lives. They are in fact already marginal to their group. Such active participation simply isolates them further from the majority and further fragments the solidarity of the group. A good example of this circumstance has been repeatedly seen among American Indians, who select such marginal people to represent them with outsiders. The selection is not made because such individuals can really represent the group. Rather, it serves two purposes. It can serve to get rid of the individual, further isolating that person from the group. Because dealing with government and outsiders is always difficult, it also provides the group with someone to take all the unpleasantness associated with that while they continue doing what they have always done. This further supports the idea that there are leaders and there are leaders.

Many of the role characteristics that arise from the culture change context for focal groups revolve around motivation Motivation can be tied to traditional culture, direct and indirect benefit. People change because there is a recognized need for it or they perceive some benefit in doing so. Within the focal group there may already be a felt need to change something in response to some problem requiring resolution. This will determine group response to the proposal. When the group members themselves seek assistance, this can indicate a willingness to change. Some care is essential with such solicitations, for they also may indicate ulterior motives. Motivation can be tied to practical benefits, as may be demonstrated in economic areas, education, or simple convenience. It can also encompass indirect benefits tied to social acceptability, enhanced status, increased competitive edge, or rewards derived.

Practices

The last group of focal group characteristics to be considered is those loosely identified as practices. These characteristics are tied to traditional culture but are not easily handled in that context. As already demonstrated, most traditional behaviors are tied to core areas of culture. They stem from the existing economic, religious, social structural, or organizational systems of the group. Other practices emanate from other things, even seem to defy logic. Patterns of consumption may actually go against economic maximization. Recreational choices may also be in direct contradiction to avowed economic goals of groups and individuals. It is also important to note that many practices in focal groups do not fit the traditional categories of the agent. In some culture groups, a great many more things come into play in the economic system than are provided for in the traditional boundaries for this part of culture. What would normally be seen as a religious concern or a social consideration, not generally included in economic contexts, might be the real core of the economic system of the focal group.

For both of the major participants in culture change, the agents and the members of focal groups, learned beliefs and practices represent the culture characteristics which they bring into the change context and that become part of the process aimed at bringing about change. How they become involved in that process points to the dynamics of culture change. Each element of this "cultural baggage" brought into culture change is accompanied by role characteristics that will also become part of the process. How these become part of that process will become understood within the dynamics of interaction. In addition, both participants in change will assume or be assigned roles because change is being proposed, implemented, or attempted. Such role characteristics become part of the change, again to be understood as part of the dynamics of the change process.

SUGGESTED READINGS

This group of readings will provide some appreciation of the various participants in the change process, as well as of the motivations of Americans within the context of culture change.

Arensburg, Conrad M., & Arthur H. Niehoff (eds.).1971. *Introducing Social Change: A Manual for Community Development.* 2nd ed. This work remains one of the best presentations on the characteristics of participants in the directed change process, and the importance of understanding culture. The volume also presents valuable insights into the cultural baggage of American culture change agents.

Foster, George M. 1969. *Applied Anthropology.* This work, although focusing on applied anthropology, provides some useful descriptions of innovating organizations, change agents, and focal groups. Discussion of the problems of change agents is of particular significance.

Henry, Jules. 1966. "A theory for an anthropological analysis of American culture." *Anthropological Quarterly.* Although somewhat dated, this work presents a solid discussion of the ideal and real values that tend to characterize American culture, along with insights into some of the values and feelings that tend to motivate Americans.

Hsu, Francis L. K. 1972. "American core values and national character." In *Psychological Anthropology.* Francis L. K. Hsu (ed.). This work contains some very insightful observations of members of the American culture. Written by an outsider, it provides useful and thought-provoking ideas for American change agents to ponder before becoming involved in directed culture change in multicultural settings.

Niehoff, Arthur A. (ed.). 1966. *A Casebook of Social Change.* The first part of this volume characterizes the innovation process, the characteristics of the participants in the process, their interaction, and the kinds of forces that can impinge on the process.

Chapter 6

CULTURE CHANGE STRATEGIES

In addition to the cultural characteristics of participants in culture change, other aspects of the process must be considered before moving to address its dynamics or the interactional setting where all of these come together to determine outcomes. In the model of directed change proposed in Chapter 4, strategies were identified as important aspects of both planning and interaction. It was pointed out that change agencies select particular strategies to accomplish their goals, although actual participants in the change process devise their own plans and strategies for coping with each other in the interactional setting and the circumstances that have brought them together. Probably nothing is more significant than the many strategies that become a part of the actual change process and context. Unfortunately, important distinctions between plan/approach, implementation, and responsive strategies have not always been made clear. In the first instance, there are the strategies of the change agencies, and in the second, the strategies of the change agents. In the last instance, there are the strategies of focal groups, generated in response to the plan strategies, implementation strategies, and the change context in which they find themselves. The plan, implementation, and responsive strategies that are generated as part of the total process are all related, and together they will impact every aspect of the effort. The three types of strategy are obviously not the same and must be kept separate.

Change agencies will select a general strategy as part of their planning to propose or introduce a culture change. In the development of a plan and the selection of the strategy to accomplish a change, agencies may provide for some involvement and contribution from working agents and/or members of the focal group(s), or they may simply be dictated/determined by circumstances or forces quite apart from the parties involved in the change. In the selection of plan strategy as part of designing some change, the interactional strategies of agents and members of focal group will be impacted. Change agents will develop their own working strategies as part of their efforts to move members of a focal group in the direction of the goals or objectives that have been established by the change agency. Their strategies which will focus on implementing the intended change or bringing it about as designed by the change agency, must be developed within the constraints imposed by plan strategies. Elements of change agent strategy have been discussed in the literature under the category of role characteristics. As active participants in the change process, focal groups develop their own responses to proposed change, their own strategies to respond to what they are being asked to do or accept. The strategies generated by the face-to-face participants in the interactional context will play a large role in the outcomes, but only after the change agency has originated an idea for some change and designed a plan for accomplishing it. The plan strategy will ultimately condition both the implementation strategies of change agents and the responsive strategies of focal groups. From the first planning of change to the interactions that produce a result, strategies will loom as a large part of the process, as will the cultural characteristics the various participants bring to the change setting. Change strategies and cultural characteristics will be closely interrelated, and this will surface in the plans for culture change and in the interactional strategies of the participants in the process.

PLANNING FOR CULTURE CHANGE

The idea to change some belief or practice of a specified group has to come from somewhere. Coming up with an idea is not however the same thing as bringing it about. Few if any changes have ever occurred simply because someone had an idea for it that was good or desirable. An idea for change can originate from many quarters, including the group to be impacted by it, change agencies, change agents, or some combination of these—or it can originate quite apart from any of the actual participants in the process. In the context of directed culture change generated by agencies staffed and funded for the purpose, an idea to change something in a culture originates outside the group for which it is intended, with some group motivated by its own assigned, avowed, or elected objective/goal/mission. Because of this fact, ideas for change frequently are generated quite apart from specialists who are expected to implement or bring them about, or those for whom the change is intended.

In the modern context, an idea to change something can originate at any one of the many government levels of the complex nation-state (community, city, county, state, province, or national level), or with any of the many agencies that exist as part of the bureaucracy of the modern state. It can be generated within the international community (United Nations, World Health Organizations, World Bank, etc.), as the community of nations assumes more and more responsibility for the conditions and well-being of people throughout the world. It can originate out of the issues, interests, or concerns of any number of religious, political, social, or economic organizational groups. In modern nation-states, ideas for change can originate from any of the specific, constituent, or scene culture groups that make them up. In the culture of the United States, for example, ideas for change can originate with any one of the many organizational, ethnic, business, academic, religious, gender, age, professional, or special interest groups represented within its immense diversity.

Once an idea for change has been originated, plans must be formulated to bring it about. Strategy is a major component of this planning process. The primary characteristics of the plan strategy center on goals, implementation needs, costs, and timetables for completion. Although strategy on this level can take into account questions of timing, this usually means that someone has determined that its time has come, as in the case of bringing marginal groups into the mainstream of the nation-state culture. The question of fit usually means that it is necessary in the larger context, as in the case of business or industry making a change to ensure that a corporate culture remains competitive in the marketplace. Neither change agents or members of focal groups are necessarily involved in generating the idea for change or in the design, or in planning for it. This means that neither will necessarily have any input into the selection of the strategy used to bring it about. Change is being introduced simply because someone, somewhere, said it will be introduced.

People responsible for working to implement change as it has been decided upon by some change agency are usually not involved in the actual design or planning of the change; they are only hired to implement it. These people, who become the change agents, are the experts or professionals acquired by the agency to implement the change plan by influencing members of the focal group in the direction desired by the agency. They work at the pleasure of that agency. In many cases, the change agent is a late add-on, secured after the idea, design, and plan have already been developed. They are merely the specialists or experts to whom the agency turns in keeping with its established goals or program. As late additions, hired as employees or perhaps contracted experts, they will have no hand in the decision to change something or in the choice of general strategy to bring it about. They will simply be expected to implement the program or the specific change within the time frame and fiscal constraints already established by the agency that hires them.

Questions of timing and fit, always identified as important aspects of change, are as important in the planning stage as they are for change agents. In nearly all discussions of change agents, timing and fit have been identified as significant matters requiring attention. Anyone working in the context of change knows that if a proposed change is timed properly, and if it fits into the context or patterns of those for whom it is intended, there is a greater likelihood of success. But there are important considerations and differences between these aspects as they come into play in the change equation during the planning process and as they come into play during the implementation stage of the effort. For example, fit may not be given serious consideration by a nation-state government or one of its agencies that has assumed the goal of generating a change for all members of the state culture or any one of its constituent culture groups (e.g., bringing a "subcultural" group into the mainstream of national life). A change may be proposed to solve a social problem of the state that has been identified by someone. Whether the change fits into the cultural context of the group may have little or no bearing on the decision to implement it. It is something that is going to be done or must be done. Few decisions to change American Indian cultures were based on the fit of such change to their cultures. Change in the culture of business can be seen in much the same way. For example, instituting information technology in a corporate culture may be seen simply as a change necessary to ensure competitiveness in the business world. Any question of whether a proposed change fits the context of the local culture group is really not part of the decision to do what somebody has decided must be done. Experience has repeatedly shown that if the question of fit is not considered, the work of the agent is made considerably more difficult.

The same thing can be said for the timing of a change. The question of the timing of a proposed change has nearly always centered on change agents addressing whether a proposed change is appropriate in terms of the state of development of the culture group for whom it is intended. But timing has also meant something else when change agencies have been involved in the planning and design of a change. For change agencies developing plans or designs for change, timing has also meant timetables for accomplishing the change. In this, timing means something quite different from timing as a consideration for change agents. From the perspective of agencies of a government, it has meant that the time for a change has arrived, and it will be done within a specified time frame. Timing a change to fit local conditions is rarely a primary consideration.

In the case of governments and certain other types of change agencies in power positions over groups to be changed, timing generally has meant that the idea or change will be pursued and implemented regardless of the timing or fit of it to local culture. Goals have been set and timetables for accomplishing them have been established. The change agent has been no more than the hired representative of the originating agency who has been given the task of accomplishing the change as determined by the agency, within the limits of funding and according to the schedule already established. Change agents never have much influence on a plan or design for change that originates within change agencies. Unless an idea for change is developed in concert with members of the group for which it is intended, members of focal groups will fare no better than agents, in that they too, have no input or influence over plan strategy, timing, or fit. This may account for the tendency to see focal groups as merely recipients of change designed for them and implemented by change agents. A case in point is the Indonesian government plan known as Operasi Koteka, aimed at the rapid and massive development of Irian Jaya in the early 1970s (Operasi Koteka 1973). Irian Jaya (translates in English as Glorious Irian) was formerly known as Dutch New Guinea, West New Guinea, and Iran Barat (translates in English to West Irian) (Naylor 1973b, 1974).

Operasi Koteka was initially formulated to elevate, with due urgency, the social, economic, and political conditions of inland peoples of the Indonesian province of Irian Jaya, so that locals could become an integral part of the Indonesian society. "Stone Age" people (e.g., the Dani of the Balim Valley) were to be brought into the mainstream of Indonesian society and the modern world. The Dani were first contacted in the 1930s, but permanent contacts were not established until the mid-1950s. Operasi Koteka (a free translation would be Operation Clothing) was a comprehensive development plan formulated in Jakarta at the highest levels of government. Its goal was to bring about radical change in a very short period of time. In that comprehensiveness, the plan exhibited a decided lack of understanding of local conditions. The plan included the building of roads and fishponds, the introduction and wearing of clothes and the introduction of new agricultural practices, crops, animals, and fish. It also provided for activities aimed at improving literacy among adults and children. The field personnel expected to carry out the many provisions of the plan (the actual change agents) were recruited from the military, the civilian administration, and local universities. Operasi Koteka personnel were divided into teams that were strategically located throughout the highlands and the Balim valley. Each team was assigned specific tasks that were to be accomplished within specified timetables.

The plan revolved around education, practical training, and speed. It also required significant amounts of community inputs for reaching its objectives. The entire project was scheduled to be completed over a two-year period. Because every objective of the plan represented changes of kind, away from traditional practices to those of the wider Indonesian society, it was clear that neither the fit nor the timing of many of the proposed changes to local cultures was given serious consideration. People such as the Dani of the Balim Valley, exposed to the outside world for less than twenty years, could hardly be expected to change so much of their culture, so dramatically, in so short a period. In terms of the existing Dani culture patterns and the sequencing of the changes, most of the specific objectives considered neither timing or fit. Many changes outlined in the plan were contingent on the completion of other changes that were not made part of the overall effort. As designed, they were inappropriate and out of sequence. The time allocated for reaching all of the plan's objectives was clearly unrealistic, as were goals that depended upon things not considered. Many aspects of the plan involved these considerations of time and fit (Naylor 1973b, 1974).

For example, Operasi Koteka provided for the introduction of new agricultural practices, cash crops, and the wearing of clothing. Without the development of a market-exchange system, wage-labor jobs, and knowledge of money, these changes had little chance of being implemented. The requirement that the local people wear new styles of clothing was clearly out of step with economic reality. It simply did not fit with local conditions, let alone traditional culture. Clothing had to be purchased and cared for, both things requiring money. Although the concept of money had been brought by the Dutch, Indonesian money was a recent introduction into the lives of the Dani. As their traditional culture had neither markets nor money, the Dani had little understanding of money, and, just as important, they had little of it and even fewer opportunities to acquire it. The need for money to purchase clothing and provide for its upkeep was not lost on the Dani. Without the necessary money or the means to acquire it, they could not adopt the practice of wearing clothes. Also working against the idea was the fact that the Dani lacked motivation for it. Traditional clothing did not have to be purchased, and little effort was necessary to obtain it. These same kind of limitations could be seen in the ideas to introduce new foods and cash crops into the agricultural practices of the Dani.

Part of Operasi Koteka provided for the introduction of new foods, animals, fish, and cash crops into the agricultural practices of the local people. Although such changes, at least theoretically, could provide the people with a means of acquiring money, they were clearly alien to local cultures and out of sequence with economic reality. The plan provided for the redesign of gardens, the building of fishponds, the introduction of new animal husbandry practices, and the idea of cash crops well before local conditions might have ensured their acceptance. The new crops and foods to be introduced, were mostly for the benefit of immigrant Indonesian nationals and other outsiders, not the local population. There were no provisions for the acceptance or integration of the new foods into the diet of the local people. The idea of a cash crop was inappropriate because there were no local markets for the cash crops, nor were there efficient means of getting them to existing outside markets. A local market would depend upon the local people and the immigrant inhabitants who came with contact, a small number of missionaries, government administrators, and immigrants from other areas of Irian Jaya and the nation. This group was hardly sufficient to sustain a cash crop. The most serious flaw in the plan was the lack of roads to outside markets. Although the plan provided for road building within the Balim Valley, there were no provisions for roads to the coastal areas. This meant that the only means by which a cash crop could be gotten to the outside markets was by air. Because of the high costs involved, crops grown in the interior and transported to the coast could not be competitive with similar crops grown closer to such markets. This same kind of scenario played out with objective after objective of Operasi Koteka. Questions of timing and fit obviously had played a major role in these changes beyond the simple timing and fit of the changes to the local culture. Both ended up as major factors in the failure of the program to reach it goals and in its termination.

Operasi Koteka demonstrates a number of significant points with regard to change agencies and their plans and strategies for change. It was a classic example of an outside agency imposing change on a group of which it had little understanding. The decision to introduce changes was made at the highest levels of government, among national leaders with little or no understanding of local conditions. It was based more on the national agenda than on the needs of the local group expected to adopt them. Local people had no input or influence on the decision or its design, nor did the change agents expected to carry out the provisions of the plan. The change agents were secured after the program was planned and designed. This case demonstrates the limitations imposed on change agents by agency plans. It also highlights the importance of both fit and timing. Such concerns are significant to change agents, but they go beyond simply fitting or timing a change for traditional culture.

As demonstrated in Operasi Koteka, time and fit are significant in planning change as well. This case strongly suggests that the question of fit must also incorporate the question of whether the proposed change fits into the overall scheme and goals of the planners. If a change is out of sequence with other changes that have to be made, or have to be accomplished first, the change is neither a good fit nor well timed. The example also points out the dual nature of the time consideration. Timing is more than a question of appropriateness given the stage of development of local culture. Timing also refers to the timetable and schedule imposed by change agencies and planners for accomplishing the change. It looks at the appropriateness of a proposed change within the larger program or agency goal, at its placement in the total sequence of changes to be introduced. The final disposition of Operasi Koteka was, in a great many ways, largely determined in the initial planning, which did not recognize many of these things.

GENERAL PLAN STRATEGIES

In the design or planning for change, in the decision of how a proposed change will be accomplished within any restraints or limitations, the plan strategy surfaces as one of three strategies to impact culture change contexts. Plan strategy represents the entire change project, program, or effort from the point of view of the change agency. It is more than a statement of proposed change; it reflects the goals and objectives of the change agency, outline the agency's position as to what will be done and when, by whom, and under what conditions. It details the contributions and involvement of the agency, particularly in terms of the resources (fiscal, material, personnel) it will provide. It outlines the expectations the agency may have for members of focal groups, and it may detail how outcomes will be evaluated. In the final analysis, the plan will determine a great deal of what will occur in the actual process. It will condition the interactions of participants in the process by influencing the strategies of change agents hired to implement the project or program, and the response strategy of the targeted group.

Warren Bennis (1966) and Gottfried O. Lang (1973) recognized four basic approaches to culture change, which they identified as strategies for induced change: the paternalistic strategy, the engineering strategy, the community development strategy, and the facilitative assistance strategy (Lang 1973:45). These types of strategies (see Figure 6.1), are roughly comparable to strategies in business and government circles that are labeled authoritative, assertive, and participatory leadership styles (Hersey et al. 1987), and in other circles as re-educative, persuasive, and power strategies (Zaltman & Dugan 1977). The approaches can be distinguished on the basis of agency imputs and the locus of authority (who makes the decisions) (Niehoff 1966; Batten 1969; Bennis 1966). The first distinction relates to agency investments in the project, the level of material and/or financial resources and expert personnel to be provided by the sponsoring agency (see Figure 6.1). The second distinction relates to whether an approach is directive or nondirective. In the directive approach, all decision-making authority resides with the change agency and by extension, the change agents. In the nondirective approach, decision making is shared among agencies, agents, and members of focal groups who become partners in the effort. Using these basic distinguishing characteristics, the types of plan strategy can easily be distinguished. The paternalistic strategy requires a low level of agency investment and is essentially directive. Community development requires a low level of agency investment and

Figure 6.1
Strategies for Planned Change

Material Inputs Invested	Locus of Authority	
	In Change Agency (Directive)	In Local Community (Nondirective)
Low Amounts of Material Investment	Paternalistic Approach	Community Development Approach
	Superior knowledge and skill of the change agent determines the acceptance of change.	Emphasizes "self-help" and community resources in problem solving.
High Amounts of Material Investment	Engineering Approach	Facilitative Assistance Approach
	Stress is on the building of facilities needed for development without provisions for teaching the people how to use them.	Local groups solve their own problems with the assistance of change agents.

is nondirective. In the engineering approach high amounts of material investments are required and all authority is monopolized by the change agency. In the facilitative assistance approach, high level of material investment are required and the strategy is nondirective. In the community development and facilitative assistance approaches authority is shared with members of the groups involved.

Paternalistic Approach

In the paternalistic approach, all decision-making authority resides with the change agency. This particular approach to change is perhaps the most familiar and widely used throughout the world. Its use has been documented in all types of cultural contexts. It is a mainstay strategy of nation-states and, those in a dominant position over other culture groups, and is the strategy of choice of cultural groupings whose existence is based on shared and strongly held beliefs (e.g., religious and political groups). Paternalism is a directive change approach in which all decision-making authority rests in the hands of the change agency, which decides what is best or necessary for the focal group and assumes a condescending attitude toward those it seeks to change. It can be likened to a "do as I tell you, I know better than you what you need" model. Members of the focal group are perceived as "childlike" or "backward." The approach is particularly appealing in situations where capital is limited and the people may not be aware of the opportunities open to them (e.g., in developing nations with limited resources). Without serious drain on limited national resources, change can be brought about by legislation, decree, or fiat. The paternalistic approach was very popular with early missionaries and colonial administrators, and it remains popular with nation-state governments attempting to bring about change without any substantial commitment of resources. Paternalism also exists in organizational cultures (e.g., business and academic) and in culture groups where power is monopolized by a few.

As a strategy for change, paternalism depends primarily on the power of the agency to force the acceptance of a proposed or designed change. This can be accomplished through coercive power based on fear; connective power based on the utilization of influential people; expert power based on expertise, skill, and knowledge; information power based on the possession of valuable information; legitimate power that accompanies status and position; referent power based on personal traits; and/or reward and punishment power based on the ability to provide either of these. The paternalistic approach does not necessarily require huge amounts of financial or material resources on the part of the change agency. It is an approach that assumes the superior knowledge, or simply the power, of the agency will accomplish the proposed change. In determining what might be required or is in the best interests of the focal group, paternalism equates with what Zaltman and Dugan (1977) have termed a re-educative strategy in which leadership will be authoritarian (Hersey et al. 1987). The change agency or innovating group decides what change is necessary and informs the focal group through a representative or intermediary that it will be done, because it represents what is best for them. In some cases, it can amount to little more than a decree by the agency—change by fiat. It is assumed that the expertise, superior knowledge, or legitimate power position of the agency will be sufficient to convince members of the focal group to accept a change. It assumes that expertise of the change agency will be readily accepted because members of the focal group are seen as either backward or considerably less knowledgeable as to what is in their best interests.

The paternalistic strategy has been widely used by governments and other change agencies in dominant positions over those they wish to change. Being directive, it is basically uncritical and a one-way approach, from agency to focal group. Governments frequently utilize this approach when attempting to change constituent and scene cultures. For example, this particular approach has been used extensively by the government of the United States in its dealings with Native Americans and other constituent groups making up its multicultural national culture. Agency paternalism has been the dominant and constant theme of Indian/white relations (Spicer 1961:255). The government, through one of its agencies or representatives, decides on change for the Indians or their cultures, and then imposed its will on those people through the Bureau of Indian Affairs, the army or local agents. This same paternalistic strategy dominated the business or corporate world, including academia, for a great many years. In some instances, it still does. Paternalism in these organizational cultures can be equated with management from the top down. Responsibility for change brought about using this approach rests squarely with the change agencies but it is rare that other than successes are credited to them. Negative results or consequences are not generally assumed to be the responsibility of the change agencies; rather, they are nearly always attributed to some other cause. Failures may be considered the result of a faulty perception or definition of a problem, a shortcoming of the implementing agent, or a lack in the focal group. More often than not, failures are laid at the feet of the focal group rather than of the agency or the change agent provided by the agency.

Proposed changes using the paternalistic strategy are frequently unsuccessful because the approach does not provide for local input, the utilization of local leadership, and the attitudes that members of the focal group develop toward the innovating organization (Spicer 1961:257). Change programs attempted using this strategy are frequently seen as agency programs, for the agency's benefit and not that of the people. This results in a lack of commitment on the part of the people expected to adopt the change. Despite its obvious limitations, there are occasions when the choice of a paternalistic approach is justified. It is a particularly good strategy in change programs requiring significant levels of formal education (e.g., any project involving scientific or technical procedures). In fact, any kind of education or instruction is paternalistic by definition. Thus, any change project that involves some level of instruction will have elements of paternalism associated with it. For this reason, elements of paternalism are, and should be, incorporated into any plan for culture change. Education ensures, at least in part, that an introduced change will continue long after a project has ended and the change agents have left the area. In the true paternalistic approach, however, the entire effort, from beginning to end, will exhibit its main characteristics of being directive, authoritarian, and relying on coercive power centered on reward or punishment.

Engineering Approach

The second of the directive approaches concentrates on changing belief and practice by providing some infrastructures for change, essentially physical structures that require large amounts of capital and expertise beyond the capability of the local people to provide for themselves. Unfortunately, this approach usually begins and ends with providing such expertise and structures. For this reason, it can be characterized as a "here is the structure, you figure out how to use it" approach. Change agencies opting for this strategy tend to see their prime responsibility, frequently their only responsibility, as providing the infrastructure. Their responsibility ends with the completion of the construction effort. The approach is characterized by huge investments of money, material, and expertise by the agency. But it is also characterized by limited direct contact between project personnel and the people expected to benefit from the project. It centers on providing complex structures in response to identified needs, and little else. There is a widespread belief that economic and social opportunities will simply follow as the people begin to utilize the facilities or structure. The people for whom such structures are designed are left to figure out how to utilize them. Few provisions are made to teach the people how to utilize the structures, for the agency nearly always has become focused on the complexity of the construction effort and providing sufficient resources to bring it to completion. In this approach, local decisions are minimal, if not precluded altogether.

This particular strategy can be found in many national or international change programs where particular facilities are required but are outside the abilities and resources of the local groups to provide, (e.g., a dam, irrigation and road systems). It does not always involve large structural or engineering feats such as the Aswan Dam. It also has been used to provide such things as community centers, health centers, and other physical structures considered essential to local communities (e.g., for Native-Americans in the state of Alaska). Its selection is determined by the inability of local groups to respond to their own needs and the need for significant amounts of capital and material investments. Because of the high costs, many restrictions and controls nearly always accompany this approach. This usually results in the project being viewed as for the government, the change agency, or some special group. It is not viewed as a project for the people. At the heart of the approach is the assumption that over time, the people for whom it is intended will learn how to use it. Unfortunately, this is not always true or as automatic as assumed. In essence, the approach centers on providing the engineering expertise and the materials for the physical infrastructure necessary to address a problem or need. The human factor is usually not considered in other than the most general terms, nor are any accompanying cultural consequences. Contextual considerations and preparations for the use of the construction are addressed minimally, if at all.

There are obvious circumstances where the engineering approach is useful, if not necessary. It is appropriate when the needs of some group far exceed the ability to respond to those needs. In such cases, this approach may be the only viable alternative. The limitations and difficulties of the strategy come with the minimal involvement of the people for whom such projects are intended and with the lack of attention to educating the people on the use of the resulting structures. It is a very directive strategy wherein the agency decides that a major undertaking is necessary, based on the agency's belief that it meets a local need. In this sense, it is paternalistic as well. The agency decides to provide it with no input from the focal group, although the idea may have been generated within the latter. The focal group may have requested a structure in the belief it will solve one of their pressing problems. In either case, agency responsibility usually stops after the structure is completed. Because the approach assumes a top-down stance, little attention is paid to the cultural context of the people for whom it is intended. For example, most engineering projects require changes in the lives and cultures of the people beyond those associated with their use. They can require changes in both belief and practice. New cooperative behaviors may be required, or perhaps new customs for regulating access to resources must be instituted. Or the people may not be able to use the project's result because of local cultural constraints or its lack of fit to local custom and tradition.

Agencies electing the engineering strategy rarely take such considerations into account, focusing, as they must, on the massive resource requirements. Their major concern is to provide the physical structures or expertise that is required. History has demonstrated that many projects done under this particular strategy have impacted or benefited only limited groups within the focal group population. In some cases, they have ended up providing preferential treatment to an already privileged group which has a direct relationship to or stake in what the construction made possible. It other cases, projects done with this strategy have benefited only a relatively few people within the focal group who have sufficient resources to take advantage of it. Potential outcomes such as these have rarely been included in the thinking of the change agency. Finally, there is always the question of the ability of the focal group to maintain such projects after they are completed. These potential outcomes or considerations have not normally been seen as being within the parameters of the change agency's charge. As far as the agency is concerned, its consideration of a human element begins and ends with the belief that the people need the project, and they will learn to use it and capitalize on its perceived advantages. This general strategy is a power one resting on the possession of expertise and resources. Addressing some of the shortcomings of the approach may have the net effect of maximizing the value of the engineering strategy when it appears as the only viable alternative.

Community Development Strategy

Perhaps the approach to culture change most widely used in the industrialized and developing world is the traditional community development approach. This is certainly true in the American culture, where it has been utilized at all levels of the society with apparent success. In developing nation-states, the strategy has been extensively used where money for development is in limited supply. In this context, the strategy has had mixed reviews. As a strategy for change in a complex society, with a relatively high standard of living, it has a good chance for success. In the developing societies where resources are limited at all levels, it does not. The approach is basically a nondirective one in that decision making is shared between the agency/agent and the focal group. Change agencies, agents, and members of the focal group all participate in the planning and implementation of the change. The approach centers on developing within the local community the ability to identify and resolve local problems or needs with locally available resources. For this reason, it has been characterized as the "self-help" approach, which indicates the "catch" in the strategy. Material and fiscal inputs on the part of the change agency are minimal in this approach, whereas focal group investments are usually considerable. It relies heavily on the voluntary contributions of resources, both money and labor, from the focal group to meet project goals, foster community development attitudes and self-reliance.

The community development approach to culture change has been widely used, for in the short run, projects done under it have looked like successes and, even better, it has not required much from the change agency (Niehoff 1966). The development of local leaders and self-reliance is an important aspect of the approach. Given the involvement of members of the focal group in the actual decisions to undertake some change project, to contribute their time, resources, and effort to it, they are usually more committed to accomplishing its goals and objectives than they are with directive approaches. Outside experts and/or a locally educated elite are heavily relied upon in this strategy. On the other hand, although it may appear otherwise, local communities are not always in a position to provide the resources necessary to undertake and complete projects. When they do make the necessary commitments, focal groups have found that ultimately they have to pay a cost, either in terms of traditional activities and pursuits, or in the continuing outlay of funds. In the case of developing nations, local communities more often than not exist at a subsistence level and can ill afford to devote time and energy to a project rather then to traditional labors. They may have the resources to initiate a projects but not to sustain it over any length of time, or not without severe hardships in other aspects of their lives.

Change agents hired to work with members of the focal group frequently find themselves involved only with selected or willing members of the group, those who are part of the emerging elite or are dissatisfied marginals. Either way, agents will be working only with limited segments of the entire group. Thus, the result is usually a mixed one, frequently increasing existing inequalities and distrust. This creates a cynicism that will impact and subvert the trust required to implement additional programs or projects. When utilized in situations where strong factions already exist, it can foster additional dissatisfactions and disillusionment among important members of the focal group. Many examples of this kind of situation can be found in communities where bipartisan stands are assumed on development issues and projects.

Under certain circumstances, the community development approach to culture change is a viable one (Singh 1952). Where local interest can be identified and sufficient resources are available, it frequently can produce desired results. It is probably best utilized in complex societies as opposed to developing ones. In the latter, because the people live so close to the survival line, all their energies must be devoted to that surviving. This means that the necessary contributions of material and labor are not available for the project. Devoting time and energy to the project will threaten their survival. From this perspective, the costs represent too high a price to pay. Yet the strategy may be useful, even the only viable alternative, for developing areas where the government may not have the resources to undertake many change programs. For example, Indonesia was simply not able to provide significant funds for the development of Irian Jaya up through the 1970s. Within restricted nation-state budgets, the approach may represent the only way the agency can become involved in a change or development program. This approach requires significantly more time to reach project goals than do some of the others discussed, but with realistic expectations it can produce continued change over the long run where it is required.

Facilitative Assistance Strategy

The last type of approach strategy available for culture change is the facilitative assistance approach, sometimes simply referred to as the facilitative approach. Although viewed as very promising, this particular strategy has not been widely used (Dalton 1971; Niehoff 1966; Choldin 1968; Lang et al. 1969). Facilitative assistance is concerned with local groups solving their own problems with the help of the change agency (Gearing et al.1960; Holmberg 1955, 1958, 1960). In this approach, the emphasis is on local decision making, but it also calls for relatively large material and nonmaterial inputs by the change agency. Although such inputs can be necessary, providing information to the focal group is of greater importance to the agency. Helping to develop new skills among members of the focal group and mediating between them and the change agency are the central tasks of the change agent. Whereas decision making lies primarily with the focal group, providing information, capital, and expertise is the task of the agency and its agent(s). The contextual fit, timing of the change, and obtaining a significant level of focal group participation are absolutely critical in this strategy, so that the people learn the use and accompanying behavior changes that go along with the acceptance of a change. The primary task for the change agency is to facilitate the efforts of the focal group and provide the personnel and resources necessary for successfully completing the change task.

The facilitative assistance approach is most appropriate where members of a focal group either recognize, or can be led to recognize, a need that is greater than they or an employed agent can respond to within their limitations or abilities. It is also appropriate where sustained growth is desired or required. It is based on the assumption that change which promises an immediate and highly visible reward will be more readily accepted and integrated into the patterns of the focal group, once it is broken down into its component parts and addressed accordingly. A fundamental belief underlying this strategy is that a complex change has a better chance of being adopted if done in stages. The approach recognizes and assumes the inevitably of stress, conflicts, and perhaps disappointments. Because of such things, the emphasis is directed toward the teaching/learning continuum and providing the structure within which this can be done. Members of the focal group develop a commitment to the effort, become accustomed to handling responsibility, and acquire new skills.

IMPLEMENTATION STRATEGIES

Change agents are specialists, professionals who influence innovation in a direction already determined by a change agency (Zaltman & Dugan 1977). As such they serve as the link between the change agency and the focal group. The agents stimulate and guide the actual implementation of change. Although they function at the pleasure of the agency that employs them, and are thus controlled by the agency and its approach to change, they do have some measure of control over the actual change process by virtue of their implementation strategy. As indicated previously, it is not always the case that the change agent's strategy and that of the agency will be the same, so it is very important to distinguish the general approaches to change of the agency and the functional or pragmatic strategies that agents adopt in their attempt to implement change. Although a great deal of what agents do may be conditioned by the general approach of the agency, the agents are still left with the task of selecting their own strategies for working with the focal group and to meet the goals of the program or project. The strategy of the change agency may influence or determine the kind of interactional relationships the agents must assume toward the focal group, create the perceptions people will have of their role, and impact their ability to fashion the program to fit local needs and context, as well as the style of approach the agents will take with regard to the project and members of the focal group. All of these things become part of the strategy of the agents, along with the cultural baggage they individually bring to the interactional context by way of membership in all the cultural groups of which they are a part, their own skills, and their personality traits.

After a change agency has generated an idea for change and opted for one of the approach strategies, it is up to the agents to establish the working relationship with those being asked to change and to work toward the accomplishment of the project's goals and objectives. Because of their role, the tendency in the past has been to refer to role characteristics as opposed to implementation strategy (Foster 1969; Niehoff 1966; Arensberg & Niehoff 1971). The consequence of this has been the misinterpretation of the actual input of agents into the change context. The plan strategy elected by the agency, and forced upon the agent will dictate the thrust of the agency and the resources available for the task, but it is through the efforts of change agents that attitudes and practices are actually changed. Such change will hinge on their personalities, personal habits, skills, and actions (perhaps things they fail to do). In the working strategy of the agents, the first concern will be the kind of relationship to be established with the focal group and its members. Agents can interact directly with the members of the focal group or indirectly through intermediaries.

If the change agency has opted for the engineering approach to the change project, the agents are pretty much relegated to an indirect relationship. Their efforts will probably be channeled through intermediaries (e.g., government officials, department heads, midlevel administrators or supervisors) to the focal group. Their primary responsibility will be on communication and providing information. Their ability to complete the task will be tied to the others through whom they must work, and will depend on their personal expertise, skill, or knowledge regarding the project to be undertaken. Assertiveness or persuasion, delegating or telling, will likely characterize their interactions with those they must work through.

If the agency has planned the change project around the paternalistic approach, the agents' strategy will not be very different. The agents, in a legitimate power position, simply tell the focal group what they will do, as opposed to engaging in activities designed to persuade them. As a result of the employing agency's opting for either the paternalistic or the engineering approach, agents are pretty much relegated to an assertive persuasion strategy based on the coercive power of reward or punishment. Their implementation strategy will be characterized by the use of logic or reason to bring the change about. The agents forward the idea, relate what must be done and how it will be done. They will use evidence and argument, as opposed to raw power and authority, to persuade members of the focal group to accept/adopt a change. Unfortunately, as has been pointed out, people in change contexts are not always guided by logic or rationality. Given multiple cultures already in conflict, the change context is one of stress and high emotions. Sole reliance on the paternalistic strategy usually produces more resistance to the effort. Reward and punishment strategies are characterized by the use of pressures and incentives to produce the desired change result. They can mean the exercise of naked power or the use of more subtle or veiled pressures. In this strategy, agents communicate what is expected and what ultimately will be judged for the purposes of approval or disapproval, praise or blame, and in the final analysis, rewards or punishments.

In the community development and facilitative assistance approaches, agent relationships are quite different than in the directive strategies. In these cases, direct relationships are common as the agents attempt to bring a change about. These approaches require that they collaborate with the members of the focal group but retain some power to impact the circumstances by virtue of their possession of or access to information. They are the experts whose interactions will depend on their skills of compromise and accommodation. Under these kinds of approaches, participation and trust are significant and personal traits become much more important. In the facilitative assistance approach, the agents' ability to reach successful outcomes will rest on their developing the many connections required to ensure an ongoing program. They must share a common vision with those with whom they work, both agency and focal group. The agents' primary role is to bridge the gap between the agency and the focal group, in essence to serve as broker between the two. For the agents, these approaches means teaching through demonstration, and creating the circumstances wherein the assistance of the agency is no longer be required and the expert becomes obsolete. In short, the task of the agents under these particular strategies is to establish the climate for mutual learning and teaching while helping to build a self-maintaining system.

The challenges to agents using such these approaches are perhaps greater than with other strategies. The agents must believe in themselves and the procedure. They have to assume responsibility for what they do, and perhaps for what they do not do, either of which can influence the effort, its successes and failures. They must be willing to become teachers whose primary goal is to make themselves obsolete. For example, as a result of having to work under either of these plan strategies, change agents are more apt to rely on the participation and the trust implementation or common vision strategies. Both rely on involving the members of the focal group throughout the change process, building trust and open relationships. In the first instance, decision making is shared, thus establishing local commitment, and direct intervention is kept to a minimum. Fostering participation and decreasing outside supervision is the key. In the second instance, the agents work to identify the common goal and mobilize local energies and resources—in essence, to facilitate action. The major thrust of the agents is to communicate clearly. It is directed at emotions rather than logic, and at building enthusiasm for the project.

Personal Styles

To be sure, the plan strategy elected by the change agency will directly influence the implementation strategy of the change agents. But what agents do, both consciously and unconsciously in the course of their activities, will also play a major role in implementation strategy. Change agents are first individual humans with personal characteristics that, directly or indirectly, become part of their particular change strategy. In many cases, these characteristics will be an extension of the cultural baggage they bring to interactions, for the vast majority of them are created and conditioned by their cultural affiliations. For example, if their affiliation is with a culture like that of the United States, where the individual and competitiveness are highly valued, agents will likely be assertive in their direct contacts with members of the focal group. On the other hand, if they are representatives of an American Indian culture group, they will likely be introverted in their relationships with focal group members. Cultural baggage will also impact other personal styles of agents that become part of their strategy of implementation, whether it be conscious or unconscious. Such personal traits as sensitivity and feeling, thinking and intuitiveness, perceptiveness, ethnocentrism, and judgmental tendencies are also culturally connected.

Beyond personal characteristics that have already been culturally impacted, what the agents do directly to bring about the change is an important part of implementation strategy. Remembering that these actions can be influenced, even determined by the general strategy approach of the agency, the agents can still pick and choose from among alternatives. In a change project with paternalistic strategy, they can choose between persuasion and reward/punishment. The expertise, skill, and knowledge of the agents are expected to "carry the day." They do not worry about management styles because the reward/punishment accomplishes the task. The agents simply utilize a coercive power to accomplish the change goal. Those who change are rewarded; those who do not, are punished in some way. In the engineering type of change program, the agents again rely on expertise, skill, and knowledge to accomplish the objective, which amounts to providing the necessary physical structure or facility. The assumption in this general strategy is that the use of the facility will naturally follow its completion. The agents assume the connection will be made by the people for whom the structure is provided and that gradually they will attempt to use it. More often than not, the agents are the experts who provide the engineering structure and little more. In the absence of direct relationships or contacts with those for whom the project is designed/intended, the agents' task in developing an implementation strategy is negligible, if there is one at all.

In the projects designed under the community development and facilitative assistance approaches, more responsibility for implementation falls on the agents. Both require local participation and direct contacts with change agents. In projects done under the community development strategy, personal traits are far more important than in the first two strategies. Expertise, skill, and knowledge are again important to agent's strategy, but the agents also must develop a level of participation and trust among the members of the focal group. The agents are in a unique position in this respect, for they have persuasive power and legitimate power by virtue of their monopoly, possession, or access to essential information, and their actual position. In projects based on facilitative assistance, the circumstances of the agents change once again. The agents' strategy will revolve around personal traits, a common vision with members of the focal group, developing trust, and their participation within that group. Their characteristics of expertise may influence their interactions with the focal group, but their personal traits (e.g., willingness to collaborate, compromise, and accommodate) will have greater impact on their involvement than will any other form of approach. In this circumstance, agents' sensitivity to concerns of the focal group will be paramount. Rather than be assertive, change agents must be cooperative.

Obviously, the ability to obtain a high level of focal group participation will depend upon the communication skills of the agents. Local leadership is utilized to the maximum degree, and developing motivation for the change is critical. Although the program may be initiated on the basis of the needs the people themselves recognize, demonstration and ascertained needs initiated by the agents have to become significant elements of their implementation strategy. At this point, the agents must consider the fit of the change to local values, social forms, and economic realities; timing; and the sequential fit. Agents must demonstrate as much motivation as the focal group with which they work. The thrust of the agents' activity centers on questions posed to the focal group. The strategy of the agents emphasizes this in attempting to stimulate people to think about their needs and what changes may be necessary to meet them. This can lead to questions of how to organize themselves for what they want to do, and when and how they want to do it. The agents also assist the members of the focal group to think through difficulties they may encounter in dealing with each stage of each problem in the course of what they intend to do.

Through each of these general approaches, the agents are somewhat constrained in the development of their implementation strategy, and conflicts are inevitable. Most of these will focus on areas of responsibility, resources, reward/punishment, and the attainment of goals. Agents are going to be assertive or cooperative, and their management style will be related to this. In opting for a competitive style, the agents' own objectives are paramount and relationships with members of the focal group will be minimal. In this case, the agents gain while the focal group loses. In the accommodation style, the expectations of the agents are low but the chances of good relations and success are increased. Compromise management styles require the agents to give and take, and their own expectations are moderated. In the collaboration style, the agents' expectations must be high, relations with the focal group produce a circumstance wherein both the agents and the group come out well. In avoidance, the agents' own objectives are low, relations are low, and neither the agents nor focal groups come out very well. Competing and collaboration are very assertive whereas avoidance and accommodation are least assertive. Compromising lies somewhere in the middle.

Many scholars of change agree that in the change agents' implementation strategy, questions of communication, the fit and timing of the proposed change, adaptation to the local culture pattern, and the kind of interaction with the focal group are all important considerations. Communication can be directed at the psychological barriers that develop with regard to the proposed change, or it can focus on the establishment of communication channels between agent and focal group. Effective channels of communication can lead to essential exchange of information, play a role in the interaction contact of agent and focal group, be the essential means of learning about the change, and serve as a feedback mechanism. In this regard, agents can choose to use the local language, which helps build rapport with the members of the focal group. Agents can utilize mass media technology (if available) for aiding in the contact interactions or they may choose demonstration as a channel of communication, showing the pragmatic advantages of the change. Interpersonal communications are tied to the personal image that agents project. Even group communication channels, such as gossip, may be included in the implementation strategy.

In the implementation strategy, adapting the change to the local patterns is a crucial concern. If not precluded by the general approach of the agency, agents can select changes for their adaptive value, as additions or replacements for already existing practices. They need to incorporate local leadership in changes aimed at administration, religion, education, and civic affairs. In a change aimed at social behavior, agents must keep in the mind the integrated nature of things, especially kinship, ethnicity, politics, and any central authority. Economically, the agents want to consider the usual patterns for allocating resources, behavioral questions of work groupings, proprietary rights, distribution and consumption patterns. Of course, timing and appropriateness of the change are related to these considerations. In changes aimed at belief patterns, the agents must recognize that all customs have associated beliefs tied to them. According to some authors, among all these considerations, the level of participation achieved, flexibility, timing, continuity, and maintenance are significant concerns that must also be included in the implementation strategy of the change agents.

FOCAL GROUP STRATEGIES

Whereas plan strategies focus upon the general approach to be taken to proposed change, and implementation strategies are oriented toward a working relationship oriented to successful completion of a change task, members of focal groups develop strategies of their own that impact the process. Members of focal groups are not passive participants in the change process. They are not simply targets for change, nor are they merely recipients of change. Focal groups are active participants in the process and develop responsive strategies as part of the total process. Naturally, focal group strategies will be directly related to what change is proposed and who has proposed it. Of prime importance to them is whether the change impacts a part of their culture that is directly tied to survival, but any proposed change in their learned beliefs or practices can be perceived as threatening. Focal group strategy will evolve in response to the agents with whom they will deal most directly, and how these persons attempt to introduce and implement change. It will be tied to their perceptions and motivations for change in general, and with regard to the specific change they are being asked to make or accept. The key to understanding focal group strategy centers on perception, it will be based on all the perceptions held by members of the group.

Perception

Within directed culture change contexts, focal group perceptions will be tied directly to motivations, attitudes, and the general change climate. Culture initially provides the basis for the perceptions held by members of the focal group, and thus the foundation for whatever strategy the focal group elects in response to any proposed change. This remains true whether the change is proposed from inside or outside the culture group. All cultures make provision for change, have established beliefs and practices with regard to it. Culture groups must be able to respond to changing conditions if they are to remain viable and survive. At the same time, most cultures are conservative with regard to change, simply because of the process whereby individuals are made members of their groups, how and what they are taught. This circumstance points up one of the most striking paradoxes or contradictions of culture and culture change. The fact that both physical and social environments are always changing necessitates that cultures constantly change to ensure their survival. On the other hand, as the members of the culture are taught the correct way to think and behave, a strong element of conservatism is introduced. As discussed earlier, it also produces the ethnocentrism of culture groups, the tendency to judge others based on the particular brand of "truth" that has been learned. Members of focal groups have already learned the correct way to think and behave. They bring this ethnocentrism to bear on any change they are asked to make. They judge the change against what they have learned and practiced. On top of this, in being asked to change cherished beliefs and practices they are being asked to admit that what they had learned in becoming a member of that focal group was not correct. This kind of paradox or contradiction can be readily seen in the case of the American culture.

Both Jules Henry (1966) and Francis Hsu (1972) have noted that Americans place a great value on change. In some areas of American education (e.g., instructional technology and some areas of curriculum), changes appear so frequently as to lead one to conclude that in this arena, change is for the sake of change and little else. As consumers, Americans are conditioned to change clothing styles, cars, and other material possessions on a regular basis, but suggest eliminating any of these (e.g., changing from a mid-size car to a small one, or eliminating the use of an electric can opener to save the environment), and great resistance is encountered. American businesses change almost on a daily basis in order to respond to changing business conditions or to stay competitive. To change American business practices to be less ethnocentric would not be easy. Most Americans readily accept almost anything delivered to them as a development. On the other hand, Americans, like most nation-state culture groups, are almost obsessed with preserving their culture and traditions. For Americans on a national level, change speaks to modernization, development, and improvement, all of which justify change as a normal and highly desirable process. To change means to move ahead, improve, progress, keep up, and so on.

Here again, it is important to remember that nation-states are artificial and arbitrary culture groupings. Because they are made up of other culture groups, on the more limited levels, attitudes regarding change may not adhere to the national norm. Even though change is highly valued by most Americans, some constituent and scene groupings do not share in that belief. Most American Indians and many ethnic, religious, and academic cultures place far greater value on maintaining traditional beliefs and practices than on changing them. Proposing change across American culture as a unit can be quite different from proposing change for specific, constituent, or scene cultures.

Most groups as a whole will be resistant to change from the start. Whether a proposed change originates within or without the group makes no significant difference. Whether it has been decreed or has originated with some level of group participation will make no significant difference. Change of any kind threatens to disrupt the status quo and people's satisfactions. In the multicultural environment of the nation-state, or the more limited environment of a constituent group or scene, some members will feel more threatened than others. In the nation-state, change is usually introduced for the good of the majority. This means it may not be good for all the constituent groups making up that culture. Based on this reality, even within a focal group on the level of the nation-state, there will not likely be unanimity. A benefit to one group will mean a cost to some other group. There are no benefits without costs. People's response to change will be determined by where they perceive themselves on this cost/benefit continuum. As pointed out by Appell, "The costs and benefits of any innovation or planned change are not going to be distributed equally throughout the population; some people will benefit and some will lose. What has to be kept in mind is whether the distribution of costs and benefits is fair or desirable" (1988:272).

The perceptions of members of the focal group are not always linked directly to the proposed change. For example, although most can agree that the change is necessary, and they subscribe to the goal or objective, they may still respond negatively to it. The Equal Rights Amendment can serve as a good case in point. most legislators, and presumably most Americans, agreed with the goals and objectives of the amendment, but it was not passed by the required number of state legislatures to become law. Equality, equal opportunity in employment, equal pay for different sexes doing the same job, fit quite well with basic American values. Most legislative representatives probably recognized that despite the equal opportunity laws already on the books, there was great disparity between the sexes. Women were not receiving pay equal to that of men doing the same jobs. Few women were rising in the male-dominated corporate business community. Women were barred from many career fields traditionally reserved for men, and so on. Nevertheless, the amendment went down to defeat. It can be suggested that the major reasons for this defeat lie in perception, not directly of the change to equality, but of that change as necessitating changes elsewhere in the culture and society, changes many felt were totally unacceptable. Although most elected officials could agreed with the equality goal in the amendment, they saw it as threatening another part of their life deemed more important. The trade-off of what they could characterize as symbolic equality against a more central area of their personal lives was not possible. Some voted against it because it would adversely impact their religious views and practices. Others voted against it because it would dramatically alter the economic system of the society or mean that women would have to fight in war, just like men. Still others voted against it because it would change the basic family structure, something they valued more than what they admitted was a valid but less important part of their lives. The interrelatedness of culture came to bear on the proposed change.

Based on the idea of integrated culture, members of focal groups will respond to proposed changes on the basis of their economic, political, enculturation, or religious organization, or their social affiliations, simply because those are related to whatever the proposed change might be. Even in situations where they may have participated in the generation of the idea or its planning and design, members of focal groups will avoid, where possible, changes that promise to negatively impact core areas of culture that are essential to group survival. When faced with a proposed change that directly or indirectly impacts such areas, some level of avoidance response is inevitable, particularly from those most closely associated with the area to be impacted. The culture also has provided members of focal groups with role characteristics that will indirectly become part of any strategy in culture change contexts. For example, in some cultures there are established traditions for dealing with people who are not members of the group. There may also be established principles of interaction between members of focal groups and nonmembers. Eskimos are well known for telling outsiders what they think the outsiders want to hear. Culture may prescribe how members of the group should reveal their motivations, if at all, and even how they are to communicate with outsiders. In some culture groups, members are to use only their group language when dealing with nonmembers. In other cases, given the variety of language, or of levels recognized and used by particular groups of people (e.g., formal, consultative, casual or intimate), further limitations on communication, are introduced and become part of the strategy of focal groups.

To propose a change for any group is to ensure some level of conflict. Beyond the conflict between those asking for a change and those asked to accept a change, competition between the traditional and the new is conflict in itself. Those lining up on each side of the issue will come into conflict. "Turf" battles are also sources of conflict in change circumstances—for example, agents working directly with people without regard to local leadership patterns can easily involve conflict. Local leaders perceive the change not as good or bad, but as a threat to their traditional power status and position. Where conflict is evident, those who perceive that they are threatened by the change being proposed, will be negative to that change.

Motivation

Directly tied to perception is motivation. No change will occur unless there is a felt need to change. If people are obtaining their satisfactions by following traditional practices, there is not likely to be a felt need to change anything. Cultures are sets of problem-solving solutions selected from among alternatives within the environments in which people have found themselves. As long as they are successful in surviving, or in obtaining their satisfactions, then they perceive no need to change: "If it ain't broke, don't fix it." This extends into situations where the group may have achieved only a marginal success in attaining their satisfactions. In fact, the felt need to change may be even more remote given this marginality. People barely surviving are less apt to support a change because their existence is already tenuous. From their vantage point, a change could mean the difference between surviving and not surviving. Why take a chance? It is essential to the successful accomplishment of a proposed change that the people themselves recognize the need for the change. Even if they ask for it that does not necessarily mean they are motivated for it. Second to this felt need can be any number of other motivations. Reward, punishment, novelty, even competitive advantage can serve as secondary motivations.

Attitude

The strategy of the focal group will also involve the question of attitude, for this is tied directly to perception. From perception come individual attitudes toward the suggestion or effort to introduce change. Cognitive attitudes are consequences of perceptions. Affective attitudes are covert responses to perceptions held, as are behavioral attitudes. The individual who knows the right way to do things, has knowledge of the correct way of thinking or behaving, will perceive any shift or change in that way in a negative manner. From the point of view of a change agency or agent, a change may have a rational basis. The plan for implementing it may be based on sound logic. But the focal group may not share the logic of it. The change may actually be perceived as irrational. Focal group responses to any change, more often than not, will be emotional ones. This affective attitude is the norm. Initially, people will generally respond emotionally to a proposed change in their cherished beliefs or practices. As might be expected, such an attitude translates into a behavioral component, one the agency and agent will judge as irrational. The bias toward rationality on which the planning and action of most change agencies and agents is based, will be in direct contradiction to this emotional response.

Climate

All of the perceptions, attitudes, and motivations of the focal group create the climate for change, both in a general sense and in the case of specific change. In a sense, perception, motivation, and attitude create the climate for change and influence the strategy of the focal group to the proposed change. Felt need will reflect attitudes and motivations. Motivations are based on perceptions of what focal groups are asked to do or accept. Attitudes are how perceptions surface in the individual and the group. How open members of the focal group are to change reflects cultural learning and whether the change is perceived as a threat to either the group or the individual. This is tied to the group's capacity for change. Perception, attitude, and motivation are products of how members of the group see themselves in the effort, how they perceive control features of it, their past experiences with the agency or agents making the proposal. Of course, all these things can also lead to group recognition of the importance of the proposed change in either positive or negative terms. How they see it in this sense translates into commitment or lack of it within the focal group.

FOCAL GROUP RESPONSE STRATEGIES

Irrespective of perceptions, attitudes, or motivations on the part of the members of any focal group, one can start with the assumption that any proposed change is not going to be readily accepted by everyone for whom it is intended. Where the culture of the focal group is oriented more to traditional belief and practice, the strategy of the focal group will be based on resistance or avoidance. If people are asked to change any of their valued traditional beliefs or practices, they will attempt to avoid doing so if they can, and minimize the impacts at the very least. In situations where the change is being forced upon them, the negative response will be greater than if they have some measure of input in the generation of the idea and in its implementation. In the first instance, the strategy will quite likely be active resistance. In the second instance, it will more likely be passive resistance. Both are means by which such groups attempt to avoid the change they are asked to make.

Another strategy for focal groups is perhaps best referred to as superficial acceptance. To take the pressure for change off themselves, members of the focal group appear to accept the change, at least behaviorally. They go through the day appearing to have accepted the change, although out of sight of the agent or agency they continue to believe or practice as they always have. Side-stepping is another strategy of avoidance. In this strategy, members of focal groups develop their own plans for averting the change. It can involve developing a new pattern of behavior that will off set what they have determined is an unacceptable situation. For example, among the Dani of the highlands of New Guinea, marriages of young girls were chronologically advanced in order to avoid the loss of the girls to school when the national government made school attendance mandatory. Married women were exempt from attendance; unmarried girls were not. Thus, marrying young girls earlier side-stepped the new requirements.

Another strategy on the part of focal groups concerns additive acceptance, producing what outsiders usually refer to as a form of syncretism. In this strategy, members of the focal group appear to accept a change when in fact they simply add it to their existing patterns, pigeon holing it to circumstances involving those who asked for the change. In another version of this strategy, the focal group accepts the change in behavior but alters it to fit into their own system in such a way that substantive change is not required and impact on traditional patterns is minimized. Still another variation involves limited acceptance of behavior but not the idea behind it. All change involves both behavioral and ideational change to be complete. A environmental change invariably necessitates a behavioral change, and so on.

Another strategy selected by focal groups can probably best be termed *coping behavior*. In this approach to change, members of focal groups simply cope with proposed changes in traditional cultural patterns. For example, if the culture of the group is a particularly strong one, they merely fit the change to the new environment that is being created for them. The Maori of New Zealand can serve as a case in point; they were able to adjust to a new environment yet preserve their cultural core. The Tibetans, on the other hand, well adjusted to a specific environment in which they live, were able to save cultural patterns. The thrust of this strategy is to use what you have to respond to the suggested change while reinforcing traditional beliefs and practices. How a change is being introduced also results in strategy moves on the part of focal groups. If the change is being introduced under forced draft (fiat or decreed), the people will choose one type of strategy, usually resignation if they have no alternative, total resistance if the power behind the proposal is insufficient to enforce it. If they themselves asked for the change or assisted in the development of the idea and generation of its planning, they will opt for another response (e.g., willing participation or active participation). In both cases, the direct response of members of the focal group will be based on their perceptions of the entire change context as well. In the first case, they will evolve a strategy out of response; in the second, they will generate a strategy tied to their participation in both the generation of the idea and the planning for its implementation.

SUGGESTED READINGS

This group of works will provide some understanding of the kinds of strategies that are used by change agencies and agents to induce change.

Appell, George N. 1988. "Casting Social Change." In *The Real and Imagined Role of Culture in Development: Case Studies from Indonesia*. M. R. Dove (ed.). As one of a large group of Indonesian case studies focusing on the role of culture in development programs and projects, this work provides some insightful and thought-provoking considerations on strategies for inducing social change.

Batten, T. R. 1969. *The Non-Directive Approach in Group and Community Work.* This work provides a discussion of the nondirective, facilitative assistance approach to directed culture change.

Bennis, Warren G. 1966. "A Typology of Change Processes." In *The Planning of Change.* W. G. Bennis, K. D. Benne, & R. Chin (eds.). This article provides a clear and concise discussion of the various strategies for change that have been used. The four general strategies for inducing change are distinguished on the basis of locus of decision making and amount of fiscal or material inputs required by the innovating agency.

Lang, Gottfried O. 1973. "Conditions for Development in Asmat." *Irian: Bulletin for West Irian Development.* This article provides a concise summary of the advantages and disadvantages of the general strategies available for socioeconomic development and change. It also contains a good summary of the nondirective, interactional, or facilitative assistance type of strategy.

Niehoff, Arthur H. (ed.). 1966. *A Casebook of Social Change.* This volume discusses some of the most important elements of strategy that must be considered by culture change agents working in multicultural settings.

Chapter 7

DYNAMICS OF CHANGE

Throughout this volume, the process of culture change has been presented as a necessary component of all cultures, the means by which culture groups adjust or alter their beliefs, behaviors, or products in response to changing sociocultural cultural or physical environments. Although some of the alterations or adjustments are absolutely essential if a culture group is to remain viable, not all culture change is tied to survival. Some can amount to no more than pseudo change, alterations that do little to impact the basic core systems of culture or are changes in degree, a little more or less of something. To gain some increased understanding of and control over culture change as a dynamic process, it is necessary to look to the actions, forces, or powers that produce it. Most scholars of culture change point to some specific thing(s) as "the" major force(s) that produce(s) change, help(s) or hinder(s) the efforts of people to implement or impact it. Some point to various social, psychological, or generalized "cultural" factors from the cultures of the participants as the major forces influencing the process and helping to produce the outcomes. Still others suggest that the specific actions, usually presented as the role characteristics or strategy of participants, especially those of change agents, are the more significant forces in the process. The position that has been taken in this volume brings all of these things together in the interactional context, suggesting that without interaction, there would be no change. The interactional setting like culture itself, can become a force of its own in the process of change. Putting the emphasis on interaction more clearly focuses on change as a dynamic process. Change is presented as the result of a progression of action and reaction. Perhaps the end result is the intended or designed one, or perhaps it is something else.

Voluntary change and directed change are the real processes of culture change, for only these refer to how an innovation can become a culture change both in the context of a single culture and across a number of them. Voluntary change refers to that which occurs without specific efforts on the part of anyone to introduce or implement it. Directed change is that which requires some form of coercion to get other members of a culture group to adopt a change in their beliefs or practices. These processes can be seen to operate within cultures, as internal change, and between culture groups, as external change. In internal change, there is no outside contact or interference. In external change, the context is a multicultural one in which contact and outside interference or pressures are involved in changing beliefs or behaviors. In the combination of process and context, the dynamics of change become somewhat clearer.

Having assumed a culture-centered stance throughout this volume, it should come as no surprise that culture is presented as the starting point for gaining a better understanding of the dynamic forces of the change processes in both internal and multicultural settings because change plays such an important role in the lives of people. Students of culture change have long recognized its cultural foundations. Such things as conservatism, cooperation, competition, coping behavior, opposition, conflict, motivations, fit, and timing—all identified as major forces of change—are directly related to culture in one way or another. Some of these are characteristics of culture itself, serving as general forces of change, whereas others are tied to specific patterns of belief and behavior. Specific cultural characteristics of participants can serve to stimulate change just as easily as they can serve as barriers to it. Throughout the previous chapters, many of the characteristics and strategies of agencies, agents, and focal groups have been discussed, any one or all of which can positively or negatively impact the change goal. Although such characteristics have been discussed as part of the context of change, as contributions of the participants, their dynamic qualities have only been suggested and it is important to identify them. But it is equally important to understand how these characteristics interact with each other and produce outcomes in the change effort.

In the interactional context, these characteristics can represent the most significant forces whereby some result is achieved. General and specific forces are related because they interact with each other, but there are other forces as well. It is important to keep in mind that change does not occur in a vacuum or isolated from other things, just as most cultures of today do not exist in isolation. Any change program or proposal can be subjected to any number of internal and/or external forces that can impact its progress and produce particular results. Internally, history can play a significant role in any change effort, as can the relationships among the various core systems of any culture. Political, economic, religious, or social considerations can significantly impact any proposed change. Externally, these same considerations, along with seemingly unrelated events far removed from the change context itself, can have tremendous influence on the change process, in some cases even determine the final outcome. Individually and collectively, all of these things can be seen as forces of culture change that surface in the interactional change settings. A force implies energy and power to influence, and these are significant forces that impact the change process. In this chapter the goal is to examine much more closely those things that can serve as dynamic forces which operate in the culture change context and produce its outcomes. Of particular importance is the consideration of the dynamic forces of the directed change process in multicultural settings, where change hinges on coercion and contact.

CULTURAL FORCES OF CHANGE

Creating culture, and then using it to mediate between themselves and the environments is a uniquely human characteristic. It represents a set of problem-solving solutions to the environments, and it is something that must be taught and learned, shared by groups of humans. In the most general sense, it represents the major adaptation for the human group. Because of what it represents for humans, and what it is, some of its general characteristics are quite germane to the change process. Conservatism, competition, and cooperation are characteristics of all cultures that serve to generate responses, to guide actions and reactions in the change setting (Foster 1973). In a very real sense, conservatism, cooperation, and competition are complementary characteristics of humans and their cultures. In many cases, they will be the determining forces generating a group's response to proposed change. They can serve to stimulate change, or they can underlie a group's reluctance even to entertain the possibility of change. They tend to guide the specific actions and reactions of participants in both internal and multicultural settings. In change involving culture contacts, cultural characteristics become even more significant influences because contact means culture conflict.

Conservatism

Conservatism is a basic characteristic of all cultures and serves as a major underlying force in the change process. Individuals and groups require continuity. People need to know how to get from one day to the next. In acquiring culture, people are taught the right way to do this. Initiates taught what to believe and what to do as they become members of cultural groupings. This is how members of culture groups get to know the right way for them. Because people use culture to respond to the pressures of their environments, any suggestion of changing that adaptation represents a threat to them and the group of which they are a part. To suggest an alteration in culture or any of its parts threatens the "knowing" so essential to human activity, and the security that comes with it. Human personality, so pliable at birth, hardens as the cultural patterns are acquired. The resulting shared cultural pattern becomes engraved in people's minds and hearts, and it emerges as the ethnocentric attitude characterizing all individuals as members of groups. It results in a basic conservatism that also characterizes all individuals and culture groups. This conservatism comes with knowing the "truth," the "true and correct ways" to think, believe, and act. This satisfies the need for continuity for individuals and groups. People have to believe their culture does this. In fact, it may or may not do it very well. This suggests that conservatism is closely linked to ideal culture, form of culture they acquire during the enculturation process. There is little argument with the fact that cultures are basically conservative, and this cannot help but influence any suggestions about changing them, whether the suggestion comes from within the culture or from outside it. The intensity of culture's role in the change process can increase in multicultural settings because of ethnocentric

ethnocentric attitudes acquired by members as they had to learn it.

Ethnocentrism, the tendency to judge other beliefs and practices on the basis of one's learned culture, is tied to the basic conservatism of culture. Once a culture, or the right ways to think and act, have been learned, ethnocentrism can surface as a major force of change within a culture, just as easily as it does when another culture's beliefs or practices are involved. Within cultures, suggested innovations, alterations, or modifications are going to be judged against what is already known and practiced. In multicultural settings, ethnocentrism becomes a major force as contacts produce conflicting truths. Change agencies and agents act according to their truths and the belief that the change they suggest is the right one. Members of a focal group respond from the belief that they are already doing the correct things. Giving up one's truth is a very difficult thing to do. Ethnocentrism can play a major role in the formulation of a change, in the plan and implementation strategies, and it will most certainly play a role in the responses of the focal group. Conservatism and ethnocentrism are significant cultural forces that can produce consequences for change programs and projects.

Competition

Despite the conservatism that seems to go along with culture learning, humans are competitive, both as individuals and as groups. All animals are competitive within the environment. Whereas most animals rely on physical adaptations to enhance survival, humans use culture. Whether it is for satisfying basic needs within the limitations of the physical environment or satisfying derived needs generated out of their cultural adaptations for meeting basic needs, humans compete with other animals and themselves. In competing with other animals in the natural or physical environment, humans have gained the edge through their culture. In competing with other humans, culture again provides the edge. In this sense, the "superior" cultures, those with the more successful adaptations, have always dominated those with less successful adaptations. Competition characterizes the interaction of specific constituent and scene cultures. It characterizes the world of business and organizational cultures as each group vies for position, prominence, or success. It characterizes political and economic cultures, which vie for prominence and power within cultures and on the international scene. Where religion is characterized by diversity, each form competes for dominance. In complex societies, the organizational systems can even compete with each other (e.g., political with economic, religious with political and economic, etc.). In the social structure of societies, competition begins with the family, and characterizes the interactions of families, minority groupings, and social classes. The struggles between minority, racial, and ethnic groups in complex societies are well known. On a worldwide level, the artificially created nation-states vie for dominance, positions of influence and status. As physical and sociocultural environments change, these specific, constituent, and scene cultures constantly change to enhance their survival, to better position themselves to compete with others, and to achieve their own goals.

Competition is a characteristic of all cultures, and by extension, this becomes a major underlying force in the change process as it functions to ensure continuous change. One of the ways the competitive edge is maintained by humans is through cooperation, another dynamic force in the change process.

Cooperation

Cooperation is another human characteristic that is integrated into the learned culture patterns of people as they become members of cultural groupings. The human animal needs to associate with others of its kind. The fact that culture itself is shared introduces the idea of cooperation into culture as one of its main characteristics. Cooperation is obviously tied to both the conservatism and the competitiveness of culture in positive and negative ways. First, a cooperative effort is required to get things done that societies must get done if they are going to survive. The more complex the system, the more cooperation is required. Recognizing this, culture groups make group cooperation a major tenet of the culture transmission and acquisition process. For example, in the educational system of the American culture, "socializing" the individual to the group is a major consideration during the first few years of school. It is critical to teach the elements of the group's social relations, to convey the rules of social behavior and the expectations people within the group have with respect to one another. This results in conformity to a set of prescribed social beliefs and practices expected of all members of a culture group. These two things create the cooperative setting which then enables the group as a whole to do what they must. It also ensures the continued viability of their shared culture. People have devised all manner of social groupings to foster cooperation, for it enhances their competitiveness as individuals and groups. It represents one of the most significant ways that humans remain competitive. From the smallest of human groupings of kinship and association, to the larger, artificially created nation-states and the world of nations, human groups cooperate to maximize their goals in meeting all kinds of needs. Proposing any change is tied to this general characteristic of human groupings and their cultures. It is also related to the conservatism of groups as they come to believe their particular way of believing or doing is the right or only way.

SPECIFIC FORCES OF CULTURE CHANGE

Just as any conceptualization of human evolution must provide for both general trends and specific circumstances, any consideration of the change process must do likewise. General or underlying forces only serve to generate specific human responses in the interactional settings of change. On the more specific culture level, such things as motivation, timing, fit, coping behavior, and strategy can become the more significant elements or forces of the process, germane in producing outcomes. All of these things are influenced by the culture's conservative, competitive, and cooperative characteristics. The conservative nature of culture directly affects motivations and strategy, and these can be affected by questions of timing and fit. Competitiveness and cooperation are directly related to motivations. In directed culture change, where conflict characterizes the interactions of participants, these things become even more powerful in influencing outcomes. Earlier discussions of change almost automatically focused on these kinds of specific forces of the process, and rightly so.

Unfortunately, such discussions focused so much on these that other forces were almost totally ignored and became footnotes. The dynamics of change became skewed in the process. The emphasis on these kinds of forces was understandable, because they readily surfaced in the interactional settings of participants in the process, most particularly where cultures were in contact. But they may have been only symptomatic of the underlying forces. Despite the tendency to emphasize these things as the major forces of change, it is not always easy to separate them into neat and orderly categories that serve as barriers or stimulants to change. All the specific cultural forces are interrelated, and each, on its own or in combination with others, has the capacity to become a dominant force in a change program or project. In the final analysis, any one of a great many specific characteristics of a particular culture can become a major power to produce change. Left unattended, they can become significant impediments to proposed change.

George Foster (1962, 1969, 1973) provides us with a number of ideas on forces associated with specific culture that can serve to restrict or inhibit culture change. According to Foster, these forces fall into three categories; social, psychological, and cultural. Social barriers are identified as those things rooted in social relations. Psychological barriers come primarily from the perceptions of people, and cultural barriers are those things rooted in tradition. These distinctions are significant, to be sure, but they are all related. Culture is a holistic phenomenon, each of its parts related to all the other parts. What Foster really does is point out several aspects or parts of culture that can serve as barriers to change. This is fine as far as it goes. He simply does not go far enough. To separate, distinguish, or divorce social and psychological aspects from "cultural aspects" is misleading. In the distinctions made by Foster, core areas of culture are only suggested. They should be made important considerations in their own right.

Core areas of culture are too significant to be ignored. The social relations of which Foster speaks are in fact part of the culture, just as are its other traditions. The psychological is part of culture, in that culture has shaped and molded the mind-sets and perceptions of its members. These are potential cultural forces that will influence the change process and outcomes, there are more. By focusing on a cultural category of change forces, such things as traditions and values, social structure and social organization, the psychological and perceptions, belief and behavioral practices, and all the remaining parts of culture can be addressed. This also allows us to maintain the holism of culture and the interrelated nature of the parts making it up. All core areas of culture are related within the culture context, each impacts the other. The perceptions of people come from their cultures. Social relations are maintained within the context of culture. Beliefs and practices are given to the individual by culture. In this sense, there are many aspects of culture which can serve as barriers to culture change, just as they can serve to stimulate it. Such forces of culture change can come from any of culture's parts, ideationally or behaviorally, and from either its ideal, real, or construct versions.

Cultural Values and Traditions

There are potential cultural forces rooted in tradition, and in the learned beliefs and practices associated with them. As pointed out by Foster (1969), barriers to change can come from the value people place on their traditions, what they were taught as they became members of the culture, what they learned as true and behaviorally correct. Such things produce the pride in being identified with the group and with knowing the right way. In other words, the cultural forces consist of all those things that exist within the integrated culture and the logical order of things as they have been learned. It has become very clear, over many years of study, that the greater resistance to change comes where people place the greatest value, in association with core areas of culture. The social system of culture is such a core area of culture, if for no other reason than that humans group together. The enculturation system, which emphasizes cultural transmission and acquisition within a culture, is another core area on which great value is placed, for it ensures that the culture survives. Culture is reproduced through learning. Worldview provides the members of the group with some understanding or perception of the world around them. Economic and political systems assist them in adapting to the resources with which they have to work and the social order within which all these things must exist. Changes that suggest altering basic beliefs and/or behaviors with regard to any of these core areas of culture, directly or indirectly, come into conflict with established patterns of belief and practice. In such circumstances, any of the traditional patterns can turn into barriers or stimulants to change. This is why it is so critical to understand the cultures involved in a change setting, not just as they may be ideally portrayed but as they actually exist and as individual members live them. For example, in the American culture, the gaps between these versions of culture can be substantial.

Ideally, Americans portray their culture as one in which great value is attached to the individual, freedom, equal opportunities, an educated electorate, and so on. These specific characterizations will nearly always appear in discussions of American values and dominant themes. Ideally, most Americans want to believe such things about themselves and their culture. On the other hand, as with any culture and society, the individual is always sacrificed for the good of the majority. Freedom is never absolute. Individual freedom must always be secondary to the group and its need for social order. Equal opportunity is always contradicted by the existence of a stratified system, where inequality can be based on economic class, occupation or specialization; ethnic, religious, or sexual groupings. Although much is made of maintaining the educational system, actual support for it waxes and wanes consistently. The real themes of the culture stem from its economic and political systems. A much greater value is placed on these systems of American culture than on enculturation or social systems. The value of the individual is subverted by the economic needs of various constituent or scene culture groups. The majority group can subvert the needs of the smaller constituent groups. The oscillating support for the educational system will always be determined by the oscillating economic system (as opposed to support tied to the value of the system). The achievement of equal opportunity will always be subject to economic and political feasibility. The political system gets its drive from this sociopolitical tradition, and the worldview of its members keys around economic considerations.

Thus, although ideal culture values are taught and learned within a culture, the true dominant values can stem from any one of its organizational patterns. Individual culture members have to function somewhere in between the ideals they learn and the realities within which they must live on a day-to-day basis. Individuals accommodate the ideal and real cultures by formulating their own individual versions of culture, constructed lifestyles based on their personal limitations in living up to the ideals or in coming to grips with the realities they must face. Some people turn to any one of their cultural affiliations for their personal construct. Actual culture forces that become the barriers or stimulants to change can come from any of these culture versions. At the same time, in the case of American culture, competition remains the major underlying cultural force for both the individual and the group. In other cultures, the dominant themes may be quite different, and thus the underlying forces will be different.

In some cultures (e.g., Pueblo Indians of America's southwest), the social system takes precedence and group harmony underlies all actions and reactions. In these cultures, cooperation is the dominant underlying force impacting change. In others, the dominant traditions and values can be based on political beliefs and behavior, as within the still predominantly communist nation-states. In the Communist and socialist political states, willing or forced cooperation within the group becomes the thing most highly valued. In still other cultures, religion can permeate everything (e.g., in the Islamic Republic of Iran or other predominantly Islamic nation-states). In these cultures, scene and constituent groups, social, economic, and/or political decisions are subservient to religious teachings and dogma. Social structure and organizational systems revolve around religious teachings and practices. Religious values are of the highest priority. Given the nature of such cultures, the primary underlying cultural force in change is conservatism.

In addition to the ideal and real values of particular societies are the values of the various cultures that make up the multicultural reality of most nation-states. As pointed out a number of times, the world's nations are actually made up of a number of culture groups that were forced into the state by one means or another. This means that in addition to the orienting values espoused in the ideal cultures of the state, or in the real values as they are practiced, there are those of the constituent and scene cultures. Because of the inequality ever present in multicultural groups, the values, beliefs, and practices of the dominant groups will take precedence over those of subservient groups. Depending upon where change is directed, and who will be most impacted by it, the relationship between the dominant group and the subservient group will produce traditions and values that will have repercussions in the change context. Most of these will be born out of the conflicts between them. In change settings where these circumstances predominate, the most influential underlying culture force to change will be competition.

Values and attitudes are identified and strongly held with regard to all those things with which any society or group must concern itself. Great value can be placed on traditional ideas about social, political, economic, religious, and enculturation systems. The attitudes people have on such things come from their learned belief that their system is the most correct one. If such ideas and practices have been followed over considerable periods of time, and if the people continue to meet their needs by using them, they become traditions or the "natural" order of things. The integrated nature of culture introduces the idea that such things must be considered in a contextual framework and not as individual values or ideas.

Standards of modesty, group and individual pride, dignity, motor patterns, customary body positions, customary greetings, and norms of polite behavior are other cultural traits and traditions that can become barriers or stimulants to change (Foster 1969). All of these kinds of traditions can become significant in change contexts, as can the value placed on the individual or the group, material possessions and wealth, practical and esoteric concerns, the minimum and maximum social groupings, the here and now, past and future, right and wrong. The bottom line forces us to recognize that all of the things that are learned and practiced as part of culture can serve as barriers or stimulants to change. In directed change, where culture contact is added, the cultural values of change agents and agencies come into conflict with focal group values, and the impact of the culture forces on change takes on even greater significance. It is at this point the traditions of the agents and the traditions of the members of the focal group can conflict dramatically. The conflicts can be so great as to bring about a less than successful result.

Organizational Systems of Culture

The very nature and character of culture's organizational systems serve to stimulate or inhibit change. Studies have repeatedly shown that political systems and leadership patterns can have tremendous influence on the direction of change programs. Local political leaders frequently work against change they perceive as threatening to their status or position. This resistance can surface with regard to the proposed end result, or it can appear during implementation, as a response to that series of events. The same can be said for leaders in any of the core systems. Religious and economic leaders can be very important players in the direction or result of change to any of culture's parts, not just in those directly related to their interests. By the same token, the nature of the organizational systems can work to stimulate or restrict change (e.g., with an economic system). In the case of an economic system based on capitalism and competition, the values associated with them ensures a certain amount of continuing change. Change on almost a daily basis has long characterized the business and industrial sectors of the American culture. Enculturation and religious systems can inhibit change simply because they represent two of the most conservative areas of any culture. In the American educational system, change appears to be a fact of life. On closer examination, one finds significant amounts of surface change but little change in basic goals and curriculum. When it does change, it is a slow and very painful process for all participants. Religious systems are even more reluctant to change. Changes in these systems of belief or practice are nearly always totally resisted, simply because any change threatens their very existence and their totality. The interrelated nature of culture, and the fact that it can include a number of constituent or scene cultures, must always be kept in mind. As should be obvious, the culture also provides the context for the social and psychological barriers/stimulants.

Structural Systems of Culture

Some especially powerful culture forces producing or inhibiting culture change come from the social structure of culture. These forces originate from the social relations or the traditional claims and obligations people have to one another as they attempt to live together in groups. The system of social relations of any group can serve as a barrier or stimulant to suggested change. More often than not, social forces act to maintain the status quo and preserve social equilibrium. Put another way, there will always be conflicts of interest, status and class conflicts, and conflicting channels of command or authority. In the corporate world, this can boil down to expected relations between management and employee, established channels of communication, or recognizing formal leaders (managers, CEOs, supervisors) and functional leaders (the ones who set the tempo or are looked to by their fellow workers to show the way). Social inhibitors are rooted in the formal and informal social obligations and expectations of people. For example, in the acculturation studies of the past, researchers repeatedly found that a change or shift in a culture group's economic base is almost always followed by significant changes in the nature of family organization. Such change strains traditional family relationships and even the nature or role of the family within the society. Introducing cash crops takes away from subsistence crops and practices, and it tends to destroy cooperative work patterns. Rapid change promotes factionalism and divisive tendencies within the group. Wage labor fosters independence as opposed to family interdependence. Family structures in a state of strain will frequently become the focal points of resistance.

Psychological Aspects of Culture

Psychological forces, important in the change context, are tied to perceptions held by individuals as members of culture groups. Psychological considerations are determined or constrained by culture. Managers and employees, blue-collar and white-collar workers, blacks and whites, men and women, finance and advertising specialists, will all perceive things differently. There is no doubt that people from vastly different cultural backgrounds, especially those of the nation-state, will see many things quite differently. An individual of the developing world will simply not see things as someone from the developed industrialized world, or from a subsistence-based economy does. Experiences with various global problems provide evidence that perceptual disparities can minimize efforts to solve such problems. From the point of view of the industrialized world, global problems are becoming crucial issues deserving the attention of people throughout the world. Many solutions have been proposed and attempted in an effort to respond to them. People in the developing world simply do not see such concerns in the same way. Even if they recognize the problem(s), they may not assign it (them) the same level of priority. They may be more concerned with surviving on a daily basis or meeting their own needs. The solutions offered by the industrialized world may work in that world, but in their world, they may be seen as threatening their very existence. The Green Revolution to combat starvation, family planning to combat overpopulation, and efforts to stop the loss of tropical rain forests have all largely failed to reach their goals because of such perceptual differences.

On the more limited scale of the constituent cultures within the artificial nation-states, perceptual differences can loom very large as well. Perhaps the greatest misconception held by people nearly everywhere, is that most members of such cultures tend to think basically the same way. This may apply to smaller cultural groups as well. Perhaps this is a consequence of enculturation systems striving for national unity or consensus through standard curricula. It may also reflect the nature of the curriculum, most of which is oriented to the way things ought to be, as opposed to the way they actually are. For example, academics and nonacademics certainly view things quite differently. The academic researcher is convinced of the value of research and the need for it as part of the decision-making process. On the other hand, most others are not oriented to research and thus are far less convinced of its value. Their priorities are focused more on their everyday needs than on something in which immediate and tangible results are not necessarily possible. There are comparable differences in business. From a CEO's vantage point, a particular change may be justified, whereas from the vantage point of the production line, a proposal for change may be nothing more than a pseudo change, one that simply asks them to do more, or the result of some manager justifying his or her continued employment by thinking up new things for everyone else to do. None of these perceptions would justify the proposed change in their minds, or the efforts that must be expended to achieve it. Just because all company employees go through the same orientation (enculturation) process, this does not mean that they all think and perceive things the same way. Another fact to keep in mind is that people may be employed by a particular company, but they come to that company with many other cultural patterns fully engraved in their minds, those acquired from all the other groups with which they identify. This is the "cultural baggage" people bring to the job. Employees of any corporation or business represent a wide range of constituent and scene cultures. The beliefs and practices to which they subscribe in their daily lives, outside of the workplace, are not left at the company door. The corporate culture is assumed as they go to work, but not at the exclusion of all the others that make up their individual identity. Each of the culture groups represented by an employee may have different perceptions of many things that impinge on business operations.

Another important aspect of perceptual difference that can lead to successful or unsuccessful change effort comes with the perceptions of a specific change. The perceptions of a change held by an agency, its change agent, and the members of the focal group do not always coincide. Consider the various projects associated with the global issues discussed earlier. Agencies and agents of the developed world may have sincerely believed that they were addressing overpopulation, starvation, deforestation. Based on their cultures, the introduction of a new food crop was a reasonable solution to the problem of food shortage. By their cultural standards and logic, their drive to limit population growth, they saw reducing the number of children per family in order to slow population growth as a reasonable solution. In the efforts to stop the destruction of tropical rain forests, people in the industrial world might have believed that reducing the number of acres cleared for agricultural production would help resolve this problem. From their particular cultural vantage point, all of these proposed and attempted solutions were logical and reasonable. The necessary changes in lifestyles of the people that would be most impacted would be minimally disruptive. The changes were necessary because the problems would ultimately impact people everywhere. National ethnocentric ideas about progress, modernization and development were injected into the solutions for solving global problems. The agencies and agents came into the change circumstance believing that change meant progress or a shift toward a better or more efficient way. Changing from an old way to a new way, particularly in technology, was a desirable thing. Their jobs and livelihood were dependent upon it. From development came the idea that change is always for the betterment of everyone. Just who actually benefits from so-called development projects was never quite specified, but it was probably the agencies and agents of change.

Further exacerbating the problem of perceptual difference is the difference between ideal and real change: what the agencies and agents tend to believe they are attempting to accomplish and what they are really asking people to do. Many change agencies and agents believe they are simply introducing *a* social change, *a* technological change, *an* economic change, *a* political change, whatever. After all, "that" is what their agency was established for, or what they as individuals were hired to do. Naturally, *the* change being proposed or introduced appears simple enough, is singular and reasonable. That it may be biased or intricately related to their own cultural beliefs, or that it is actually part of a larger integrated system, is apparently lost on them. Like most specialists, change agents are prepared to deal with specific processes as practiced and taught in their cultures (e.g., in agriculture, economics, or in technical specializations). Because they were trained in and represent narrow specialties, most agents of change have never had the chance to become versed in the holism of culture or the idea that all things in culture are intricately related one to another. Few are exposed to the idea that changing anything in a culture's beliefs or behaviors will likely impact other areas not directly related to what they propose, or perhaps all the rest of the culture.

Agencies and agents can believe they are introducing only a very small change into someone's beliefs and practices. For example, the introduction of cash crops into areas of Irian Jaya, Japan, Latin American, and North Africa would not seem to involve dramatic changes for people in these areas were already farmers. Introducing more sanitary cooking methods and facilities in Rhodesia would only make things better and more efficient. The introduction of powdered milk in Venezuela would only improve health conditions, particularly among the young. Introducing the steel ax to the Yir Yoront would only make their work easier. The building of the Aswan High Dam would enhance agricultural production and benefit everyone by improving production capacity. Many businesses and corporations introduce modern technology into their operations based on the belief they are only responding to changing market conditions. In the vast majority of cases, change projects are directed at very specific things, with little regard to how they may fit into the context of the larger culture. In the introduction of cash cropping, change agents actually impacted family structures, cooperative work patterns, and diet. In the introduction of more sanitary cooking methods and facilities, agents actually changed social interactional relationships. In the introduction of powdered milk, agents actually caused severe health problems among people unaccustomed to it, and overtly challenged the role of women in the society. In replacing a stone ax with a steel one, agents were responsible for the demise of a culture. The Aswan High Dam benefited only a very privileged few. Introducing modern technology into business actually requires the alteration of nearly every aspect of doing business.

All of these outcomes were the direct result of the narrow perspectives taken into the proposed change task, being unfamiliar with local culture, and a failure to understand the integrated nature of culture. Members of focal groups sometimes fare no better for they are grounded only in parts of their own cultures. Although they may know more about the context within which a change is being considered, they, too, will generally not consider the holism of culture. Native peoples of Alaska wanted government help in constructing community centers in their villages, but they clearly did not perceive the other changes that accompanied them. They did not anticipate the disruption to families and family relationships that followed. Agencies, agents, and members of focal groups tend to view their activities and goals in a very narrow sense.

In the analysis of the many projects undertaken in the efforts to resolve some of the global issues facing our world, perceptual differences have been painfully obvious. New crops were introduced in an attempt to combat increasing starvation, yet the very people for whom the program was designed refused to support it. In some cases, the refusal was tied to the group's definition of food; in others to their perception of the program as of limited benefit to them. The winners, from their point of view, were the small numbers of already privileged people within their societies. In other cases, changes were refused because the people did not have the resources to implement them. Introducing cash crops into marginal subsistence areas would seem to be a reasonable solution to poverty. When it has been done, the immediate impact has been to disrupt social relationships, particularly within families. Reducing destruction of tropical rain forests ultimately keeps individual families from clearing and planting crops for their own survival. The introduction of sanitary or new cooking methods and facilities may be important, but as demonstrated, it eliminates opportunities for social interaction. Limiting family size helps reduce population, but it can also restricts the ability of families to meet their current needs, and it reduces the parents' chances of having someone to take care of them when they are old.

These circumstances are more than mere possibilities; they have appeared in change projects that have been tried and have had limited success simply because of the perceptual differences of the participants. A great many failures can be attributed to perceptual differences between the agent/agency and members of focal groups. Project failures can be tied to the inability of agents or agencies, even members of focal groups, to perceive what they actually ask people to do in accepting a change. Nearly always, it will go well beyond project goals and objectives. Proposed changes always impact things in the lives of the people that appear quite unrelated to project goals.

In the highlands of New Guinea, the Dani of the Balim Valley were asked to wear clothes (Naylor 1974). To accomplish the goal, the government planned to give each Dani a set of clothes. The idea seemed a reasonable and not overly complicated way to bring the Dani into the mainstream of Indonesian society and the modern world. For the Dani, the government request was more involved than simply putting on clothes. They realized that more than one set of clothes was necessary. What would one do while the only set was being washed? How would one wash these clothes without soap, and how would soap be obtained? That it could not be purchased without cash, or some means to acquire it, was not lost on the Dani. In another case, the government required that all young Dani attend school in order to become literate. On the surface, this requirement seemed to be rational and logical because the government was attempting to develop a national consciousness and bring the Dani into the mainstream of Indonesian life. What it failed to take into account was the position of females in Dani subsistence activities. To the Dani, sending young girls to school would take them out of the subsistence system, and this would limit their ability to produce enough food to sustain the high population density of the valley. It was also seen as a potential threat to traditional marriage patterns.

That these things were not recognized by the change agencies and agents points to the importance of psychological forces (perceptions) in culture change contexts. Agents and agencies must have a good grasp of what it is they are asking members of focal groups to do, and they must recognize that any proposed change can impact other areas of culture, even the integrated whole of it. They also must realize that their own perceptions of what they are doing will have impacts on the settings, for perceptions come from the cultural groups they represent. More than likely, they will be biased according to the views of those cultural groups. The perceptual differences of representatives of different cultures in the change context can be counted upon to be significant factors in the change process and its outcomes.

INTERACTIONAL FORCES OF CHANGE

Besides the cultural forces, in change contexts there are other change forces to be considered. Some of these are specific to the interactional context of change. Interaction lies at the heart of the culture change process and is absolutely necessary for the diffusion of any change. The interactional setting is created as the people involved in the process come into contact and set into motion the processes that result in change. In all the discussions of change throughout this volume, interaction has been assigned a key role in change, regardless of the source or circumstances. The premise of this volume has been that all change results from interactions; of people and environments, of physical environment and social environment, of cultural groups and individuals. Interaction has provided the means by which cultures developed, regardless of whether they borrowed from one another, generated change within their own culture groups, or directed its course across cultural groupings.

Interaction has always assumed a position of prime importance in the change process where people from differing cultures are primary participants. It has been in the interactional setting that the actions and reactions of participants have produced the many outcomes that we identify as cultural changes. Whether one is dealing with change by way of innovation within a culture group, or planned and directed change involving people from outside the group, interactional forces make culture change the dynamic process that it is. A cause of change, a pressure for change, or someone coming up with a new idea is only the necessary first step. To bring change about, something has to interact with something else, someone interacts with someone else. The innovation must spread throughout the group or across groups, and this requires some human interactions. The settings for these interactions can become either barriers or stimulants to desired outcomes. The character and quality of the interactions will be directly related to the culture forces because individuals bring their cultures to these settings.

In voluntary change, interactions are primarily associational and the dynamics of the process are tied to cooperation, competition, and conservatism. In planned and directed change, interaction is tied to coercion. In both types of change, the interactions emanate from the culture beliefs and practices of the people involved. They determine actions and reactions, influence communications and perceptions, produce the stress and emotions associated with change. In both internal and multicultural settings, the interaction will be based on oppositions and conflict. *Conflict* is the best term for referring to what happens within the interactional setting, for it denotes the strife for mastery among competing interests, the hostile encounters and prolonged struggles between participants that arise out of the clash of opinions or interests that come with cultural change.

Cultural Conflict or Opposition

Whether one is addressing culture change within a culture or across cultures, the cultural component of interaction is unavoidable. For change within a specific cultural grouping, a proposed new trait nearly always comes into direct conflict with established patterns. As discussed earlier, people learn the right beliefs and behaviors as they become members of groups. They learn the social structure and the organizational system used to meet the needs of the group. Their view of the world is structured, and their values and attitudes are provided. Proposed change in any of this learned pattern comes in one of two forms: it can be a change of kind, as with something totally new to the culture, or it can be one of degree, more or less of some things with which the group is already familiar. In either case, it comes into direct conflict with a learned way and produces oppositions or conflicts. A proposed change will always be in conflict with established practice and/or beliefs, and it will always put people into conflict with one another; those for and those against the change. The proposing individual—agent as opposed to innovator—is set apart from the group in one way or another, creating another kind of conflict and opposition.

In multicultural situations, the interactions caused by these conflicts are more intense, because of the differing cultural patterns of the participants. Questions of the status, power, dominance, or subservience of the cultures represented in the interaction will inevitably arise. The culture truths of the participants clash, and the stress and emotions that then characterize the settings will emerge. Whether the change is one of kind or of degree does not seem to make any difference when the pressure for change comes from outside the group. In proposing change and in attempting to implement it, the beliefs and practices of both agents and members of the focal group are challenged. In the suggestion of change, the members of the focal group are being told that what they believed or did as part of their culture was incorrect or wrong. In the process, the agent's expertise, beliefs, and practices can equally be challenged in a context for which they were really never prepared to function. This brings to the forefront the ethnocentric attitudes that are given to people during the acquisition of culture, and these will clash. The pride and dignity of participants, the value they place on tradition, norms of right and wrong, motor habits, and all the other things that make up their own culture will surface and become significant forces in the dynamics of interactions and the ultimate outcomes.

In the actions and reactions of people, individually and in groups, the needs, motivations, and even forms of communication will all be constrained, if not determined, by the differing culture patterns represented in the interaction. Perceptions, both real and imaginary, will serve as impetus for participant actions and reactions, in essence defining the quality of the interactions. The quality of the communication between the participants will be determined and guided by the cultural backgrounds, perceptions, and preferences of the individuals involved. The strategies that come together in the settings—the plan, implementation, and responsive strategies—will be culturally specific and as such, will conflict. The strategy of change agencies focuses on what will be done and why, when it will be done, and with what contributions of the agency. Change agent strategy focuses on implementing change, on elements of motivations, timing and fit, participation levels, use of local culture, flexibility, continuity, and maintenance. Focal group strategy revolves around the response of the group to what is being proposed, how it is to be implemented, and the person(s) with whom they will most directly relate and interact in that effort.

Motivations

As has been discussed, nobody will change anything without a motivation to do so, and this applies to both change agents and members of a focal group. In successful change, agents must be motivated, just as those being asked to change must be motivated. In the latter case, motivation means there must be a felt need to change. In the case of agents, it means they must be motivated to their task, convinced of its appropriateness, and willing to do what is necessary to carry it out. For focal groups, motivation can come from their own perceptions of need, solicitation, consultation, or persuasion. Motivation focuses on the presence or creation of a felt need to change. In cases where focal groups recognize that they must change, the felt need is already present. In the case of someone directing or implementing change, this can mean creating the felt need among those with whom that agent is to work.

George Foster (1969) suggested that the most powerful motivations are to be found in people's desire for status and prestige, even more so than economic considerations, which he saw as secondary motivations. Arensberg and Niehoff (1971) suggested that motivations are tied to needs people themselves recognize, demonstrated needs, solicited needs, or those developed through consultation. They suggested that competition, punishment, reward, and novelty are all tied to secondary motivations. In any case, motivation exists where people recognize a need. If there is no real, imaginary, or created need, there will be no motivation and no change. This could suggest a relationship between the change that is attempted and the ease or difficulty that can be expected. The change easiest to accomplish might appear to be that which the people themselves solicit. Their motivation for it seem apparent. Additive changes, which do not compete with traditional beliefs or practices, might be viewed as the next easiest to motivate. These would be based on a change satisfying a new need or representing a required response to changing conditions. The more difficult change to motivate is that which replaces something in an established culture. But just because people ask for a change does not automatically mean that all of the group's members are asking for it, nor is its acceptance assured. First, the group may not realize all that may be required of them until the change is actually initiated and implemented. Even additive changes require adjustments because of the integrated nature of culture. A replacement change can actually be easier than the others if traditional practices jeopardize the people and their culture under changed conditions. Although there may be a great temptation to expect certain responses, the circumstances do not always work out as expected.

In some cases, a motivation for change may already be present in the culture— as for example, within American culture, where change has unquestionably become institutionalized. In this culture, some level and quantity of change has become a fact in the day-to-day life of its people. Members of the culture are quite accustomed to change and are willing to accept it. It may even be seen as being in the natural order of things. Take, for example, the changes associated with the economic system. Almost any change is acceptable if it promises to satisfy material wants and needs, which are given high priority in this culture. Because of the competitive nature of the culture, changing to maintain the winning or competitive edge has become highly desirable, if not an accepted necessity. This can even be seen in the more conservative religious, political, and educational systems, in where variant groups compete with each other. This is not to say that change is regular and acceptable throughout all of America's constituent culture groupings. Nor does it necessarily mean that change is acceptable in all of its aspects. In the ideal belief systems upon which behavioral and product systems are based, Americans are as conservative as members of any other culture group. In societies and cultures oriented around cooperation or another organizational system, change as a normal fact of life may be far less obvious or acceptable. Interestingly, the smaller and less complex the society, the less focused on change it will be. This means is that the larger and more complex groups are more likely to have some motivation for change built into their culture system. That it may not appear so, is going to be tied to smaller constituent or scene groups that may hold sufficient power to maintain the status quo.

When a culture group perceives that it is no longer competitive with others, the necessary motivation for change is present. The same thing can be said for individual members of scene cultures or constituent cultures of the most complex nation-states. In some cases, where the competitive culture characteristic is a predominant underlying force of the culture, the motivations can be tied to simply keeping ahead of the competition, change itself becoming the felt need of the individual and/or collective group. Felt needs will always be tied to basic or derived human needs as they are defined by the culture of the individual. The shift from basically a conservative stance to one more conducive to altering some belief or practice can also come from a changing physical or sociocultural environment. In the case of felt needs based on a changing physical environment, change simply increases one's chances for surviving within the shifting conditions or new limitations imposed by the environment. In needs associated with sociocultural environments, change enhances status and prestige, comfort or efficiency, political or economic advantage, and so on. Of course, the novelty of an idea, practice, or product in some contexts is sufficient as a felt need for a change. With changing sociocultural environments, there is also the possibility of needs generated by internal conflicts or oppositions. If an environment produces conflicts wherein the members of the group are faced with contradictory choices, motivation to change may already be present, for a choice must be made. The people will want to change from the present condition to something else. It can be to something new, or it can be a change back to the way it used to be (e.g., nativistic and revitalization movements). In the context of modern and civilized states, this surfaces as movements to return to "the good old days." This is a very real possibility when the contradictions are in beliefs and practices associated with any of the culture's most valued traits.

In directed culture change and in situations of unequal culture contact, motivation will quite likely have to be imposed on a group or created through persuasion. In these contexts, motivation will be tied to some form of coercion, force, reward, and/or punishment. Such coercions can be powerful motivators for change. The change agents are the key players in creating or developing the felt need among those to be changed. It is the responsibility of the agent or agency to ensure that a felt need for the proposed change is present. If not, it must be created. The catch to this comes with how the agent attempts to do this. Some may choose to impose or force the change in an either/or circumstance. The conflict created by such a choice almost always ensures that the end result will not meet the expectations of the agency or change agent. Members of focal groups in these circumstances will respond because they have no choice. The consequences of not responding as directed may be more disastrous than maintaining ongoing reluctance to a proposed change. A lack of commitment to the change will inevitably be present as well. The real motivation may be to subvert, sidestep, or minimize the change the group is being forced to accept. At the very least, when members of focal groups are faced with forced change, there is minimal effort on their part to accept it or make it work. All the efforts to implement change must fall on the shoulders of the agents responsible for bringing it about, not on those asked or told they must accept it. In forced change, motivations will be passive at best. Motivation can be created through consultation or reasoned persuasion (as opposed to forced) in directed culture change. In essence, the necessary felt need is developed as the change agent interacts with members of a focal group. Again, the major responsibility for this falls on the agents or agency. Either motivation is present or it must be generated through some form of persuasion. It may amount to no more than the agent pointing out to members of the focal group something they may not have seen or perceived, or it may mean the agent has to convince the group that they need the change. The direction and context of the agent's argument will be determined by the nature of the culture as well as the nature and extent of the change. Theargument can be based on demonstrating the advantages or value of it, or it can revolve around reasonable persuasion. This second thrust is perhaps the more difficult, for conflicts regarding "reasonable," even reason and logic, may be culturally specific and thus conflicting.

Alexander Leighton (1945) perceived that in directed change, the sentiment of the focal group is the key, sentiment based in history and tied to a current social equilibrium. He saw that the agent's interaction with members of the focal group was characterized by stress created out of social organizational conflicts of the agent and the focal group, the sentiments (attitudes and beliefs) of the participants in the process, and their reactions to the stress being created. From this, Leighton concluded that members of focal groups are motivated to change more by emotion than by rationality. He directed our attention to the elements of conflict and stress created by the circumstances of the change context, and he cautioned about expecting too much of "reasoned persuasion." Leighton, Foster (1969, 1973), and Arensburg and Niehoff (1971) all recognized that motivation is essential in culture change and represents a major force in the process, particularly during implementation. It already exists, or it is the product of the interaction required for any change, as a consequence of contact and the actions of people. Without this human interaction, there can be no culture change, only new ideas that do not "catch on" for some reason. It may simply have been a bad idea, or it may be that the people could not be convinced that it was worth accepting. But by itself, motivation does not ensure that change will occur. Tied closely to motivation are questions of timing and fit. These also can become major forces in the success or failure of a proposed change.

Timing and Fit

Although timing and fit were discussed as important considerations of strategy, in interactional settings they assume an even greater position of importance. If a proposed change does not fit into the cultural context of the focal group, chances for implementing it are reduced substantially. If the change is ill-timed for the focal group, its chances of success will be reduced. Fit involves an assessment of whether a proposed change is adaptable to existing values, social forms, economic reality, and so on. Adapting a change to fit the existing cultural patterns, whether it be the introduction of an innovation or the result of a perception that it is valuable to do so, obviously indicates fit better than something that is not adopted. Clearly, a change is stimulated if it is, or can be, adapted to patterns already in existence—say for example, within the context of local leadership, existing social structures, and/or belief patterns. Timing can become a stimulant if the change is introduced at the right or most appropriate time. Attempting to introduce a change before the people are ready for it turns timing into a barrier that ensures its failure. In internal change involving only members of the focal group, these considerations will loom large. In external change and directed culture change with cultural contacts, they become even more significant. Like most implementation forces, timing and fit are primarily change agent or agency considerations. Left unattended, these forces can doom change efforts to failure or minimal accomplishment, just as easily as other forces that tend to serve more as barriers than as stimulants. There are additional questions of timing and fit that must be considered, particularly those which address fit and timing in terms of the plan and overall goal of the change agency. As discussed earlier, when changes are out of sequence or are expected in too short a time period, these questions tied to the agency and agents become just as significant as when they are applied to the local culture.

Timing change for focal groups addresses both the stage of their development and their readiness for the change. In many ways, timing is really a question of fit in this sense, but one deserving special attention. For example, introducing information technology into a business before the people expected to utilize it are ready to accept it would be an ill-timed change. Attempting to introduce a democratic system of government to a group with no experience or traditions required for it would be ill-timed. Introducing behavioral change into some aspect of culture that is dependent on other changes being accomplished first, would put it into jeopardy. For example, among the Dani of Irian Jaya, the introduction of clothing in place of traditional dress without the presence of a money-dominated market-exchange system upon which it would depend, simply put the cart before the horse. Introducing cash crops into areas where only a marginal subsistence agricultural base exists would also be viewed as poorly timed (Naylor 1973b, 1974).

Timing can also be factor where many changes are being proposed—in essence too much too soon. The same could be said for established timetables for implementing change. The 1970s plan of the Indonesian government to totally alter Dani lifestyle in a very short period of time is certainly a case in point. To accomplish such a total revision of a culture was unrealistic. Many changes fail because insufficient time is allocated for them to be implemented and integrated into the cultural patterns of the focal group. To come up with or introduce a new trait does not mean that a culture change has been accomplished. Culture change involves the spread of the new trait to the majority until it becomes institutionalized within the culture of the group. Seeing associated behavior among the group does not necessarily mean that it has been done. Change requires shifts in both behavior and belief systems, and these may require significant periods of time. As in the case of many of America's native groups, some are able to withstand massive change pressures to their cultures for a great many years.

Although fit usually means the selection and adaptation of a change to fit the local context, it can also mean that a proposed change should fit reasonably into the overall plan of both the change agency and the agent. Fit addresses an adequate consideration of the cultural context as well. Change agencies and agents need to design change, and the implementation of it, to realistically fit aspects of the existing culture. They need to consider the use of local leaders from political, religious, and economic areas of the culture, remembering that there are formal leaders and there are real leaders. Their plans must take into account the belief and behavior patterns associated with the core areas of the culture. For example, they need to be cognizant of social structure and the behavior associated with kinship groupings, ethnic group identifications, and stratifications. They need to plan their changes around existing elements of the economic system, (e.g., resource allocation, organization of labor, and distribution patterns). As changes are being designed, it is important to recognize that behaviors have related belief systems associated with them, and these must be considered as part of the question of fit. For example, the supernatural and health-related behaviors frequently are closely related For change agencies and agents, questions of timing and fit may have to include all these considerations and more. It means they must design and implement change according to existing local culture and in their own plans for accomplishing it.

Communication

The role of communication in culture change is recognized by everyone. It may be the single most important force of change, particularly in the directed process. Foster (1969) identified communication as a potential barrier to change. Arensberg and Niehoff (1971) listed communication as a potential stimulant to change. The importance of change agents establishing good communication channels with members of the focal group is generally accepted by all these authors, who see them as a means for exchanging information; important in the establishment of working relations between the participants; serving as the means of learning about proposed change; and a feedback mechanism about the progress of the project or program. Between agencies and focal groups, agents and focal groups, between members of the focal groups themselves, communication can become either a barrier to change or a significant stimulant for it. Communication is directly related to the cultural forces already discussed, many of which will influence the type and quality of communication that actually occurs in the change setting. There must be good communication between those asking for change and those asked to accept it. This allows for the interchange of information critical in its implementation, especially in the interaction context of agent and members of the focal group.

From the point of view of the change agent, communication is a major tool. It serves as the means of interchanging information and as part of the working relationship with members of the focal group. It is the means by which members of the focal group can learn about a change they are asked to adopt. In all change, there must be an educational component, and this rests on communication. Communication can also serve as the feedback mechanism to inform agents on the progress of the project or program. Any one or a combination of channels can be a part of communication. Use of local language can characterize the interaction, as can formal lectures or addresses to impart knowledge about the change. The use of local language serves to build rapport with members of focal groups. Formal presentations are useful in providing information on innovations or changes. Demonstrations can be used to show members of the focal groups the practical or pragmatic advantages of the change. Whereas using a local language can be used to impart information about the change, demonstrations allow for showing the members of focal groups the pragmatic advantages of the change. Demonstrations can do more to stimulate change than all the verbal arguments or presentations that could ever be given by a change agent. Demonstration can be a very effective means of communication.

Communication is more than words exchanged between the participants in interactions; it also involves nonverbal communications, things communicated by actions and personality. Image communication projects age, sex, expertise, and affiliations, all of which can become important in a change project. Interpersonal and intragroup communications have their roles to play as well. Communication between the agent and focal group members, between group members, and even gossip channels within a group can be useful in feedback, learning, and information processing. The communication between the person responsible for implementing change and those asked to adopt it is a crucial element that can in a large measure determine a program's success or failure. Communication on this level can be between agent and members of focal groups, or it can involve the communication between members of the focal groups. Gossip channels already exist in all culture groups and organizations, and these can be used quite effectively by change agents as an element of communication about change. One cannot overestimate the value of communications between the agent and the members of the focal group. In this one area, nearly all of the other elements of communication are brought to bear on the proposed change. The agent will convey an image to those with whom he or she works; then important cultural differences on age and sex, social and personal interactions, beliefs and practices will either be worked out or they will collide in cultural conflict. The agent conveys expertise, affiliations, commitment to the effort, and willingness to work with members of the focal group. Members of the focal group convey their response to the proposed change. Unfortunately, a great deal of the nonverbal communication is not conscious; rather, it is simply the extension of what people have learned in their cultures. In terms of change dynamics, communication looms as perhaps the most powerful force in stimulating acceptance or in serving as a barrier to it.

Strategy

The various strategies of all those involved in change will conflict in the interactional setting. General strategies adopted by agencies can by themselves serve as barriers or stimulants to change, as can the specific implementation strategy of agents. As suggested in Chapter 6, some general approach strategies are better than others, depending upon the circumstances of the focal group. To expect members of a focal group to commit the time and resources required for a community development approach to a change does not make much sense when the group is already existing on the subsistence margin. To provide a physical facility without education as to its use would be acceptable in complex cultures but probably not in small-scale ones, especially if it is directed at a change of kind as opposed to a change of degree. Using a paternalistic approach has never been very successful in any kind of change program.

Strategy is a question to be considered in the dynamics of change during implementation as well, for in many ways the entire discussion of this chapter needs to be taken into account by change agencies and agents. Minimizing the potential barriers to change and maximizing the potential stimulants must become as much a part of planners' strategy as the introduction of the change idea itself. What will be done and perhaps why it should be done; considerations of when it must be done and with what inputs from the agency; questions of timing, fit, motivations, and even strategies for implementation made possible by the plan—along with how this will be communicated—must be considered. All that is considered in the design and planning of a change will directly impact what change agents will do, perhaps even how they will be viewed in the interactions that will produce a result. Change agencies must anticipate and consider the reactions of those being asked to accept a change, and they must anticipate the strategies of those people that will develop during the interaction necessary for its implementation.

In the implementation of change, the most direct interaction will occur between the agent of change and the focal group, singly or in groups. Agent strategies focus on many of the same considerations as those of agencies, but on another level. They act on the personal level, whereas planning agencies tend to be far removed from those who will be asked to change some part of their culture. Motivation, timing, fit, formal and informal communications must, of necessity, assume central roles in their strategies. These will represent the points of potential conflicts that must be gotten over before there can be any expectation of a successful result. The interactions of agents and members of the focal group will revolve around these; the actions and reactions of both will be generated by them. Whereas the design or plan for change is rarely flexible, agent strategies are not unalterable, not set in concrete. Agents act, but they also react, just as members of the focal group do. Agents react to the situation in which they find themselves and how they perceive the people are responding to them and what they are doing. Consciously or unconsciously, change agents respond to their perceptions of these things, and to what they may see as challenges to the accomplishment of their task, their expertise, skills, or personality. Their own cultural values, beliefs, and practices may be challenged during the course of interacting with people who believe quite differently from themselves, behave quite differently, and respond to them in a negative manner. The strategy they develop in an effort to bring about the change designed by the agency can be also be challenged in the interactional setting, and how they respond will impact the setting and the outcome. It becomes a force in the process.

The strategy of focal groups depends on what they are being asked to accept and the strategies of the asking agency and the implementer. It can be based on what is being proposed, and it can be tied to the conditions under which it is being tried. It can be developed in response to how it will be implemented and by whom. It will change as the process unfolds, as a consequence of the actions and reactions of those with whom they will interact in the process. With focal group input into the planning and design of change, there may be a little less conflict, but there will be conflict nevertheless. Where they are not involved from the very beginning, the success or failure to reach project goals does not rest with them, and they know this. Success or failure rests with the change agency and the agents. The idea for change was not theirs, so no responsibility can be laid to them. Their responsibility will be to oppose what they did not ask for—at the very least, to minimize its impact as much as possible.

The responsive strategies of focal groups can be quite varied. They can even vary within a focal group itself, depending on the specific group or individuals involved. Agents may find themselves having to respond to several strategies at the same time. For example, formal leaders may respond quite differently than informal ones. Different minority groups may respond differently, depending on their status within the society. Dominant groups can respond differently than do minority groups, and political interest groups quite differently than social or religious ones. The cause of the responses can be as varied as the groups that generate them. Some will respond to the idea of change, and some to the agency that proposes it. Some responses will be a product of group ethnocentrism and their beliefs that what they are already doing is the most correct for them. Some will result from the kind and quality of interactions or the communications that occur within them. Some responses will be based on the change agents: what they do or do not do, or simply people's perceptions of them. Whatever its source, focal group strategy is a product of interaction and a significant force in the change setting.

EXTERNAL FORCES OF CHANGE

The last force in the dynamics of change is perhaps the most difficult to deal with, but its importance is no less than any of the other forces that have been discussed. External forces can impact culture change at any point in the process, and their sources can be quite varied. External forces can be instrumental in the initiation of change, in the planning and design for it, or they can operate during the attempt to implement it. External forces are those powers that can influence the direction of culture change that come from the larger context. This goes beyond an interrelated culture pattern and points to forces beyond or outside of the particular group context that can become involved in the change process and the direction that process might take. No cultural group lives in isolation from other groups. In the modern nation-state, specific, constituent, and scene cultures all exist within the context of that artificial creation. In the global context, all culture groupings are increasingly dependent upon others that are frequently far removed geographically and ideationally from themselves. All cultural change is susceptible to forces that are related to that dependency. Some people would even suggest that this dependency is the first step in the development of a global culture. Whether or not a global culture is on the horizon, it is very clear that the largest nation-state and the smallest of culture groupings must respond to the influences and pressures that modern world development has occasioned. What happens in the smallest group—whether small-scale, underdeveloped, or even the most primitive by modern standards—can significantly impact the change process of others, even the most modern, industrialized, and complex nation-state.

Although external forces of change are nearly impossible to predict, because they can come from a wide variety of sources, there are areas where such forces are likely to develop that can have a direct influence on the change process. The power of international corporations, frequently equal to that of nations, touches every group in the quest for raw materials to sustain the industrial complex, or in efforts to develop markets for products. The developing global economic system now touches nearly every society and culture group in the world, all of which must directly or indirectly participate if they are to continue to survive. Modern states continue their drive to incorporate or assimilate specific and constituent cultural groups within their artificial boundaries and to a uniform culture. Specialization and differentiation, the continuing centralization of political and economic decisions, complexity and stratification, the nucleation of human populations, and the conflicts these things bring have the power to impact culture change, its origins, and attempts to implement it Despite the best efforts of participants in the process, these external forces have the power to subvert any attempt, to determine its course and final outcomes.

External Forces and Nation-states

Perhaps the most difficult grouping to deal with is the complex nation-state, for, as pointed out, such groupings tend to obscure many actual cultural groupings that have been brought together in their creation. Although many people might prefer to see such contexts as primary cultures, and they are ideally presented as such, reality is something else. The state may have incorporated many distinct culture groups within it, and they may even be well along in the development of a consensus culture, but that is not the same as saying that the culture is homogeneous and its members subscribe to a single pattern of beliefs and behaviors. As already discussed, in the multicultural context of nation-states, the change process will nearly always involve culture contacts. In the nation-state context, external forces can be those associated with the national consensus culture, or the core systems of that culture imposed on the constituent cultures that are part of it. For example, a change project or program aimed at any of the ethnic or native cultural groups of the United States will be susceptible to many social, economic, religious, and political forces originating in the consensus culture. Economic forces associated with the national culture can become an effective force determining the course of a proposed project. The project design may have provided for substantial inputs from a federal agency, but a reduced budget may alter that and subvert the final objective, or a compromise budget may come out of Congress that is very different from that originally requested. A political decision, or lack thereof also can influence the course of project implementation. In the U.S. culture, economic and political considerations frequently combine to seriously impact the process of directed change. The special interests of a particularly strong religious group may become the determining factor in the final outcome. For example, in the effort to reduce pregnancies among teenagers in the United States, efforts were initiated to increase the amount of sex education in the schools was introduced. The program has been only minimally effective because of the opposition of religious groups.

Changes in the social structure are frequently subverted by those who have the most to gain by maintaining the status quo. Efforts to improve the system of taxation are repeatedly subverted by people who have the most to lose with any change in the current system. Either they hold the actual decision-making power over any changes in the system, or they hold significant influence over those who have such power. Efforts to improve how the country utilizes its natural resources are frequently subverted by corporations that have gained the most from their exploitation. Examples such as these demonstrate how conflicting interests of "the" system and particular cultural groups can serve to generate forces that directly impact change attempts and outcomes. Although it is tempting to suggest that in the context of the nation-state, this simply points to the interrelatedness of culture traits, given the context, it actually points to the diversity of such cultures, and the external nature or settings for most cultural changes within them. It also directs our attention to the fact that most cultural groups exist within larger contexts, as part of larger settings in which there can be forces that impact the change process.

Forces in the Global Context

The kind of circumstances that produce external forces in the nation-state can be seen on the global level. International politics, relations among nation-states, the economic and ideological competition among industrialized nations, can also produce forces that impact change proposals, designs, implementation, and final outcomes. Although the world has become more interdependent, it has not become more homogeneous. The same competitive, cooperative, and conservational forces identified for individual cultures function on a worldwide basis, between nations competing for status, power, and influence. International bodies have arisen to exert very powerful influences on the change process, no matter what it might be, or where it might be attempted. An economic system based on money and market exchange is sweeping across the globe. Nation-states and other cultural groups are increasingly being forced to participate in that system or face the prospect of not surviving. The development of the international or multicultural corporation, with power and influence that can surpass even that of the nation-states that spawn them, exerts tremendous influence on cultural change throughout the world. The resurgence of religion, ethnicity, and race as guiding forces of nation-states increasingly play major roles in world affairs.

The emerging global economic system and development of international corporations have become a major forces for cultural change, originating it and affecting that already being undertaken. The international corporations have promoted the diffusion of technical and cultural knowledge to the non-Western and preindustrial societies to such an extent that Alvin Wolfe (1989) considers them a new social force in the world. With their power and influence, international corporations can significantly alter the course of events in any society and by extension, the course of change processes of those societies. The extent of their influence is seen in the example provided by Paul Shankman (1975) in his study of the changes introduced into Western Somoa by a multinational corporation. The emerging global economic system, with its interlocking markets, products, and services, has caused rapid change, and its elements have impacted change programs throughout the world, as seen in the experiences of the Soviet Union and Eastern Europe, China, the United States, and Japan. The contact between nations under this economic pressure has produced economic crises, even more contact, and has created new aspirations, all of which have impacted culture change.

International politics, economics relations and competition exert considerable influence on the change process and its directions. On the level of international relations, politics, ideological differences, and national self-interest serve to generate change and the outcomes of change attempts. Although international bodies such as the United Nations and World Bank have been created to facilitate the relations among nations, provide a forum for the exchange of ideas, reduce world conflict, and help improve the living conditions of people everywhere in the world, such bodies are not evidence of a developing world culture or a willingness on the part of member nations to lay aside their individual interests. The compromises that characterize nation-states will also be found in international bodies, where consensus determines what will be done and how it will be done. The individual self-interests of member nations determine these. Conflicts among nation-states and competing constituent groups within member nations have continued unabated. Most international bodies are actually change agencies involved in the planning, design, and implementation of culture change throughout the world in the name of development, human rights, and humanitarian aid.

The United Nations Development Program (UNDP) is a good example. Within the programs undertaken by this agency, changes aimed at nearly every aspect of culture are funded and designed. Through contracts with affiliated agencies such as the World Health Organization (WHO), the United Nations Educational, Scientific and Cultural Organization (UNESCO), and countless others, assistance, expertise, and money are provided for the sole purpose of changing conditions, beliefs. or practices of people throughout the world. Under the auspices of the UNDP, the Fund for the Development of West Irian (FUNDWI) established a development program for the Indonesian province of West Irian (now known as Irian Jaya or Glorious Irian) that covered the entire spectrum of political, economic, and social development. In concert with the Indonesian government, but none of the cultural groups to be effected, a comprehensive and very complex plan for the development of the area was designed. Experts from around the world were hired to implement the various components of the plan. Not only were local people and cultures exposed to a multitude of changes in their way of life, but the change setting created was excessively multicultural. Experts represented cultures from around the world and conflicts were many. The goals of the plan and the specific activities of the experts who assumed the role of change agents were at the mercy of the constantly changing political climate within the U.N. General Assembly, which had final say over the project. The activities of most international bodies involved in change activities can be characterized in much the same way.

The relations among nation-states can also produce significant forces that impact change programs and projects In these circumstances, the ethnocentrism of the interacting states, even that of constituent groups within those states, can be the major force in determing change outcomes. For example, the U.S. Agency for International Development (USAID), and the Peace Corps, both oriented to change, are at the mercy of national self-interests, the interests of particular cultural groups within the United States, the changing political climate within the country, the fiscal debates of the United States Congress, various social debates, and specific relations with the particular country involved. For example, a program aimed at family planning might be at the mercy of legislators, powerful constituent or religious groups, debates on the foreign aid program or on birth control, and so on. In addition, the activities of the Peace Corps might be severely impacted by the deteriorating relations between the United States and host countries which can result in the termination of programs. All these examples demonstrate the presence and potential power of forces external to any specific project or program that can be operationalized to impact final outcomes.

Global political, ethnic, and religious trends have also become forces in the change process. Contradictory ethnic and religious trends in pluralistic societies can become powerful forces affecting the change process. As the complexity of nations increases, leadership is not always able to keep in touch with the local populace. As a result, nations increasingly appear fragmented along ethnic lines. Separatist movements in Africa, Europe, South America, and elsewhere seem to abound. This trend has caused significant change, and it has impacted specific change programs that have been contemplated and/or implemented. Religious trends have always been a force in change, but now there are conflicting trends in this aspect of human culture. On the one hand, secularization has accompanied the development of industrialized societies. On the other hand, religious institutions have remained persistent, even revitalized, because of secularization. As global changes have introduced sweeping changes into the cultures of people, and as these changes have threatened traditional beliefs and practices, religion has become a means by which people can react to the threat.

Global trends are impacting the way of life of people nearly everywhere. Global industrialization, population growth, resource depletion, environmental change, multinational corporations, and the emerging economic system have become major players in cultural change, frequently determining its direction and outcomes. Political, economic, and religious trends all are as such forces. For people directly involved in the change process, such forces can surface at any point in the process, from generating ideas for it to how it will be done. Because of the multicultural settings for most change today, settings wherein culture plays the major role in the dynamics of change, global forces magnify the conflicts in interaction. In the final analysis, it is quite impossible to predict which of these forces will prove to have the most influence on any particular change program. The important thing that needs to be remembered, is that such forces are out there, and any one of them, or any combination of them, can determine the course or outcome of culture change. It is impossible to control most of these kinds of external forces, perhaps impossible even to be aware of all of them. They do operate. In the dynamics of change, however, there is no substitute for developing an awareness of the possibilities and thinking about how such forces might become involved in a particular program. Of all the unpredictable aspects of culture change, this area of external forces is the most chancy. Despite the best ideas, good design and planning, adequate funding, and skilled agents to implement change, these external forces can operate to impact the process at any point in time, at any stage of the process, and produce serious consequences.

SUGGESTED READINGS

This group of readings will provide a more in-depth treatment of the dynamics of culture change as seen by various authors. In combination, they provide a fairly balanced treatment of directed culture change dynamics.

Arensberg, Conrad and Arthur Niehoff (eds.). 1971. *Introducing Social Change: A Manual for Community Development.* 2nd ed. In their chapter on culture change, the authors discuss conservatism, competition, diffusion, and planned change as the dynamic forces of change. Conservatism is tied to enculturation and its accompanying ethnocentrism, and competition accounts for the fact that cultures change.

Foster, George M. 1962. *Traditional Cultures: And the Impact of Technological Change.*

————. 1969. *Applied Anthropology.*

————. 1973. *Traditional Societies and Technological Change.* All these works contain discussions of the various social, psychological, cultural, and economic forces that can serve as barriers and/or stimulants to change, and how these are interrelated.

Hogbin, Ian. 1970. *Social Change.* 2nd ed. This work contains a discussion of change in the context of continuity, translating into the conservatism and competition of other writers. The thrust of this volume is to look at change in the context of continuity.

Leighton, Alexander. 1945. *The Governing of Men.* The work discusses the role of stress and emotion in the context of change in multicultural settings, as opposed to some kind of rationality.

Chapter 8

ACCOMPLISHING CHANGE

Having discussed culture change in general terms and from a historical standpoint (Chapter 1), concepts of culture and change (Chapters 2 and 3), processes of culture change (Chapter 4), and the various aspects, participants, and dynamics of the directed culture change process (Chapters 5–7), it is now possible to turn our attention to the all-important question of accomplishing change. Of course, this is the question that haunts all those who at some time in their lives are asked to design or plan for change, are assigned the task of implementing change, or are placed in the position of having to consider the adoption of change in their existing beliefs or practices. In the modern world, no individual or culture group will be untouched by this all-important process. Most of the major elements and considerations of the culture change processes, or how an innovation becomes a culture change, have been identified and discussed at length. Voluntary change is the least predictable. This process is not something that can be controlled, for it happens without specific, conscious efforts to spread a new trait throughout a culture group or across cultures. It happens as someone comes up with a new idea and others choose to adopt it for themselves. Because change is inevitable, and because there are always better ways, this process will always be present. Planned and directed change is a much more complex process centered on conscious efforts to bring about a culture change.

It is on this process, its planning, implementation, and dynamics, that attention is focused in an effort to gain some measure of control over it, whether the change is to be directed within a culture group or across culture groups. Many of the same considerations will be involved in nearly all change settings, whether that of nation-states or of specific, constituent, or scene cultures. What holds for ethnic grouping, also holds for corporate cultures. It has been strongly suggested that because culture can be applied to all manner of human groupings, as groups of people learn specific beliefs and behaviors that distinguish them from others, most change today will occur in the multicultural setting, where people representing more than one culture interact. Based on this inescapable fact, interaction is the key to understanding the dynamics of directed change, and crucial to gaining some measure of control over the process. All culture change ultimatley comes down to people interactions.

The model of directed culture change proposed throughout this volume is based on culture difference and the cultural conflicts that arise in the change setting. Because of culture and culture conflicts, directed change in multicultural settings is a complex system of interrelated elements that together make culture change the dynamic process that it will always be. It is from the content, form, and quality of the interactions of the participants in the process that most results and their consequences flow. While the concept of culture is not always easy to grasp, but without some better appreciation and understanding of it, and the role it plays in the lives of humans, any hope of better control over the change process will remain illusive. As a distinctly human creation, culture is a set of problem-solving solutions to the pressures and demands of the environment(s). It serves as the mediator between people and the environments in which they attempt to survive. It is the primary means of adaptation for humans. Recognizing that humans must adapt to both the natural environment and the sociocultural environment they created with their culture is likewise important, for the sociocultural environment has now replaced the physical one in importance and in the necessity for continuing, perhaps never-ending, culture change. People must continually adapt to this environment, just as they must continually respond to the changing physical environment, but with cultural and world development, the sociocultural environment clearly exerts the greater pressures for shift in human beliefs and behaviors.

Cultures exist as systems of belief and behavior and their resulting products, as sets of problem solving solutions created by people as they have sought to survive and provide for their needs. It applies to any group that learns a way which is specific to them and which distinguishes them from others. It exists as something taught and learned as truth by each new generation. It makes all humans the same, and it makes them different. It is the basis for the vast majority of what people will think and do during the course of their lives. It will come in an idealistic version, reflecting what a group would like it to be, as it ought to be, as they tend to think about themselves, or want others to think of them. Real culture focuses on how people really think and act in everyday life. Construct versions of culture come into existence as people attempt to understand others, to speak of the difference between ideal and real culture, and, as individuals with their own personal limitations play out their roles as members of the group within which culture is shared.

In any of its versions, culture is not a haphazard collection of beliefs and behaviors but an integrated system, with each of its elements interrelated to all the others. Once established, it does not remain static but changes constantly, as the environments change. In today's world, changing culture has fallen to individuals and groups of people in agencies that plan change, design it and implement it. No cultural group is immune to the effects of change agencies. In today's rapidly changing and interdependent world, the importance of this process looms large. Culture change suggests an alteration in the thoughts, behaviors, or products that together define a culture. When it is obvious that a change is needed, or someone has determined that a change should be made, the question arises as to how one goes about the task. The question plagues all culture groups, from the largest nation-states to the smallest special interest or organizational cultural groupings. It must be faced by individuals and groups given the task of changing someone else's beliefs and/or behaviors. It must be faced by individuals and/or groups who will be asked to change some aspect of their culture.

Taken within the culture context, change can mean subtraction, addition, or modification in any of a culture's beliefs, behaviors or products. Because of the integrated nature of culture, a change in one aspect of it will quite likely mean change in other parts. In today's rapidly changing world, the constancy of change is assured as culture groups are forced to respond to constantly changing physical and sociocultural environments. This need for constant change applies to all manner of culture groups, especially the artificially created nation-state groupings. It applies to the former Soviet Union and the United States, African-Americans, and Asian-Americans, Serbs and Kurds, Native-Americans, Berger King and McDonald's, the Republicans and Democrats, the Christian and Muslims, and all the other cultural groupings that can be identified. The largest nation-states and smallest culturally identifiable groups must now participate in a world increasingly dominated by a global economic system. For nation-states, and the specific, constituent, and scene groups identifiable within them, this translates into finding their place in this system or facing negative and inevitable consequences. For business cultures, this translates into changing how they do business, organize to accomplish their goals, or stay competitive in the marketplace. For ethnic groups that exist within nation-states, it means changing to become equal participants. For the individuals and the many special interest groups associated with scene cultures, it means changing to successfully pursue their goals. Culture change is as inevitable as the constantly changing environments, with planned and directed change now the primary means by which humans of any culture grouping go about that task.

CULTURE CHANGE MODEL

Coming up with a proposed change for one's own group or some other group is only the beginning of the change process. For a new idea to become a culture change, it must be implemented or spread to the majority of the group's members and integrated into their culture pattern. Before addressing this all-important question of how actually to bring about change, it may be wise to review the directed culture change model that has been advocated throughout this volume, discussed at length in Chapter 4. The model proposed (Figure 8.1) approaches directed change in a slightly different manner and with a significant change in emphasis than has been the case with earlier models. In the proposed model, the chief area of concern is the interactional context, where the participants come together to act and react, where a plan or design for change materializes out of the efforts to implement it. Out of the interaction of the participants who act and react, and any number of outside forces, there will always be a result, and there will always be consequences tied to the result. The model does not offer a textbook

Figure 8.1
Directed Culture Change

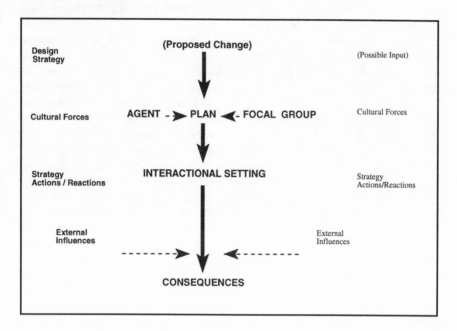

solution for directed culture change, for there are no step-by-step procedures that can ensure or predict successful attempts.

The basic components of the proposed model are not very different from those of all of the earlier models of directed change. All of existing models identify the same basic components: the plan (idea for change), participants in the process (change agents and groups for which change is intended), a setting where these participants come together, and a result or consequence. It is not in the identification of basic components that the proposed model differs from earlier ones; rather, it is in specifics of these components, and in the shift of emphasis to interactional settings, that the model provides a different perspective on the process. The planning or design of change represents an important element of the directed change process that must be dealt with quite apart from either of the participant groups. Planning change and the attempts to implement it are very different.

Earlier models tended to blend the activities of change agencies and change agents, clearly putting the emphasis on the actions of agents. This tendency was justified at the time, because those proposing change were frequently the same individuals or groups that attempted to implement it. That this was not always so was readily admitted, but agents and agencies were collapsed into a single component of the process. As directed change has unfolded, and as so many agencies have been created, funded, and staffed for the sole purpose of pursuing change, the need to distinguish the change agency from the change agent has become clear. Change agencies plan and design change. Change agents are responsible for implementing it. Although they are clearly related, and both are concerned with many of the same basic considerations of timing, fit, strategy, and funding, the specifics are quite different.

The planning and design of change by change agencies revolve around generating the ideas for change, planning how it will be accomplished in general terms, and with what contributions of funds and perhaps personnel that will be required. Timing and fit may or may not be significant considerations. Politically or economically, a particular change may be pursued regardless of whether the timing is appropriate. The same can hold true for its fit into the cultural pattern of the focal group. Altogether, the answers to these questions will impact, and ultimately produce, the general change strategy of the agency. Change agents are given the task of implementing what an agency has designed, usually under the limitations of that plan. Sometimes an idea to change is simply generated, then left up to the agent to implement. Although agents are also concerned with timing, fit, and strategy, in their particular case such things are tied to their activities aimed at bringing about the change as intended. Change agents do not merely respond to the dictates of a change agency and its plan for change; they also develop their own strategy for working with members of the focal group. Timing, fit, and strategy take on quite different meanings in the context. The strategy of the change plan can loom large for both agents and members of focal groups, for it can place significant limitations or restrictions on what change agents can do in their attempts to implement change. The wrong general change strategy can have as much negative impact on a change proposal as an ill-conceived implementation strategy of the agent given the task of accomplishing it.

The main emphasis of the proposed model is on the dynamic interaction of the participants in the process who come together in the change setting, an interaction characterized by stress, emotion, and conflict. Both change agents and members of the group to be changed bring their learned cultures into the change setting, as well as characteristics that are products of their role and participation in the change process. Change agents are characterized by their nation-state cultures and any number of ethnic, specific, religious, or special interest cultures, including their own specialty. Agents also being into the change setting those characteristics, beliefs, and practices associated with the role of change agent and their own personalities: interpersonal skills, living habits, affiliations, implementation strategy, and their own motivations.

Focal groups will be characterized by their particular culture(s) and their role in the process as well, but the content of these will be very different from those that characterize the change agent. As with agents practicing in a culture other than their own, the learned ways and behaviors of members of the focal group become highlighted in the change process. In their case, it is some already accepted belief or practice of their culture that agents want to change. The proposal represents a challenge to that accepted truth. Role characteristics, as a result of being the focus of change activities, will revolve around responding to the proposed change and its implications. The main focus will be on activities that balance cultural expectations and actual behavior under the stress of the change context. The focal group will develop a strategy tied to the change setting, much as the agent does, but their strategy will revolve around how to deal with the agent and what he or she wants. The basic goal of members of the focal group is to respond to the new circumstances or conditions by using proven and traditional ways. Given a choice, they probably would not change, so minimizing the impact of change becomes the primary concern. Consciously or unconsciously, the ideal, real, and construct cultures of the participants will underlie their actions and reactions in the interactional settings where their acquired cultural truths conflict. Directed change is more than just these participants interacting, for, has been shown, any number of external influences can impact the process at any point in time.

Although this appears to be somewhat complicated, it really is not, when broken down into its basic parts. Someone has an idea to introduce or change an idea, belief, or practice. In today's world, this most often comes from a change agency. A plan is developed by the agency to bring it about, a plan organized around a general strategy approach, funds for its undertaking, personnel, and stipulations as to how and when it will be completed. Change agents, hired specialists in the area to be addressed by the proposed change, are hired and expected to implement the change as intended. These agents of change come into some form of contact with those for whom the change is designed. They interact with those people, and some result is achieved. Although the result is usually the product of the interaction between those most directly involved in the implementation effort, the result is sometimes the product of forces or events far removed from the actual change activity. It may simply be out of the participants' hands. Seen in these terms, the process itself is not very complicated. Operationalizing change, or actually bringing it about, is another matter. There are a great many things to be considered by planners, agents, and members of focal groups.

CHANCES OF SUCCESS

From the very beginning, it is important to recognize that there are some very chancy aspects of culture change, at any level and in any of its forms. In directed change, the ability to achieve a desired result depends on a number of factors, some of which, as we have seen, are outside of anyone's ability to control. Because of this, there is no program to be applied that can ensure success. There is no pat answer, school solution, no set of guidelines or series of steps that one can learn to ensure that a proposed change will be become a culture change. As suggested in earlier discussion, however, there are things that can be done to increase the chances of success. Developing an awareness and appreciation of the cultural context of change is the first step. This goes well beyond knowing about culture in some general sense, or the fact that it plays such an important role in the lives of people. It means understanding the general and specific underlying forces of culture that will directly impact attempts to change it. It means understanding the integrated nature of belief and behavior patterns, especially those associated with core systems of culture. It means understanding the different versions of culture that are learned and characterize members of any cultural grouping. With such awareness and knowledge, many of the pitfalls that have led to unsuccessful efforts to implement change in the past can be avoided, or at least minimized. Beyond becoming aware of the specific beliefs and behaviors of the focal group in directed change, it is necessary to become aware of things which can become the barriers or the stimulants to change. Knowing these things and taking them into account can increase the chances for a successful outcome but will not guarantee it.

Most of the chance aspects in implementing change are associated with the "cultural baggage" of participants in the process. Whether one likes to admit it or not, culture introduces many of the most significant problems to be faced and overcome in a change project or program. Earlier, it was proposed that cultures teach their members a brand of truth, a particular way of thinking and acting. This applies equally to the group being asked to change and to the agencies or agents attempting to change them. Once the "truth" is learned as the right and only way, the ethnocentric attitude quickly develops. The members of the group judge other ideas and behavior against what they have learned as "truth." Culture is mostly an unconscious thing for most people, who simply go about living as they have been taught. The ethnocentrism acquired during the process of acquiring culture is also unconscious, not readily apparent to the individual or members of the group. Ethnocentrism underlies the actions and reactions of participants in the change process, however.

In addition to the natural ethnocentrism that accompanies the acquisition of culture, a basic conservatism develops. As with ethnocentrism, no culture group seems to be immune to this characteristic. Once culture is acquired as "truth," members of any culture are reluctant to change, for in their view, they have learned the true, right, and correct system of beliefs and practices. Proposing to change any part of it threatens the entire truth that people have learned, and threatens the security of the members of the group in knowing what is right. The competition also inherent in culture makes the problem more difficult. All individuals and groups continually compete with one another. To change what has proven itself to be competitively successful will be perceived as threatening. Because cultural groups compete, their ethnocentrism and conservatism become very powerful inhibiting forces to any suggested changes in their cultures. All participants in the change process already "know the way" with regard to just about everything. Of course, this is also followed by the universally held belief that if "they" (distinguished from "me"or "us") would just do it "my" or "our" way, things would be all right.

Unfortunately, changing ideas or behaviors is not like baking a cake. For doing that chore, one simply follows the recipe: combines the flour, sugar, eggs, vanilla, milk and eggs, pours this mixture into a pan, and bakes it at a constant temperature for the prescribed period of time. If everything is done as prescribed in the recipe, in all probability the result will be a cake. All this can be simplified somewhat if a boxed cake mix is purchased and the instructions on the box are followed. Whichever the choice, follow the recipe and there is every expectation that a cake will be produced every time. Culture change is a little different. As a process, this is more like saying that you *plan* to bake a cake, *try* to put the right ingredients together by doing all that the recipe requires, then *hope* for the best. There is no guarantee you will get a cake. You can end up with something you did not intend, perhaps something you never even thought of as a result.

This chancy part of the problem has to do with lessons anthropologists have learned in jungles, deserts, caves, and city streets. It is extremely rare that a change someone envisioned turns out the way it was intended. Every case is a unique one in which different forces can determine the results. Every individual in the world has probably spent a significant portion of his or her life experiencing this reality. In the case of change, it may have nothing to do with whether an idea for change was a good or a bad one. It may not have anything to do with the culture or the people for whom it was intended. It does not necessarily mean that the person assigned the implementation task was incompetent, or that the result was the product of what someone did or did not do. Although such things are easy targets for blame, they are not always the cause of change projects failing to meet their objectives or goals. Certainly, some projects have failed because the change was a bad idea, and others have failed because of the lack of skill of agents who have attempted to implement them. Some failures, or programs achieving only minimal results, can be the result of interactional outcomes that produced unplanned consequences. The results are not those envisioned by any of the participants in the process. At other times, the results of change efforts are a product of circumstance, the result of forces over which no one seemed to have any control.

Unplanned Consequences of Planned Culture Change

"Unplanned consequences of planned culture change," although sounding much like a tautology, actually is not. Unplanned consequences refers are those "other things," results or consequences, that can evolve from change activities that no one specifically planned for, wanted, or anticipated. External forces are not quite the same thing as unplanned consequences. External forces are those influences, pressures, or events that occur quite apart from the change setting but serve to produce a particular result. Unplanned consequences are directly tied to the change activity, produced by the actions of participants in the process or as a consequence of the interactional setting. They can be the consequences of change planners or agents not being as well grounded in the culture of those they propose to change as they should be. They can be the product of not appreciating the holism of culture, or not understanding that change of any kind will impact more than the limited area for which it may be designed. They can result from the many actions of change agents as they go about their task and they can be produced by the responsive actions of members of the focal group who did not appreciate the interrelated nature of their own culture and did not anticipate the total consequences of their actions. In essence, unplanned consequences are all of those consequences emanating from change activities that nobody anticipates. Although the term might be justifiable for any change result that is other than proposed or intended, it is probably more appropriately applied to those consequences, which always seem to accompany change, that go beyond the intended goals of the participants.

At the level of change agency and agent, unplanned consequences generally flow from a lack of understanding of the context within which they propose, plan, and attempt to implement change. It can be argued that a failure to understand the culture context is a product of poor planning, but it can also mean that the proposed change was simply a bad fit to the local culture or circumstance at the time. A culture change plan or design can be a very good one, just not appropriate for the time and place for which it is intended. In the introduction of a steel ax to the Yir Yoront, the individual who served as the change agent surely did not intend to bring about the demise of an entire culture. The idea was to simply provide a more accessible and efficient tool into their culture of these people. Because the agent lacked understanding of the role, function, and importance of the traditional stone tool in maintaining the social structure of the culture, the introduction of the new technology had the long term effect of destroying the entire culture. In the case of the Aswan High Dam, the original idea and motivation for the project were to help in the development of agriculture in the area (Kennedy 1977). In the end, the benefits of the dam were enjoyed by only a privileged few, not the masses for which they were intended. Instead of increasing opportunities, the dam produced greater inequality and stratification. In this case, the result went counter to one of the chief goals of the project because the social circumstances in the area were ignored.

Unplanned consequences are commonly associated with the activities of missionaries who perceive their goal solely as introducing Christianity to traditional cultural groups, as an alternative to some set of existing religious beliefs and practices. In reality, missionaries introduce significant changes in all aspects of the cultures with which they work. For example, in the highlands of West New Guinea, one group of missionaries steadfastly denied they were involved in changing any aspect of the lives of the local people beyond the introduction of their religion. To remove the conflict between Christianity and traditional religion, this particular group collected and burned as much of the traditional culture as they could lay their hands on. In their view, the items to be burned were representative of the religious practices Christianity was to replace (Naylor 1974). They failed to see that in introducing their religion, they were also introducing the culture of Christianity. That this would impact every aspect of traditional culture was simply not envisioned or admitted. They ignored the relationship of many of the destroyed items to the traditional subsistence and social systems, and by doing so, initiated far more changes than anticipated. Much of the culture symbolized and embodied in the items destroyed was altered in the process. These same missionaries occasioned other unplanned consequences through their personal actions. Some of their actions worked counter to the avowed goal. They delivered the message of equality in the eyes of God on Sunday, then they prohibited locals from their individual homes Monday through Saturday. The contradiction was not lost on the people, who developed considerable resentment toward the missionaries and their message.

Similar situations occur with some frequency in the business world. As business managers scramble to adopt the ever changing information technology in order to stay competitive, they frequently produce unintended consequences. Desiring to give employees the best tools to do the job, management buys them the best equipment. After a short time, management finds that personal interactions, upon which the company may depend, decrease substantially. Management changes what it wants to change, but gets something else besides. In all these cases, it is not that planners get a different response than projected; change agents and planners simply get much more than they bargained for.

Sometimes unplanned consequences are the product of human interactions, the result of those trying to accomplish change and those being asked to change coming together in the effort. Examples of this kind of situation are quite common. Someone has a good idea and its implementation falls to someone else. Unfortunately, the individual to whom the task is assigned has no particular training in culture or culture change, perhaps has an abrasive personality or uses a heavy-handed paternalistic approach in dealing with people who are perceived as uncooperative. The people can balk, not so much at the change idea as at the personality of the individual trying to implement it. They can then balk at any other attempt at change proposed by the sponsoring agency. As noted by Brian Faggan (1984), the roots of many problems in dealing with other cultures lie in past dealings. The case of the Native Americans and the Bureau of Indian Affairs serves as a good example. In many cases, the individuals hired to implement change were very skilled, but their hands were tied by the agency strategy or funds provided for the effort. In other cases, they may simply have been the wrong people in the wrong setting at the right time. The result was still the same: the Native Americans developed a distinct distrust of the BIA and anyone representing it.

Unplanned consequences are often the result of responsive actions taken by members of the focal group as well. Examples where unplanned consequences coming from the actions of focal groups can be seen in the experiences of the Alaskan Natives (Arnold 1976) and the Dani of the Balim Valley (Naylor 1974). In an effort to assume control over their own lives, various native cultural groups of Alaska came together to fight for the Native Land Claims Settlement Act of 1971. As a united group, they were instrumental in the final provisions of that act, which, from their perspective, was to ensure that their lives and cultures would be maintained. As the provisions of the act unfolded, it became clear that the real consequences involved more changes than might have been occasioned without it. The natives simply became a part of the larger system. They obtained cash payments from the government, obtained control over traditional lands and resources, and they established both profit and nonprofit corporations to handle their own affairs according to the provisions of the act. In adhering to the corporate laws of the United States, and in fulfilling their obligations to themselves, the people helped to create a climate where the very consequences they sought to avoid were produced out of the necessity of participating in the system. Many of the aspects of Native Alaskan life they sought to protect had to be altered in order to continue participation in the agreement.

In another example taken from the experiences of the Alaskan Natives, unplanned consequences accompanied the introduction of community centers in

Native Alaskan communities (Naylor 1976). Grants were made available to local towns and villages to construct community centers where people could gather, hold meetings, and engage in recreational activity such as watching television. Many communities availed themselves of this opportunity. Upon completion of the centers, unanticipated consequences were almost immediate. Traditionally, the focal point of village life was the family. Nearly all social activity revolved around family groupings on a daily basis, as families gathered to eat and interact socially. Upon completion of the centers, the traditional family structure began to fall apart as the younger people began to gather at the centers, where they were constantly exposed to new ideas, values, and practices by watching television. The people got their community centers, and they got other things they did not anticipate.

In the case of the Dani, both the government efforts and the responses of the people produced unplanned consequences. In an attempt to improve literacy and develop a national consciousness among the Dani, the Indonesian government required that all children under a certain age had to attend school. The government's actions and the Dani response produced a series of unintended consequences. The requirement that all children attend school took them away from traditional activities of which they were a vital part. Boys assisted the adult males in construction or repair activities, and many had the responsibility of caring for the family pigs. Girls had the responsibility of helping their mothers in gardening activities and the care of younger children. While they were attending school, boys nor girls could fulfill what had been their traditional roles.

The policy has also changed marriage patterns. Traditionally, marriages were arranged between families and involved bride payments. Attending school changed this system. Girls, who traditionally had no say in the selection of husbands, began to select their own husbands from among those males who attended school. The economic aspects of the system were ignored; many girls simply took up residence with their own choices in the developing urban communities in the valley. The Dani response strategy to the requirement that girls attend school produced unanticipated consequences. From the Dani perspective, sending girls to schools would seriously jeopardize their subsistence system. To preclude the loss of females so central to that subsistence, and because married women were not included in the directive, the Dani response was to marry girls off at much younger ages. As a consequence, girls were married off before the onset of puberty.

All of these cases demonstrate that unplanned consequences of planned change are usually the result of participants failing to appreciate the interrelated nature of culture. Change agencies, change agents, and members of focal groups focus on their immediate change problem, with little thought as to how what they decide to do may affect other aspects of the culture. Unfortunately, it is almost impossible to see the relationship of what is proposed to everything else in a culture. It is probably safe to say that unplanned consequences will nearly always accompany any change project or program. If there are not unplanned consequences tied to the proposed idea, there will be unplanned consequences from the actions and reactions of the participants in the interaction intended to bring it about. Being unfamiliar with the cultural context within which they work, change agents run a constant risk of doing or saying something that will produce unintended results. In responding to an idea or the actions of a change agent, members of focal groups run the risk of failing to perceive that their reactions can produce consequences even more devastating than the proposed change. In the case of agents and focal groups, unplanned consequences come from a lack of cultural understanding and limited vision. The only way to minimize the number and impact of such unplanned consequences is for agencies and agents to become well grounded in the culture(s) of the people with whom they will interact, as well as with their own. They also need to become familiar with the directed culture change process.

CHANGING CULTURE

There is no textbook solution for culture change, no set of prescribed steps to ensure the success of any change effort. Just as each culture must be understood on its own terms, so each culture change circumstance must be dealt with as unique. What works in one particular set of circumstances will not necessarily work in others. But change is not a quixotic process; it is patterned, just as cultures are patterned. Change functions in similar ways in all types of human groupings because it is patterned. Culture is a kind of environmental control. It establishes order out of chaos. Understanding the processes of change and the cultural context within which it is to be attempted puts a large measure of control over its outcomes in your hands. It can minimize some of the chance elements, but it will never eliminate all of them. Even with all the right ingredients for success, you may not get exactly what you intended. There are always forces "out there" that can seriously affect your efforts. With a good understanding of the complexity of the task of changing culture, and appreciation of all the issues and aspects of the change process—including the idea that all cultures are part of larger contexts—chances for successful outcomes are improved immensely, but they can never be guaranteed.

Knowing the Cultural Context

It has been shown that in the interactional context of change, a great many issues and aspects come together to bear on the change process outcomes. First and foremost are those associated with culture: human culture in general and those of the specific participants in the interactional settings of change. It seems reasonable to suggest, at this point, that the first step in changing any culture is to determine the actual cultural context within which it will be attempted. This means gaining as much understanding of the integrated pattern of beliefs and behaviors of members of the focal group as possible. It also means gaining a much more conscious understanding of one's own cultural background, the belief and behavior systems that serve to motivate you and your efforts. Obtaining a better understanding of culture means learning as much as you can about ideal and real cultures, which are usually quite different. The difference between what is thought or believed, and what is actually thought and done, can be significant to your particular effort. Changes in ideas put you squarely in the realm of the ideal culture, probably the area in which change is most difficult to accomplish. Change that moves a group closer to its ideal culture or its real culture, is more likely to be accepted than one that shifts the group totally away from either one.

How a group may perceive a change can arise from either of these versions of culture that people possess, and this can be important in the interactional setting. Individual members of cultures construct their own versions of the culture based on their own talents, experiences, and personal limitations. Individual knowledge of the culture will always be limited, for it is rare that an individual can know the whole of it. The most important version of culture will be the real one, but no one probably ever knows the totality of that. This means you will create and work in the construct version of culture, one that combines what the people think and believe with what they actually do. Creating such a representation of culture will help you to determine the gap between what people want to believe and what they actually do believe. Assuming that a good understanding of the culture can be obtained, in its ideal and its real forms, agencies and agents will be in a better position to know how to go about the change task.

What must be understood about culture, if you proposed to make any change in it, begins with an appreciation of cultural holism, the fact that all of its parts are interrelated. Persons who approach a specific change without understanding its relationship to the remainder of the culture, without recognizing that what they intend has far-reaching implications in other of the culture's systems, only exacerbate an already difficult problem. A change in a particular aspect of culture usually means changes in other aspects of the culture as well, perhaps in all of it. Special attention must be given to the core political, economic, social, and religious systems of culture, for these are the most important in the minds of most people. Knowing a culture goes beyond simply knowing the intricacies of its organization or structural systems, or knowing that cultures are generally going to be characterized by conservatism, cooperation, or competition. It also requires some understanding of the culture's core values and dominant orienting themes, which underlie its systems of belief and behavior.

Paying particular attention to those aspects of the focal culture most likely to inhibit or stimulate change is helpful. Finding the values shared by the members of a cultural group is important. The group you represent, and the group with whom you will attempt some change, may be composed of different constituent or scene cultures. This will certainly be important in the case of a focal group that exists within the larger nation-state cultures or within organizational cultures that are made up of constituent groups. This means you may have to become familiar with a number of cultural patterns that exist within the group with which you will work, or impinge on it by virtue of the larger context. The same goes for yourself. Even shared values within a relatively confined culture context may be given different priority from level to level, constituent group to constituent group. This will lead you to understand the cultural forces, both general and specific, that will play a role in what you do and in the final consequences of your efforts. Attempting change in the most conservative aspects of culture is much more difficult than change in areas that enhance the competitive or cooperative nature of cultures.

Obtaining the necessary cultural understanding prior to undertaking cultural change is not easy. Fortunately, cultural descriptions of most cultural groups are available for nation-states, constituent ethnic and racial groups, even cultural scenes. Anthropologists have produced ethnographies on the small-scale cultures found around the world, but increasingly they have been providing cultural descriptions for constituent, scene, and organizational cultures in nation-states. Such descriptions can serve as the beginning for developing the necessary appreciation and understanding of the cultures of those to be involved in change. They are not descriptions of the real cultures; rather, they are representations of culture based on what people say they are about and what they actually are about. They are usually based on the norms of the culture, on what people do more often than not. They do not represent all the variations that may exist within a culture pattern, and they are limited to the interests of the researcher who produced them. For this reason, they can be viewed only as a beginning step. Many of the things that they can never be, are the very things with which people involved in change must be familiar: real culture. There is no substitute for doing a cultural study on your own, talking to members of the group and making your own observations. Keeping in mind that participants in change are likely to be members of a number of cultures, it is quite likely that you will find yourself doing studies of more than one culture. People, to include yourself, are going to be characterized and biased by their cultures. Your own ethnocentrism must be curbed if you expect to work with others who believe and behave differently from yourself.

The importance and value of knowing the cultural context in which a change is to be attempted cannot be overstated. Although learning about the culture of the group you intend to change can require time, it will be time well spent. Proposing a culture change, no matter how minor or insignificant it may appear to be in the overall scheme of things, will be accompanied by changes throughout the culture, some of which you may not intend. Knowing the culture will allow you to anticipate some of those changes and their consequences. It will also help you identify potential barriers to what you propose and develop plans for overcoming them. Proceeding to introduce a change without understanding its total cultural context will make your task extremely hard and open you to potential failure. Repercussions in areas unconsidered by you can subvert your efforts. Implementing change in one aspect of culture, without some understanding of its relationship to the other aspects of the culture, can result in the destruction of the group you propose to assist. Placing the group and its culture in the larger context is equally important. Understanding the larger context can help you to anticipate some of the external forces that can impact your effort and its final outcomes. It will not eliminate the possibility of external forces significantly impacting your efforts, but it will put you in a position where you may be able to reduce their impacts somewhat.

Knowing the culture within which you will work helps you to anticipate the areas where barriers to your effort can arise, as well as to identify what may be used to stimulate or motivate the acceptance of the change. Knowing the difference between the ideal and real cultures of the focal group will help you in much the same way. There are times when working in the ideal framework will be better than working in the real one. A change that purports to move a group away from a not-so-valued reality and closer to their ideals would be a case in point. On the other hand, working only in the ideal culture of the group may get you only partway to your goals. The legislation against segregation in the United States provides a case in point. Legislating segregation away has not eliminated it. Focusing on the ideal of equality without addressing the continuing behavioral inequality, has not changed the reality of its continued existence.

Knowing culture means knowing your own as well, for it will be from this base that your own beliefs, actions, and reactions will be generated to impact directed change activities. Recognizing that your cultural beliefs and practices will be in conflict with those of the focal group will go a long way toward helping you reduce the stress—yours and theirs—that will accompany the change effort. It will also play a significant role in the actions and reactions you can anticipate from members of the focal group and from yourself in that setting. For anyone involved in change, understanding the cultural component(s) of the effort is of the highest priority. Appreciating what it is, the holism of it, and the role it plays in the lives of people, including yourself, is crucial.

Knowing about Culture Change

Learning about the change process(es) is as important as learning about culture. Becoming involved in proposing a change, designing an effort, or being asked to implement change in settings of culture conflict is rarely easy. Knowing the culture of those for whom change is being contemplated, as well as one's own cultural biases, is only the beginning. Change is more than generating an idea, introducing a new trait, or altering a practice. Change depends on the spread of the innovation throughout the group for which it is intended until that it is integrated into the belief and practice patterns of the group. Getting others to accept a change in their existing beliefs or practices involves specific coercive efforts that must occur in some direct or indirect interaction of people: those proposing change, those attempting to implement change, and those asked to adopt it. All these efforts focus on convincing the members of the focal group to accept the change because it will result in more benefits than costs. Although this objective seems clear and simple enough, the fact that the effort will occur in a conflict setting, made so by the differing cultures represented by participants who have very different goals, makes for the involved and chancy process that directed change will be. All the issues and aspects of directed culture change addressed up to this point will come to bear on the final outcome of any attempt at culture change, whether it be aimed at the most complex society or at the smallest special interest or organization cultural groupings. The more complex the group, the more difficult the change problem, for multiple cultures involved. In the final analysis, the outcome of any attempt at culture change is the responsibility of those who plan or attempt to implement it. It is never the responsibility of those for whom it is intended.

Being grounded in the literature of culture change will certainly help anyone who becomes involved with it. A number of change regularities have been identified, and knowing these can help planners and agents of directed change avoid some mistakes and pitfalls. For example, knowing that most change usually begins on the upper levels of society, from which it proceeds downward and outward, may help planners and agents know where to start or direct their major efforts. Knowing that the middle class is conservative, whereas the lower classes are more receptive to change, will help in the same way (Cancian 1980). Knowing that without the support of both formal and informal leaders of the focal group, the task can be infinitely harder, will lead to their inclusion throughout the process. Knowing what can serve as potential barriers or stimulants to change can help in both the design and implementation activities associated with a proposed change. Knowing that factionalism will almost always accompany a change effort alerts change agents to be on the lookout for it, helps them direct their efforts and avoid factional affiliations that can subvert their goals.

Knowing that nativistic movements nearly always follow culture change is also important. Faced with new ideas or practices that appear to threaten the group security, people will attempt to revert to former beliefs and practices. They strongly desire to "go back to the good old days," to return to the way it was before the change. Such a response is quite normal and understandable, for people are constantly seeking the security of knowing the correct ways of thinking and acting. With change, they become confused and disoriented. In some cases, particularly with the oldest and youngest members of the group, they come disaffected, not quite sure where they belong in the changed circumstance. This leads to disillusionment, for the truth they learned is suddenly "not quite so true." This natural response becomes a desire to return to what they knew and felt comfortable with prior to the change. Even with the successful implementation of culture change, there will always be a segment of the population that will follow this path. Knowing that directed culture change creates settings of conflict, stress, and high emotion will help you understand participants' actions and reactions during their interactions and develop strategies to minimize their impacts. This applies equally to yourself. Knowing that all change involves both benefits and costs can help you focus your attention on minimizing costs or developing measures to offset costs as much as possible. In the process, you will be able to identify potentially powerful barriers to what you propose—and this, too, will help direct your efforts. Knowing that proposed change to core areas of cultures will be more difficult to achieve, because they pose the greatest threat to the focal group, encourages agents and planners to direct their efforts first at non-threatening areas in order to develop a positive attitude toward change that can later be used in attempting changes in core areas. Massive change that attempts to alter many beliefs and behaviors all at once, or over a short period of time, will be resisted more than change that addresses more delimited areas and in small doses. Small changes in small doses have a much better chance of success than attempts at changing the whole of a culture all at once. Changes that fit the local culture and are appropriately timed to its stage of development and local circumstance have a much better chance of succeeding than those which are not. Motivation is tied to questions of timing and fit, and it is the key to successful change. Without motivation, people will resist any proposed change.

Directed culture change revolves around human interactions, and successful interaction is the responsibility of those proposing or attempting to implement change. Except for the influence of external forces over which no one can exert much control, everything in the directed change process is ultimately the responsibility of those who propose or attempt to implement change. It is the agency/agent that will determine the course of events, not those being asked to change some part of their lives. Agents must be prepared to accept the responsibility for failure or success. Although success and failure must fall on those directing the change, that does not mean the end results are simply the products of what they do—and perhaps what they do not do. Members of the focal groups are not passive participants in the interaction required for change, but active respondents to what they are being asked to accept, who is doing the asking, and how it is being done. Their reactions will be based on what they already know to be true and correct. What they do will also impact the result, but it is up to the agent to be knowledgeable enough and skilled enough to orchestrate the process to the desired conclusion. Just because a person is skilled in a particular specialty does not mean he or she is qualified to undertake change.

Changing a Whole Culture

Change in a limited fashion or in a small aspect of culture can be difficult enough. Changing the whole of any culture, be it as large and complex as a nation-state group, or as limited as a business or special interest culture group, has to be viewed as a monumental task. This is not to suggest that it cannot be done, for history strongly suggests otherwise. This appears to be the case in the creation of many nation-states throughout history, where many established cultures were simply incorporated into the state through persuasion or the force of arms. A number of modern nations are still in this process. But in the collapse of nations and civilizations of the distant past, and in many modern nation-states, it now seems apparent that the incorporation of ethnic groups into the nation-state structure is never as complete as has been assumed. In the breakup of the Eastern European states, the creation of new nations out of colonial Africa, Southeast Asia, and the Middle East, the beliefs and practices of constituent groups have reasserted themselves in quite a violent fashion. Similar circumstances very likely led to the fall of earlier civilizations and states: the Greek, Roman, Mayan, and countless others. When cultural groups are incorporated into nation-states, they are asked to trade the totality of their learned culture or truth for the consensus culture of the state. As events are now vividly demonstrating, this obviously does not happen. Although people and cultures have been incorporated into states, have appeared to change or even to have disappeared, but have remained alive and well.

Nietschmann (1987:3) has made the point that people with distinct cultures never totally accept the rule of states in which they find themselves. Some groups have successfully resisted change for a great many years, despite efforts to introduce it into their lives and cultures. In the United States, Canada, and elsewhere, many native culture groups have successfully held on to much of their traditional cultures, refusing to be incorporated into national consensus cultures. The recognition of the pluralistic nation-state, and what this really means, is unavoidable, and this has serious repercussions in the change process. If the events of today say anything to us, it is that undertaking or expecting a total cultural change in a single dose is as futile as a sixty-five-year-old person learning a new language and expecting to be as competent as a native speaker. The primary language will serve as a barrier to the acquisition of the new language, just as one's culture serves as a barrier to totally learning other cultures. The best that can be expected is that the group and individual will learn some of the new culture in order to survive in the new circumstances, while also holding on to as much of their traditional culture as possible. As long as a culture is taught and learned, as long as people continue to subscribe to a particular set of beliefs and practices, remained convinced of its truth or correctness, that culture will survive in some fashion. Given the right opportunity and circumstances, the group will reassert itself based on traditional beliefs and practices that apparently lie dormant.

Eradication (Genocide). To change an entire culture means to change all the beliefs and practices of the members of the focal group. The only sure way to accomplish this is not really a culture change per se, but the elimination of the culture. The method is based on the belief that to change the whole culture, it is necessary to get rid of everything having to do with it, particularly the people who share it. The eradication of entire human societies and their cultures can be found throughout history, and similar efforts continue at the present time. In the past, genocide was used to eradicate the aboriginal groups of New Zealand and elsewhere. Conquering groups (e.g., Greeks and Romans) frequently wiped out entire societies and, by extension, their cultures. Adolf Hitler tried to eradicate the Jewish population of Europe and its religiously based culture. A number of pluralistic societies see genocide as a solution to many of their social problems and lack of national unity. It is viewed by those with competing political, religious, ethnic, business, or special interests as simply eliminating the competition.

In many parts of the world, nation-states and ethnic groups are engaged in activities designed to wipe out specific ethnic groups in their territories who steadfastly refuse to give up their cultures and become part of a national culture. "Ethnic cleansing" is the primary objective of the Bosnian Serbs in the former Yugoslavia, and it lies behind the ethnic conflicts of Rwanda, Somalia, and Guatemala. The inability of Iran and Iraq to incorporate the Kurds into their national cultures has led to military efforts to eradicate them. At one point, the approach was used against various American Indian groups by the U.S. military. But eradicating whole societies and their cultures by killing them off is unacceptable today; the political and human costs are too great. Morally, the practice has become unacceptable as the world has generally come to accept the idea that all people have a right to live and continue their particular traditional beliefs and practices. In the modern world of universal human rights, the alarming disappearance of so many traditional small-scale societies and their cultures, and the legitimization of cultural diversity, have combined to determine that totally changing cultures or eradicating them is no longer valid or defensible options. The right of individuals and groups to exist is heard across the globe, down to the special interest and organization cultures. Cultural diversity has become very popular, if not yet totally acceptable, around the world.

Replacement (Culture Substitution). Another method for totally changing a culture is termed replacement or cultural substitution. This method is based on the belief that if the desired goal is to change the whole of a culture, substitute a set of beliefs and practices, for the one to be changed. In some cases (e.g., business organizations) it can even involve replacing people. The primary focus is on education and fiat. Members of a group are educated to a new set of beliefs and practices, traditional beliefs and practices are inhibited or forbidden. The method frequently focuses primarily on the young members of the group, not yet brought into full membership. Based on past experiences, there is no doubt whatever that by using this kind of approach, a great deal of the substance of a culture can be altered. There are many cases where this approach has been used by nation-states as they have attempted to incorporate constituent culture groups into the national consensus culture. It has been tried in changing the organizational cultures of business; and on the level of political culture, the term *revolution* has been developed to refer to it. The goal of the Nigerian, Indonesian and other governments, as they continue efforts to assimilate distinct culture groups within their territories into newly created and artificial state cultures, has been based on replacement. This clearly was behind the repeated and varied efforts to assimilate Native-Americans into the dominant consensus culture of the United States. It is the usual basis for the development of national educational goals and curricula in much of the developing Third World, newly created nation-states of Africa and Southeast Asia. Unfortunately, because education is only one means by which culture is taught and learned, and because traditional culture usually continues through parents, traditional leaders, and friends, the method achieves only limited success. More often, replacement through education has only produced generations of disaffected people who do not "belong" anywhere.

In the case of the Islamic Republic of Iran, there is a tendency to suggest that replacement has occurred as a consequence of the "revolution" and societal reorganization based on the principles of the Koran. Unfortunately, because of external forces, the total alteration of the state has not been possible, as in fact it rarely is. Iran, was dependent on other nations for many things (e.g., IBM for the operation of its government, the West for the operation of its oil fields), and such dependency did not allow for the totality of change envisioned. There may even be a question as to whether a real revolution, involving the total alteration of the basic political system, actually occurred, or whether there was simply a shift of power from one strong man to another. Goldstone (1982) provides a good treatment of revolutions. Replacement has resulted in substantial changes in the societies and cultures where it has been tried, but it probably has never reached its ultimate goal of total culture change.

Forbidding the pursuit of traditional beliefs and practices is an essential part of the replacement method. Fiat or decree has long been used by state governments to inhibit or forbid the continuation of traditional practices (e.g., in Indonesia, Nigeria, and the former Soviet Union). Various mission groups have utilized the same approach as they attempted to introduce new religious beliefs and practices. In the former Soviet Union, fiat, backed by the threat of punishment, was the order of the day for over seventy years of Communist rule. The people complied, for to do otherwise was extremely dangerous. In Indonesia, as the government obtained control over all the territory formerly under the control of the Dutch, including the province of West Irian, over 300 distinct cultural groups were instantly made part of the new Indonesian state by law. By legislation and education, the Indonesian government has continually sought to incorporate these distinct cultural groupings into the consensus culture of the state. By law, all the people within the territory of Indonesia are members of the national culture, expected to share in its beliefs and practices. That many of the cultural groupings involved share no traditional past, physically or culturally, makes no apparent difference. As in most newly established nation-states, the government immediately set about creating a consensus culture that would be required of all people within their territory. A national language and a uniform school curriculum were immediately legislated.

Despite this extensive effort, the pluralistic nature of the country continues unabated. Similar situations have developed in Nigeria and other African states, where efforts to develop a national consciousness through many of the means noted for Indonesia are still being used. In all of these examples, and countless others, the governments have sought to create a state culture that is imposed on cultural groups that have been included within their territories. At best, such groups become constituent cultures of the nation-state, but never change or forget their traditional beliefs and practices. The replacement method is frequently used in combination with relocation.

Relocation. The U.S. government and Bureau of Indian Affairs used the method of relocation in conjunction with replacement as a means of totally changing native cultures and as a means of assimilation (Carbarino 1976; Forbes 1964; Walker 1972). Relocation attempts can be documented across history and the development of many nation-states. At the heart of this approach is the belief that if you relocate people away from an environment they know, to one with which they are totally unfamiliar, you can totally change their culture by making them dependent. In the case of the American Indian, the U.S. government tried the reservation system, boarding schools, and an urban relocation program. The goal was to totally change American Indian cultures by making them dependent on the government for virtually everything, and by placing them in environments where traditional beliefs and practices were invalid. The U.S. reservation system established for Native

Americans is an excellent example of relocation and its consequences. Removing the various tribes to government reservations had the net effect of substantially changing their way of life but it did not change all of their cultures. The reservation system was based on moving cultural groups from traditional territories, to which they had adapted, and grouping them in areas for which their traditional culture provided no guidelines for day-to-day living. In essence, no longer able to practice traditional subsistence or other aspects of their culture, they were forced to rely on the government for food and other basic needs. Traditional roles and activities, no longer required, could no longer be practiced. Hunters and warriors became wards of the government, farmers, and recipients of government handouts.

As almost the entire aboriginal population came under the reservation system, the net effect was to change the cultures of these groups substantially. That they were not changed completely is attested in the continuing presence of many traditional beliefs and practices among this American population. Similar situations can be found in Canada, Australia, Brazil, Ecuador, the Philippines, and elsewhere. In all of these cases, nation-state governments have attempted to deal with their aboriginal populations by replacement and relocation. In Australia, the term *reserve* was preferred over the *reservation* to account for slightly different circumstances. The net effect was the same: a considerable altering of aboriginal culture. Of course, with the spread of human rights issues around the world, and growing acceptance of cultural diversity, traditional aboriginal culture in these nations has reasserted itself.

Relocation and replacement were at the heart of the boarding school policy for American Indian children (Fuchs & Havighurst 1972). The basic idea was that if you removed young Indians from their homes, where they learned traditional beliefs and practices, and concentrated on educating them to a new set of beliefs and practices, traditional culture would be changed. Relocating Indians in urban environments, where traditional practices and beliefs seemingly would no longer apply, was intended to have the same effect: American Indians and their cultures were dramatically changed in the process. Despite surface appearances that the goal was being reached, individuals simply carried their cultures with them and adapted them to the new circumstances. Change was accomplished, but the totality of the change envisioned fell far short of expectations, because none of these attempts resulted in the total change of traditional culture that was envisioned.

These examples demonstrate that a substantial amount of a culture can be changed by using such methods, but they also demonstrate that a total revision of culture does not necessarily follow. In totally changing a culture, all that appears to be required is the total replacement of traditional culture and the elimination of its members. Although this might be an appropriate method in the case of some scene cultures (e.g., business or special interest cultures, where member elimination means only the firing or letting go of members), it cannot be applied in pluralistic nation-states made up of a large number of constituent cultural groupings. In these kinds of cultures, the cost is too great. The need to eliminate all the members of such groups, necessary to totally change the culture, is not an acceptable or viable option by today's standards. Instead of attempting to change the whole of any culture, changing a limited idea or behavior is by far, the better choice. Limited changes have a far better chance of success. Doing this over and over again can ultimately lead to a massive revision of a culture, but rarely to a total change of it.

CHANGING ASPECTS OF CULTURE

In recognition of the fact that it may not be possible, or even desirable, to totally change a culture, it is probably best to think in terms of change on a much smaller scale. Limited changes on a much smaller scale have a better chance of being successful than those attempting too much over too short a period of time. Studies also have shown that attempts to change the more conservative aspects of culture are the most difficult, because changes in these areas will be the most strongly resisted. Even in organizational or corporate cultures, trying to change those aspects to which the people are most closely tied will mean that strong resistance will be encountered. Change that focuses only on behavior can be difficult, but probably not as difficult as attempting to change an established idea or belief. Observing that members of a focal group appear to be practicing the new behavior is insufficient for determining that the change has been accomplished. Members of a focal group expressing an introduced idea is equally insufficient for concluding that the proposed change has been completed. In any culture change, behavior and the idea behind it must be changed before one can speak of a culture change being completed. Change does not occur because someone thinks it up. Getting members of the focal group to adopt the new belief or practice results in change.

Generating Ideas for Change

Coming up with an idea for change is not very difficult. One just has to think about another way to do something—and there is always another way. Probably the first thing that needs to be considered in generating culture change is whether it is really necessary. With change agencies, the idea of generating change is institutionalized. Members of the agency are motivated, if not charged, to coming up with changes. On the other hand, the origins of such agencies is a reflection of the fact that change may be necessary, given changes in circumstances, natural or otherwise. In the culture of the United States, change for the sake of change is readily accepted. In other cultures, even within constituent cultures of that nation-state, it is not. Resisting the tendency to assume that design or construction of "better ways" will readily lead people to accept a change. Experience has shown this to be a faulty assumption. Although a change can be an improvement by all "reasonable" standards, its advantages may not be perceived. In the worst-case scenario, the change may not be "reasonable" for the particular context and to members of the focal group. In proposals for change, planners and designers must first understand the cultural context for which they propose change, then determine what kind of change they are generating and why it is being considered. It is at this start of the directed change process that ethnocentric attitudes will emerge. Planners must assess whether the change being proposed is a needed one in terms of the culture group for which it is intended, or merely a reflection of their culture bias that others should be doing the same thing they do. Planners can then address questions of fit and timing as part of assessing its feasibility. Selection of a general strategy can then follow.

If the change is one of degree, more or less of something, the efforts required to implement it will be very different from those required for change in kind. The latter requires changes in both belief and behavior, increasing the stress and conflict that come with competing truths. If the proposed change responds to a problem that is recognized by the group, the task is infinitely easier, for motivation is much easier to identify or establish. A pseudo change which does very little to alter the core areas or substance of culture will not be resisted quite as strongly. But then the question centers on why they are being attempted. If there is no good reason to undertake such changes, it may be best to terminate the effort. If the change will help in the development of a positive attitude for subsequent changes, it may be defensible. If it does nothing more than give an agency or agent a continuing justification their existence, it is not defensible. Even from these seemingly insignificant activities, long-term repercussions on change efforts can be substantial. In generating change, it is a good practice to examine the motives. This can tell you a lot about the difficulties that will be encountered, about yourself, your own beliefs and motives, and it will provide some direction to the strategy that will ensure a successful attempt.

There is no doubt that proposals for change that are generated by the people themselves have the best chances of success. This would generally mean that there is a recognized need for change, and thus some motivation for the change and willingness to work toward its implementation. Because ideas for change originate within the group to be impacted, and the all-important felt need and motivation are present, does not mean the goals or objectives will always be reached. There are still some difficulties to be overcome, unknown external forces potentially to deal with, and unplanned consequences to be minimized. People proposing to institute cultural change within their own culture must ask the same questions that outside agencies must ask. They need to be clear as to what they propose to change and why. They need to be aware of how what they want to change is related to other things in their lives, things that may be negatively impacted by the change they envision. Members of any group proposing cultural change must be as aware of their own culture in all of its forms as any outside agency should be. Gaining cultural awareness can be more difficult for members of a culture group than for an outsider attempting to gain the same awareness.

Members of culture groups "know" their culture, for they learned it as they acquired full membership in the group. What they learned was the ideal version, and although they may function from, or appreciate, their real culture, they will tend to think from and be motivated by the ideal version of their culture. Some members of the group may have difficulty distinguishing between the versions, and this will have an impact on generating change ideas. As pointed out on a number of occasions, it is rare for people to know all of their own culture. It is very difficult for members of culture groups to assess the difference between what they like to think of themselves and what they really are. It may be very difficult to see how different areas of culture are interrelated, for culture is an unconscious thing; most people simply live as they have been taught, do and think as they have learned.

Given that changes generated within the group to be impacted by them have a better chance for success, it behooves agencies and agents to include members of the focal group in the process as much as possible. The vocabulary of post-modernist anthropology speaks of this as empowerment but the idea is the same. Agencies and agents should involve them in decisions to introduce change and how it will be done. Involving members of the focal group in the process results in many of the same benefits as change being generated within the group itself, most notably in motivation. People involved in the process from the beginning will be much more committed to a change proposal than when it comes from outside the group, without any input from them. Members of the focal group will also be able to provide agencies and agents with a much better cultural awareness and understanding than will be possible without their involvement. Potential barriers to the change can be identified, along with any factions that have developed. Such things can then be incorporated into the design for change during its planning and later in implementation activities. Members of the focal group can help change agencies and agents to see how the proposed change relates to other aspects of their culture. They can be instrumental in deciding upon the general strategy of approach, the course of action to be followed during the implementation phase of the process, the selection of personnel to best fit the context, and pointing out where perceptual problems may develop. In essence, because of the multiple benefits derived, members of the focal group at should be involved at every stage of the process. It should be considered essential in directed culture change. Once a proposal has been made for a culture change, the potential stimulants and barriers can be addressed.

Addressing Barriers and Stimulants

In all culture change settings, change agencies and agents must spend considerable time and effort addressing the barriers and stimulants to what they are attempting. The objective is obviously to remove the barriers and utilize the stimulants. As previously discussed, the barriers to change can be found in culture, in traditional practices and beliefs, in social structure, and in psychological areas. Potential social barriers to change come with the traditional social obligations and expectations people follow, their claims on and obligations to one another as prescribed by their culture. In the corporate world, this can mean the expected relations between management and employees, using established channels of communication, and recognizing that there are both formal and informal leaders. Cultural barriers can come from the value people have placed on tradition, the learned truth and correct behaviors, things closely tied to the natural ethnocentrism of culture groups, the pride they take in being identified with the group, and the logical order of things as they have been learned. Psychological barriers are rooted in perceptual differences between those asking for a change and those being asked to accept or implement it. Managers and employees, blue-collar and white-collar workers, blacks and whites, men and women, finance specialists and production engineers, all tend to see things quite differently. In business, a company executive officer will see things from a different perspective than someone on the production line. In these cultures, as in traditional ones and other organizational ones, not everyone learns the same things, nor does everyone think the same. Just because all of a company's employees go through a similar orientation program does not mean they will emerge thinking and perceiving the same way. In business culture, all the employees may belong to the company, but they bring to work many cultural beliefs and behaviors learned in other groups to which they belong. Those beliefs and behaviors will impinge on what is taught by the company and is learned as its employee. These forces that serve to inhibit change can also be turned to stimulating it by skilled and culturally aware change agents.

The best time to begin identifying barriers and stimulants to the proposed change is at the beginning of the effort. Many innovations or changes are not accepted because they are not improvements or there is no particular advantage or benefit in accepting them. The social or other costs may far outweigh the benefit. It must always be remembered that there are no benefits without costs, to someone or something in the culture of focal group. Stimulants to change come primarily from motivation, fit, and timing. For the person desiring to bring a change about, this means a felt need to change may have to be developed. Without this motivation, no change will occur, nor should one be expected. This can be tied to the needs identified by the members of the focal group or created by you the agent. The important thing to remember is that whatever change you propose or attempt to implement must be adapted as closely as possible to the context for which it is intended. Making sure that you have such a "fit" means more than simply fitting it into the existing culture system; it must include consideration of the timing in terms of the culture group and the long-term goals of the agency. It also means considering these things within the larger context as well. Obviously, if the timing or fit is wrong, you may find yourself having to do other things first, introduce other changes, or design your effort in much smaller increments.

Motivation focuses on the felt need to change. Based on traditional culture, motivation can already exist, or it can be developed on the basis of traditional value placed on cooperation, competition, or conservatism. Where felt needs do not already exist, they must be generated by the change agent. In nearly all cultures, the more powerful motivations are found in people's desire for status and prestige, frequently tied to economic considerations. If acceptance of a change can be made socially or financially worthwhile, a strong motivation for the support of the change will be generated. Motivations can also be created on the basis of the competitive nature of all cultures, the threat of reward or punishment, and, in some cases, the novelty of change. Motivation exists where the people themselves recognize needs. The easiest change to motivate is that which the people themselves have sought. Additive changes that do not compete with traditional values or behaviors are the next easiest to motivate, for they will not threaten anything in the existing culture. The more difficult change to motivate is that which replaces something in the existing culture, for this is where the conflict will be generated. Fit can be a significant element of the presence or absence of a motivation for change. If the change is adapted to existing values, social forms, or perhaps the economic or political reality of the group, developing motivation is made all that much easier. If the change is timed well, fits the culture and the circumstance, motivation will be easier than if it is not. Adapting a change to fit the existing patterns, because it represents a real innovation or because it is valuable or necessary to do so, produces a better fit than something that is not adaptive. Fit also suggests that the change must be adaptable to patterns already in existence—for example, within the context of local leadership, existing social structures, and belief patterns. Timing can be a significant element of stimulation if you introduce the change at the appropriate time. Putting it into the system before the people are ready for it ensures its failure.

There are a number of steps that can be taken to overcome the barriers to change. No matter from which of the categories the barriers may come, you need to take them into account. If you are fortunate, some of these potential barriers can be turned into stimulants that will help you achieve your goal. In this process, communication will loom large. It will be the means of establishing working relationships, of learning about the new change, and of forming the feedback mechanism essential in determining whether the change is being accomplished. Another important issue to take into account is the natural conservatism and ethnocentrism of humans. Most people will naturally resist change (Downs 1975). That resistance is tied directly to the elements of ethnocentrism discussed earlier. Based on a need for continuity in the expectations people must have of one another, members of culture groups are taught what they need to know. As a change agent, you must realize that the people with whom you will work already know the "right" way. Your proposed change threatens this knowledge and the personal security that goes with it. As people learn their culture(s), their thoughts and behaviors harden into patterns that are used to judge any others that differ from those patterns.

Selection of Strategy

People wanting to introduce a change of any kind will determine, by default or design, the strategy through which it will be attempted. This will limit, sometimes determine, the kinds of actions that can be taken to carry out the project. People asked to change formulate plans of their own, basically focused on how to avoid the course of action being requested. Change agents and members of focal groups react to each other's actions. The interactional situation is a combination of the actions and reactions of the participants. When a strategy or approach is selected, it is not simply the playing out of that plan. If both parties are involved in planning the change, there is less chance that their reactions to it will be as negative as when they are not involved. Without considering this important aspect in the dynamics of a change effort, the result can be unlike anything any of the participants wanted or expected. At this point, the danger of unplanned consequences of planned culture change come into play as part of the dynamics of the change process. Unanticipated consequences produce all sorts of undesirable, unintended, and far-reaching results.

Picking a general strategy and an implementation strategy for change involves a number of prime considerations. The major differences between the general strategies available to the change agency come down to who makes the decision and the costs involved. For change agencies, the choice should fit the purpose and circumstances. As seen in previous discussions on this point, each strategy can be the best choice under certain circumstances. An essential consideration in the choice centers on choosing the strategy most appropriate for the change problem. Although agencies and agents plan what they want to do and take actions to bring it about; the people being asked to change will react to the proposal and/or how it is to be done. The interactional context is influenced by the change agent and the recipients and their interaction will alter the desired outcome for both participants. Actions and reactions of both parties over the entire project, the quality of the communication, the perceptions held or generated produce change or not, sometimes can produce something neither participant wanted. How change is attempted can be the greatest single cause of success or failure to achieve it.

Given the many issues and aspects of change to be considered in directed change in a multicultural setting, it would appear that the best strategy to utilize in most situations would be a facilitative assistance one (Batten 1969), sometimes referred to as the people-centered approach. The central thrust of this strategy is to create an environment for change. Fit, capital, and expert services are combined with participation to such a degree that the people learn use as well as behavior in the acceptance of a change. Change agents become facilitators, as opposed to orchestrators of change. Rather than emphasizing the attainment of their goals, they help members of focal groups attain the goals they have identified. A facilitative assistance strategy attempts to bridge the gap between agent and recipient, making them equal partners in the effort. Rather than focusing on the ultimate change result, the strategy aims at building a climate for mutual learning and a self-maintaining social group that can then work toward the accomplishment of their own goals.

In the interactional process, the agent basically asks questions of members of the focal group, questions that will lead to action. The agent stimulates people to think about their specific problems or dissatisfactions. The people can then be helped to think about what specific changes are necessary to deal with the problems. Timing, fit, and motivation are considered during the discussions. The change agent stimulates members of the focal group to consider what they might do to bring about changes by taking action themselves, and how best to organize themselves to accomplish what they want to do. The agent can assist them in the development of a plan of action for what they wish to do and how they want to do it. In this method, the role of the agent shifts to one of helping people do what they have planned, think through the difficulties that may arise, and consider their proposed actions within the larger context(s). The agent can then help them through the various stages of their activity. Using this kind of approach to change results in the development of satisfaction within the focal group as to the results of their of their achievement and a commitment to the change. It will also lead to the development of new skills that can be used over and over again.

Changing Ideas or Behaviors

Changing ideas or values can be the most difficult change of all to bring about. This has been the lesson of the past. Distinct cultural groups steadfastly hold on to their beliefs, even when they are no longer able to follow their traditional practices. People hold on to their values and beliefs, for these are the verbal expressions of their "truth," the codes that underlie their behaviors and thus represent the most fundamental aspects of their cultural behavior. People judge proposed change based on their ideal culture. This version of culture is the most conservative, for it symbolizes the truths they have learned. As many studies have shown, when the task is to change values and beliefs, chances of success are not very good if the proposed change is in conflict with an established idea the people already have, or if the accompanying behavior is not consistent with that idea. This is especially true if the task is to totally revise ideas and beliefs—in essence, totally change the culture. Remember that people bring with them ideas to which they have subscribed as members of other culture groups. Changing a culture means changing the people, their beliefs or behaviors. Determining whether you need to do this is the first step.

Legislative fiat is not a particularly useful strategy for changing ideas. Legislating change has been shown to be of limited value in any culture change. Coercion through the promise of punishment will fare no better; experience has shown this generally results in only superficial change. Although it appears that members of the focal group have accepted the change, in reality they are likely to continue to believe as they always have, perhaps only waiting for the opportunity to revert to the more traditional belief system. Getting members of the focal group to identify their own problems and assisting them to develop responses to those problems is probably the best approach in attempting to change cultural ideas. Gentle persuasion and relevant argument would be much better than fiat or threats of punishment. This does not mean that they will automatically accept the change being proposed, but they will not be resistant from the very beginning of the project. The approach does require more of the change agent, however. It requires that change agents be more self-aware, knowledgeable about culture and change, and skilled in interpersonal interactions and communication.

A behavior change may be easier to accomplish than one in which values or ideas are to be changed. In most change settings, behavior will change before an idea will change. Even in cases where the ultimate goal is to change an idea, the associated behavior will change first. Once people alter their behavior, get used to doing something another way, the idea (value) behind it will gradually change. The best way to obtain a behavior change is to demonstrate the benefit of the new behavior. Reward and punishment are the keys to this. One can take an either/or approach, or combine this with a reward system that encourages the correct behavior. Putting an emphasis on the punishment for incorrect behavior is not as effective as rewarding the correct behavior. The consequences of punishment are usually increased attempts on the part of those being punished to circumvent the system, or to work against it. The minimal reaction would be superficial acceptance at best. Punishment results more in avoidance than in adoption of a desired behavior. The traditional behavior will quite likely be continued when you are not around. Ignoring traditional behavior as much as possible, while rewarding the desired behavior, is the better course of action.

Constantly communicating the idea behind the behavior is also a good idea. Ultimately, culture change depends on the acceptance of both behavior and the ideas associated with it. A true change has been accomplished only when the people have integrated the behavior and the idea behind it into their culture system. This can take some time to achieve fully, and great patience may be required. There is considerable danger in assuming that the change has been achieved simply because an idea or behavior appears to have changed. If the change has not been included in the cultural system, or if no provisions for its maintenance have been made, chances are that it will disappear very quickly. Education is perhaps the best defense against such possibilities, and this will revolve around communication.

BASIC PRINCIPLES FOR CHANGING CULTURE

Although there is no recipe for directed culture change, no series of steps to be taken to ensure a successful outcome, undertaking directed culture change will be much easier if some basic principles are applied. Not all of these will be applicable in all settings, but the lessons of the past would seem to suggest their relevance. All programs for change involve someone with an idea for introducing change, those attempting to bring change about, and those asked to change their belief or behavior. These combine in the interactional context, the direct or indirect interactions of individuals and groups. They are crucial elements that must be addressed in directed culture change if you wish to improve your chances of success or to assume more control over the process than might otherwise be possible.

(1)   Assume that every change problem is unique, and approach the task as a problem, as opposed to a project or program, orientation.

(2)   Recognize that directed culture change nearly always will involve multi-cultural settings characterized by conflict, stress, and emotions, simply because people representing different cultures will be interacting as participants in that process.

(3)   Understand the role of culture in the lives of people, and in specific terms for of all those who will be involved in the change setting and process.

(4)   Consider the questions of timing, fit, motivation, and barriers and stimulations as the key elements in directed culture change.

(5)   Select changes that are readily workable and implement them in a series of small steps, evaluating each step before going on to the next one.

(6)   Select the general and implementation strategies that best fit the circumstances in which the change will be attempted.

(7)   Remember that it is the kind and quality of the interaction between participants in the directed change process that will have the greater impact on the outcomes.

(8)   Continually be on the lookout for external influences and potential consequences that can impact or accompany your change activities.

(9)   Never assume that a project is complete until both the idea and the behavior have been institutionalized within the culture pattern.

SUGGESTED READINGS

The following readings are designed to provide you with additional readings on actually bringing change about, its impacts and consequences on various peoples and their cultures.

Arensberg, Conrad M., & Archur H. Niehoff (eds.). 1971. *Introducing Social Change: A Manual for Community Development.* 2nd ed. Because of the valuable insights provided on the many issues and aspects of change that must be faced by change agents, this work could easily serve as a guidebook for change agent.

Arnold, Robert D. 1977. *Alaska Native Land Claims.* This documents the land claim settlement between the Native Alaskans and the government of the United States. The work goes well beyond the Land Claims Settlement Act itself, providing historical context, prospects for Native Alaskans, and an appreciation of the unplanned consequences of planned change.

Batten, T. R. 1969. *The Non-Directive Approach in Group and Community Work.* This work provides some discussion and guidelines for the nondirective, facilitative assistance approach to the process of culture change.

Bodley, John H. 1990. *Victims of Progress.* 3rd edition. This volume focuses on the devastation that has been unleashed upon indigenous peoples in the name of progress. The author makes the point that modernization has led to deterioration, rather than improvement, of people's quality of life. It also explores the impact of industrial development on indigenous peoples, and how the latter are organizing to protect themselves.

Foster, George M. 1969. *Applied Anthropology.*
———. 1973. *Traditional Societies and Technological Change.* Both of these works contain valuable insights and guidelines for anyone directly involved in directed culture change.

Mair, Lucy. 1984. *Anthropology and Development.* Surveys types of development policy based on the grassroots level, and the ways misunderstandings can prevent development policies, intended to raise standards of living, from working.

Naylor, Larry L. 1974. *Culture Change and Development in the Balim Valley, Irian Jaya, Indonesia.* This dissertation details the result of a study on the issues and aspects of culture change and development in the Balim Valley as the result of the government, missionary and United Nations efforts.

Niehoff, Arthur H. (ed.). 1966. *A Casebook of Social Change*. Based on an extensive use of case study materials, this volume contains many considerations and suggestions for anyone placed in the role of change agent in multicultural change settings.

Chapter 9

CONCLUSIONS AND PROSPECTS

Culture has always been both a problem and a solution. While culture provides for satisfying basic human needs, it also creates new needs and new problems for people to solve. These new needs and problems increase as the scale of culture increases (Malinowski 1944). The world continues to shrink in terms of the time necessary to travel around it, and in terms of the even shorter time to communicate across it. As people alter the patterns of their lives in similar ways in response to similar needs and problems, the world appears to be shrinking culturally as well. As the industrial societies continue to expand and draw people into an increasingly interdependent network, interconnections among the world's peoples and cultures have increased as well. According to global scholars, the reality of a global culture like system at some level is generally accepted, but whether a "world culture" now looms on the horizon is a hotly debated topic. There is virtually no doubt that the increasing dependence of human societies in all parts of the world on commercial exchange now mandates that people adjust to the presence and activities of a great many other groups of people. As international trade continues to accelerate, an even greater interdependency is assured, and this will mean that people will have to continually alter their cultural beliefs and practices to accommodate it, Global interdependence has become a major trend in the contemporary world, as have the planned and directed human responses to the natural and contemporary socio-cultural problems that occur on a continuing basis. As exchange and competition between sociocultural systems accelerate in the future, different accommodations of culture to environments, and between cultural groups, will be required.

Predicting the future is risky enough for any scientist, but predicting future culture change is perhaps even riskier. There are global trends on which nearly everyone can agree. From all indications, there are some general and ongoing evolutionary changes that will continue, with or without the specific intervention of humans. But predicting exactly what environmental, social, economic, political, ethnic, and/or religious changes will occur over the short term or the long term is something else again. Differing views about the future of humanity abound. The contradictory nature of many generally recognized global trends, and the undeniable ethnocentric perspectives being taken toward them, make predictability even more hazardous. Nevertheless, as this volume has proposed some radical changes in our thinking about culture and change, it is mandatory that some voyage into such uncertain waters be attempted. The world today is threatened on the local, national, and global levels by environmental deterioration, social and political conflict, impoverishment and inequality, increased industrialization and resource depletion.

The great diversity of culture that so characterized the world's peoples for so very long is disappearing at an alarming rate as another kind of diversity takes its place. While there are still some cultures that appear not to have changed dramatically, they have changed nevertheless, and this will continue at an accelerated pace. As people are assimilated into expanding nation-states, transnational political or international economic networks, as the ever-expanding market-exchange economic system spreads across the globe, their lives and cultures are being altered dramatically, and toward lifestyles that are becoming increasingly alike. There is some general agreement that the diffusion of the commercial system around the world reflects the beliefs, practices, and influence of the power nations, but political conflicts abound, and their consequences are causing additional changes. Such conflicts will change as technology continues to change and the integration of the world's societies continues. The future reality of some level of global integration is unquestioned. Just how much integration will occur is another matter. While the possibility of a world culture developing from all of this is being debated, that the world's societies and their cultures are undergoing dramatic change, and will continue to do so, is not. Global planners agree that now, and in the future, significant cultural changes will be required if the global system is to remain intact. The U.S. Committee on Global Change (1988) called for more interdisciplinary science for understanding this global change and its consequences. Because of its holistic approach, anthropology can serve as a model for such a science, and because of its commitment to help improve people's lives, it can play a significant role in assessing global issues, in the design and implementation of changes that will be required to resolve them.

EVOLUTIONARY TRENDS

There is every indication that some long-term evolutionary processes or trends will continue well into the future. Intensification, specialization, and differentiation will continue as peoples and cultures move inextricably toward complexity and increase their per capita energy requirements (Bates & Plog 1991). Out of the experience of the complex industrialized nation-states, it can be predicted that as more and more societies move toward the complexity that characterizes such societies, the energy requirement of the world will increase. As with nation-states, more and more of the energy budgets of all national groupings will have to be devoted to maintaining organizational institutions (universities, banking systems, stock markets, communication networks, etc.). Intensification is related to increased specialization and differentiation, both of which are tied to increasing limited productive activities of members of societies. With the specialization that accompanies increased complexity, societies will increase the number of organizational units necessary for productive activities and purposes. The kind of multiculturalism that characterizes nation-states will spread to other culture groups, new or emerging nation-states, and perhaps the global community. Differentiation, the cultural pluralism and diversity of complex human societies, will continue to increase, despite continuing efforts to assimilate more and more culture groups into fewer and fewer national groupings. Centralization, the concentration of political and economic decisions in the hands of a few individuals or institutions, will become more acute as cultural diversity actually increases and consensus becomes more difficult within the pluralistic societies that will emerge.

Stratification, the diversification of societies into groups with varying degrees of access to resources and power, will become even more widespread and the distance between groups will widen further. This will be supported by the tendency for wealth to become monopolized by fewer and fewer people, institutions or countries. The distance between the "haves" and the "have nots" will increase in all societies, creating even greater dissatisfactions, stress, and conflicts. Settlement nucleation, the tendency of populations to cluster in settlements of increasing size and density (e.g., urban environments), will continue because such centers will represent the most viable locations for successfully participating in the evolving systems. The scale of conflict that increased as societies became more complex will continue, but will be altered by changes in technology and the development of some level of global integration. The continuation of all these evolutionary trends, which have been noted across a substantial portion of human history, seems assured, given no dramatic or catastrophic event of natural or cultural design.

GLOBAL TRENDS

All of the peoples of the world face many of the same problems, occasioned by increased complexity, increased contact, and increased change. More and more, we hear of global problems that demand attention and resolution, and we are made aware of a number of global trends driven by the consumption-based market economy that influences, perhaps now dominates, all societies. Food shortages, rapid population growth, the depletion of resources, pollution, the growing number of political, economic, ethnic, and religious conflicts, and the difficulties of adapting to rapid and continuous change are global trends to which human societies will have to respond. Some of these are the costs of increased complexity and industrialization, a consequence of the close relationship of humans to the natural environment. Some are the consequences of technological developments, and others are the result of increased contacts between people of heretofore vastly different cultures. None of these things can be ignored.

Environmental Trends

The link between humans, their cultural activities, and the natural environment has been brought back to our attention in dramatic fashion. Air pollution, population growth, and technological changes in human activities have produced problems and consequences of global proportions. Mechanized agricultural practices have increased production, but they have been accompanied by the need for expensive technology, increased consumption of rapidly disappearing fossil fuels, and the production of toxic substances. While many people of the "civilized," highly complex, and industrialized world may have been lulled into the mistaken belief that culture gives humans control over their environment, culturally induced changes in the natural environment now serve to remind them that the relationship has always been a sensitive, fluid, and tenuous one. Cultural activities have now created problems of global proportions that demand immediate attention. Air pollution and a possible global warming have resulted from the development and growth of industry and the commercial economy. Resource depletion and increased competition for resources have accompanied these same developments. Acid rain and the thinning of the ozone layer are directly affecting climate, and this is disrupting agriculture worldwide, causing political and economic stress as well as population dislocations. The commercial economy, designed around resource depletion, has caused shortages which are not now shared equally around the world, nor will they be in the future. The increased stress, anxiety, competition, and conflict among individuals and groups that this has produced will become greater in the future as supply dwindles and demand accelerates.

The growing world population is another concern that has gotten the attention of many scholars throughout the world. Current population demographics show that while population increases are down in complex and developed countries, they are substantially up in Third World countries, where high birthrates and reduced mortality have combined to produce increases as they have moved more in the direction of the complex nations. Population problems and food production are related. Much concern has been expressed about the ability to feed the growing world population. While everyone seems to agree that we are quite capable of fulfilling human needs for food at the present time, at what point we will no longer be able to do this is a nagging question that lingers on. Unfortunately, one of the major difficulties in answering the question about the capacity to feed a growing world population depends on particular cultures. Capacity has not yet been defined for the world. In addition, food and the means of producing it are very much controlled by political and economic decisions in the hands of power nations with their own agendas. This will not change in the future, despite global integration at some level, for political governments must make parochial decisions to remain in power and meet the needs of their individual populations.

Technological change is now a global phenomenon rather than just a local one characterizing the technologically based industrialized societies. This change requires high energy consumption, creating many of the hazards to the environment we now face, and exacerbates the depletion of finite limited resources. As cultural groups of all kinds scramble to industrialize, or otherwise participate in the market-exchange economy that is sweeping across the world, the costs in terms of acid rain, waste, water pollution, and the greenhouse effect resulting from the depletion of the ozone layer and massive loss of rain forests will increase exponentially. David Noble (1984) suggests that the organization of commerce and industry will change even further because of the development of new servomechanical and electronic controls. Driven by new the many technological developments in biotechnology, telecommunications, microprocessor information systems, and other high-tech industries, it is hard to avoid the conclusion that the world will continue to undergo massive and rapid technological changes. The amount and speed of these changes will be greater for the small-scale societies and those at some stage of development toward the industrialized model. John Bodley (1990), Peter Worsley (1984), and H. Russell Bernard and Pertti Pelto (1987), have examined the impacts of this global-scale trend on various societies.

Some scholars suggest that all these trends combine to indicate a global crisis. They propose that the entire future of humanity and the biosphere is at risk from these environmental trends (Bodley 1994:386). For this group, it is the expanding quest for markets and resources, associated with the commercialization process, that lies at the heart of the crisis. They tend to see the commercialization process as creating the global culture that is transforming the planet we live on, and propose that only major cultural changes or adjustments will get us through this crisis. The extreme scenario hypothesizes that if current population, technology, and environmental trends continue, the result will be an ecological disaster which humans will not be able to overcome as suggested by the Club of Rome Study of 1972 (Scupin & DeCorse 1992). On the other side of this particular question, scholars such as Julian Simon (1981) are more optimistic. This group continues to have faith in the ultimate ability of humans to overcome almost anything. While both positions are extremist, most global observers agree that significant cultural changes will be required if the global human system, based on the relationship of humans, human culture, and natural environment, is to remain intact. Most of the discussions on the issue assume the world will continue as presently structured, and are based on short-term goals and technologically defined issues of warming, food production, pollution, and so on. Missing from the debates thus far has been the cross-cultural perspective, some consideration of existing political and economic power distributions, and the long-term perspective that includes a recognition that the world's structure is already changing.

Economic Trends

In addition to the development of a worldwide commercial economy, organized around the market-exchange model, the growth of the multinational corporation and restructuring of the world economic system are global trends of some significance. Market economies have shown themselves to be difficult to control, and globalization of them will only expand the problem. While factions have arisen as to relative merits of the free-market system verses those having various forms and levels of government regulation, it is hard to imagine any market system, local or global, that will not involve government regulations and controls. Special interests, monopolies, and other inequalities, inherent in all systems, belie the government-free market in any of its forms. As more and more societies are drawn into the developing global system, the controls will shift to transnational agencies or international corporations. Unfortunately, transnational agencies will always be influenced by power governments, which even now exert considerable influence on global decisions. The emerging world system was created by the global political economy, and thus it may never be possible to separate politics from economics, or vice versa. Restructuring the world economic system around the multinational corporations which have arisen and now exert considerable influence around the globe seems inevitable (Wolfe 1977, 1986). The rise and growth of the multinational corporations in recent years will continue with economic globalization (Barnet & Muller 1974). Recognizing the power and influence that have already shifted to multinational corporations, in some cases equaling or surpassing those of the power nations over world economics, one might suggest that such corporations can serve as the organizational means of globalizing the planet.

The increasing influence of supranational organizations suggests that they could also serve as organizational structures for globalization. There are both good and bad sides of this particular development. Supranational political and economic institutions or organizations now function with limited capability to shape world affairs. Since the breakdown of colonialism following World War II, such supranational institutions as the United Nations, the World Bank, and many more have taken over formal leadership of the global system. Both supranational and multinational corporations enhance further global interdependence, and they serve to organize global activities on a wide range of topics and concerns. While both types of agencies presently are under the dominating influence of the power nations, that influence has been steadily eroding. Supranational agencies have always been collectives of national agendas, with each nation pursuing those paths most compatible with its own goals and objectives. When decisions of such bodies have been contradictory to the special interests or goals of a particular national group (e.g., the United States, Indonesia, North Korea, etc.), the tendency has been for members simply to pull out of the agencies or discontinue financial support of particular activities. As long as competition among nation-states continues, the cooperative effort necessary for any organized control at the global level through such agencies will be most difficult. As resource supply decreases and demand increases with participation in the world market economy, national self-interests will serve as barriers to cooperative effort. Nations will cooperate on decisions that correspond to their interests, not the interests of others or some greater good. Supranational agencies serve as platforms for self-interest, and thus can serve only in a limited organizational capacity for the world's societies.

While global harmony has always been a vision, it has always been an ideal with little chance of becoming reality. Even with the appearance of a truly supranational agency, with political power to enforce its decisions, the diversity of humans will continue, and the competitiveness of the cultures represented in that diversity will continually work counter to the objective. It is very difficult to perceive an end to cultural groups maneuvering to maximize their particular interests, goals, and objectives on either a local or an international level. As evidenced in today's world, cultural groups assert themselves and their own identities when threatened or given the right opportunity. It is hard to imagine that cultural diversity, and what that actually represents, will ever disappear. Even in a future with some level of global integration, cultural pluralism will be increased and the competition among culture groups magnified. Nevertheless, in the world to come, the supranational organizations will play an important role, if for no other reason than that a level of cooperation around the globe will be necessary on some topics of mutual concern, or the entire system will collapse.

Development

Development, moving people toward something better than what they have, as practiced throughout the twentieth century, has systematically undermined the self-maintenance abilities of small-scale societies. Now, this is being done through international assistance agencies that provide multinational assistance (e.g. ,United Nations Development Program, World Health Organization, International Development Association, World Bank, African, Asian, and Inter-American Development Banks, International Monetary Fund, and many others). Billie DeWalt (1988) identifies four problems specific to economic development as presently defined: (1) disorder and control problems increase; (2) consumption and growth become ends in themselves; (3) societies and species are endangered; and (4) cultural material is lost. He suggests some new goals for development based on the establishment of long-term community goals, more nature-culture balance in local regions and ecosystems, the recognition of basic human needs, less centralization and more local autonomy, maintaining local cultural integrity, more justice and equity, the reduction of resource competition, gradual change, and diversity. In DeWalt's view, this would reduce the role of the global market economy and the existing international political hierarchy. These are not new goals, but many are obviously too idealistic to be achieved in other than a perfect world. Wisely, DeWalt has avoided the question of how to implement them.

Unfortunately, long-term consequences of short-run development project or changes cannot be reliably predicted from the highly centralized systems of planning and decision making that currently exist. Centralized systems seem to lack the ability to adequately anticipate long-term costs. George N. Appell (1988:272) has provided us with some principles that summarize the sorts of negative impacts that planned change occasions and that must be weighed against possible benefits. Every act of development necessarily involves an act of destruction. Any new activity is likely to displace an indigenous activity. Each act of change has the potential to cause physiological, nutritional, psychological, and/or behavioral impairment among some segment of the subject population. Modernization can erode indigenous mechanisms for coping with social stress. Costs and benefits are not equally distributed throughout a population. Some people or segments of the population will benefit more, and some will lose more. For Appell, it comes down to a question of whether the costs and benefits are fair or desirable. Of course, the real problem centers on what is "fair" and "desirable," and on whose terms. This will depend on who makes the call. The role of culture in development determines that the term "development" is ethnocentric in any language (Dove 1988).

Political Trends

As the world becomes more interdependent and integrated to some degree, major political changes will have to occur. As nations drop trade barriers, share the same material goods, and their accompanying cultural values, and as they further increase their contacts and interactions, they will take on similar appearances. But political tendencies move in the opposite direction, with fragmentation along linguistic, ethnic, religious, or other special interest lines. This kind of fragmentation is already being seen as nation-states divide into smaller constituent components based on ethnicity and religion. Ethnic unrest and tension are prevalent around the world, and among peoples who believe they share common history, origins, and culture. When set against the nation-state concept of territory, the separatist and ethnic movements have resulted in continuing and sometimes extremely violent conflict. While secularization continues to accompany cultural complexity, and as religious beliefs and rituals become separated from the economic, social, and political institutions of society to become private affairs, religion has not disappeared, nor will it disappear in the future. In fact, given the challenges to religious beliefs and practices that have come with secularization, at a time such beliefs and practices might be needed all the more, religions have tended to revitalize to meet the challenges, in some cases accompanied by a great deal of violence. This is not going to change in the future. In fact, given global integration and even more contact between groups with differing religious systems, the competition and conflict between them will increase.

ONE WORLD CULTURE

The possibility of the emergence of one world culture is based on developments in communications, travel, the links established through the spread of the market-exchange system and its products, and the transnational and multinational agencies that appear to be providing organizational structures for it. Out of the spread of the market-exchange system, some cultural similarity is being produced. As societies become involved in the worldwide economic system and engage in increased trade with others, material culture is becoming similar throughout the world. But it goes beyond simply sharing similar materials, for material items are always accompanied by the ideas and values behind them. Taking modern Western music into the former

Eastern block nations has not simply added a new and different kind of music in this area. It has also occasioned a dramatic shift in the behavior and values of the age group that has imported it. The existence of the multinational and supranational agencies would also seem to support the idea of a world culture, as would the trend for existing political units to be larger and all-encompassing. The logical conclusion of this trend would be to suggest that over time, autonomous units will be reduced to a single one encompassing the entire world (Ember & Ember 1993). Against these observations and conclusions are the convincing arguments of history.

Throughout history, it has been repeatedly observed that while societies may adopt similar material items or other innovations, they do so only after altering them to suit their own particular cultural contexts and needs. It can also be seen that large states eventually come apart, as most recently observed in the demise of the former Soviet Unit. As noted previously, many times this is the result of culture groups not being as fully incorporated or assimilated into the state as had been believed. Cultural groups reassert their identity when other groups attempt to assert control over them. Reactions to absorption by imposed states vary enormously, but they almost inevitably result in struggles with long histories. Current expansion efforts on the part of nation-states are running into more difficulty than ever before as the ability to resist has been improved by technology and a sympathetic world. The tendency for political units to increase in size while decreasing in number is being canceled out by the tendency to fragment into a greater number of smaller units. Multinational corporations, which cut across boundaries, are a force for unity in spite of political and ethnic differences, for many of them have the power to thwart the desires and wishes of governments and ethnic groups. They do draw people into relationships of a global order, but at some point they will suffer the same culture group reactions of resistance that have been noted as nation-states have attempted to incorporate culture groups. The tendency to resist will not be altered, even if the integrative economic function shifts to multinational corporations or the political integration shifts to some supranational organization.

Some argue that a generalized world culture would be desirable, given the fact that some cultures are too specialized to survive in the changed environment. But cultures can adapt, have adapted, and will adapt to the modern world without losing their identity and all or most of their culture, if they are left alone to do so. Cultural pluralism, focusing on the social and political interaction within the same society of people with different ways of living and acting, can be found. Ethnocentric attitudes, used as a charter for manipulating others for the benefit of one's own culture, result in unrest and varying degrees of violent reaction. The "greater good for the greater majority," increasingly used by governments to justify actions not universally acceptable, is becoming more widespread, as are the negative responses to it. For example, where once the value of the individual was strongly defended in American culture, and the rule was by the majority and the individual could become a majority of one, now decisions are nearly always based on the greater good for the greater number, and rule has become the dictatorship of the minority. Making the world a better place in which to live is a fine goal, but having to determine in whose terms and using what processes will always pressure against a world culture system.

It is not likely that the world could ever reach a consensus on the kind of world everyone would want, just as it is very unlikely that everyone could agree on how to get there. It may very well be that the world's societies will adopt such appearances that the existence of a world culture can be posited, but just because societies might look alike, that does not mean that their beliefs and values would be the same.

The global tendencies that move people to speak of the possibility of a world culture convincingly argue that substantial culture change will appear in the future. With or without a complete global political or economical integration, or with integration of any kind or on any level, the world's people are going to experience a great deal of change, and over a relatively short period of time. As cultural groups increase their interactions and dependencies, every one of them will have to change some of their beliefs and behaviors. In this, human societies will plan, design, and implement the changes. To do otherwise is to face extinction, for this is the adaptive mandate of today and the future.

ROLE OF ANTHROPOLOGY

Quite apart from its important role in the study of humans and their culture(s) in the classic sense, the role of anthropology in the future will revolve around applied or practical considerations. From its very beginnings, the discipline of anthropology has been concerned with the nature and development of humans and their cultures. John H. Bodley (1994:292) suggests that anthropology was the product of Western colonial expansion because the practical utility of anthropological knowledge was recognized by imperialist powers. From the 1830s through the 1870s, anthropology could be characterized as concentrating on salvaging ethnographic data that was being destroyed, while at the same time trying to determine how to increase its practical value. Bodley credits A. H. Lane-Fox Pitt-Rivers with coining the term "applied anthropology" in order to catalog a paper of Sir Bartle Frere (Bodley 1994:292), and notes that by the turn of the twentieth century, the utility of the discipline for "private enterprise" was generally recognized by all. The utility of anthropology was focused on providing information on native customs to the colonial governments which used it in the conduct of their affairs with native peoples. During the 1920s and 1930s, applied or practical anthropology shifted away from that associated with the colonial administrations, and applied anthropology became institutionalized in the discipline. Following World War II, anthropology itself shifted away from a focus on some hypothesized functional equilibrium of small-scale societies, to the study of change and the difficulties that accompanied contact, modernization, and development. Today, the applied or practical role for anthropologists has become a major focus in the discipline as more and more segments of the society have sought out anthropologists because of their unique knowledge and skills. Now anthropologists work in varied settings, from private corporations to transnational agencies working to improve people's lives around the world (Hackenberg 1988:172).

Applied anthropology, sometimes referred to as "practicing anthropology" when done outside of the discipline or academic context, is a role that is assumed by an anthropologist (regardless of specialty) when they use their skills and/or knowledge to help solve problems (Naylor 1973a). The applied role can take on a variety of forms. It can take on the form of directly participating in change programs intended to improve people's lives. It can mean contributing relevant cultural understanding and knowledge to agencies and agents planning, designing, or attempting to implement change. It can mean anthropologists participating directly in change programs, at all levels of change design, planning, and implementation, even serving as administrators of such projects or programs. Anthropologists will also be found assessing the potential impacts of change activities, or monitoring them and their effects, in an effort to identify associated problems and learn lessons that might be applicable in future activities or policy decisions. Anthropologists can now be found working with others in research efforts aimed at devising solutions for all kinds of problems that have arisen to confront modern societies (e.g., environmental, demographic, economic, medical, or any number of social problems of human society). In increasing numbers, anthropologists serve as consultants to governments, transnational, international, and private agencies working on projects aimed at improving human existence in general or the lives of people in particular places. Anthropologists can be found studying health-care delivery systems, substance abuse, and disease and curing. Anthropologists are conducting social-impact studies to assess the possible consequences of change activities in all types of communities and settings, as well as undertaking assessments of benefits and costs that accompany major development projects. They will be found working in governmental agencies concerned with international development and assistance (e.g., U.S. Agency for International Development), and they are serving in a similar capacity for transnational organizations (e.g., the United Nations, UNESCO, the United Nations Food and Agricultural Organization, World Bank, etc.). The problem for applied anthropologists in all these settings is to anticipate all the effects likely to result from change.

Ethical Issues

Increased direct involvement of anthropologists with change or development agencies has created some complex ethical issues that are not easy to resolve (Chambers 1985). William Partridge (1984) edited a collection of essays on anthropologists as consultants in development projects in which many of the potential conflicts that can arise in planning and consulting activities are discussed. Recognizing that anthropologists face serious ethical issues when engaged in such activities, a code of conduct was established for those participating in such activity in the 1940s, it was revised in 1974 (Society of Applied Anthropology 1975:34). The code mandated that anthropologists be involved in no plan or project that would not be beneficial to people, and it strongly advocated that target communities should be included as much as possible in formulation of policy. The code was structured around four main issues: (1) responsibilities to the employer and to the people to be affected; (2) the political agenda of the funding agencies and the differential costs and benefits of change; (3) predicting consequences of developmental changes; and (4) the importance of taking into account the views of those to be affected. The code made it quite clear that the anthropologist's first responsibility is to the people for whom change is being designed or implemented. Most important, anthropologists were to be concerned as to whether the change will truly benefit the target population. Applied anthropologists have the responsibility of ensuring the welfare and dignity of those to be impacted. While the code has provided some guidance for applied anthropologists, it has not resolved all of the issues, nor has it resolved all of the ethical conflicts and problems associated with applied activities. Resolving all of the ethnic conflicts associated with applied activities will never be easy.

For example, as has already been suggested, small-scale societies able to support self-maintaining system will strongly resist programs designed to integrate them into large-scale national systems. Facing resistance, most governments tend to rely on the use of force to bring integration about. This creates a significant dilemma for anthropologists, who generally disavow the use of force in any kind of development project. Change by fiat and force minimizes the participation of focal groups, and this goes counter to the code. Continuing nation-state expansion, assimilation of small-scale cultures into the state, and increasing integration and globalization also cause dilemmas for anthropologists. Integration of any kind produces homogeneity and reduces the human adaptive potential. Anthropologists are more prone to advocate a multicultural world, one that is more diverse and provides them with contexts for studying alternative solutions to the many common problems all humans tend to face. Most of the changes proposed by government and other agencies move counter to that preference. Balancing their responsibilities to all the participants in change, as well as to the academic community, is not easy either, for in many cases the choices are contradictory.

While anthropologists are not to engage in activities that go against any of their stated obligations, or that will not benefit the focal group, choosing not to participate in various programs carries an ethical burden as well. By choosing not to participate, change is left entirely in the hands of people less appreciative of culture and culture difference, less skilled in multicultural contexts, and whose agendas run counter to the stated goal of helping people improve their lives. Even if they choose not to become involved with or participate in any program or project that does not meet the various dicta of the code, anthropologists must still bear responsibilities for the consequences that evolve because they were not involved. This is the classic dilemma of "damned if you do and damned if you don't." It is probably safe to say that nearly all applied anthropology tends to be undertaken under the same conditions. In the final analysis, applied anthropologists always seem to face dismal alternatives at best. Despite the lofty intent, it might be better to suggest that when agency plans or strategies go counter to the mandates of the code, anthropologists have an obligation to attempt to ameliorate those plans already under way, or to influence the project to the benefit of the target population.

To choose to do nothing gives agencies and change agents the freedom to do anything they want, and with impunity.

Some of the basic perspectives of anthropology cause ethical problems for anthropologists who choose the applied area. Serious difficulties arise from questions of basic human rights. Making judgments about values, norms, and practices of a society goes against the principle of relativism most anthropologists strongly defend. In change programs and activities, if anthropologists continue to advocate relativism, the question arises as to how they can then encourage any conception of human rights that would be valid for all of humanity. Elvin Hatch (1983) proposes a distinction between cultural relativism and ethical relativism. He argues that understanding the values and world-views of another people does not mean accepting all of their practices and standards. He proposes intervention into cultures based on "imperative" universal standards of humanitarianism—Western notions but commonly recognized universal standards. This seems to suggest that it will be all right for the world to impose a single standard on everyone. Unfortunately, while everyone seems to favor human rights, or at least to say that they do, the definition and specifics differ around the world. There is some question as to what humans rights are basic; thus, whose standard will be used still remains problematic. To advocate universal human rights is to recognize the reality of a Utopia. It may be a worthwhile goal, albeit it an idealistic one. As with many idealistic goals, given a less than perfect world, universal human rights have little chance of becoming realities.

With different definitions and different parameters in mind, people and governments around the world are quick to state concurrence or agreement with such things. For example, given the universally accepted idea that all people should have a determining voice in their political system, as agreed by members of the United Nations, one would have to say that every nation on earth is a perfect democracy. Depending on my definitions, I can agree with most anything. Ideals are praiseworthy and established as goals worth pursuing, but there is danger in thinking they will be achieved simply by dreaming them up. Universality in anything will require consensus, and therein lies the problem. As people are brought together, and as different societies experience multiple pressures to treat each other in sensitive and human ways, the problem will not disappear. Sensitivity to some, is insensitivity to others. Human to some, is inhuman to others. The fact that anthropologists have refrained from making judgments about the correctness of values, behaviors, and ideas, has been one of anthropology's major strengths. Anthropologists have been able to maintain a level of objectivity that seems to elude others stuck in the ethnocentrism of their own learned systems. Their relativistic perspective determines that they should not make judgments across cultural lines, the right or wrong of something based on someone else's standards. This has been a major strength of the discipline.

Hatch seems to suggest that a set of standards already exists in fact and practice, that some universal agreement has been reached. If that were true, there would be no violations of basic human rights, and we know this just is not so. If all the societies of the world could agree on a set of standards, not just verbally and with different definitions, then there might be some value in what Hatch suggests. But forcing a set of standards on the entire world and all of its societies would be as unacceptable as forcing them to accept any other set of dicta determined by cultural groupings who desire that everyone be just like them. Cultural relativism must continue to be a major orienting theme for anthropologists, applied or otherwise. To do otherwise reduces anthropology to podium pounding, no matter the lofty goal or objective of an ideal world.

Future of Applied Anthropology

Despite some projections that diversity or cultural variation, upon which so much of anthropology depends, is decreasing with global integration and nation-state assimilation of so many groups into national cultures, cultural diversity is actually increasing. While the number of small-scale and independent cultures is decreasing, on local and international levels the numbers of constituent, special interest, and scene culture groupings are increasing dramatically as a consequence of increased complexity. This alone will ensure a role for anthropology far into the future. The study of cultural variation will never run out of the variability upon which anthropology depends. To be sure, there will be a decided shift in culture study to these smaller cultural groupings; the same need for understanding culture and cultural difference will continue to be significant for decision makers throughout the world, with transnational agencies or any other group that will attempt to bring people together for any purpose. The increasing interest and the need to understand and appreciate culture and culture change in a world where such things will assume even greater importance, and be highlighted all the more, ensures anthropology's role in the future. Private corporations are becoming more aware of the skills, methods, and knowledge that anthropology can apply to increasing productivity, collecting consumer data to improve marketing, and introducing effective and humane management practices. Medicine has become increasingly aware of the need for change in the treatment of members of different culture groups. Education has become very much aware of the cultural diversity of the classroom despite the continuing homogeneity of its curriculum. Businesses have become aware of the need for understanding their own organizational cultures and for involving as many people as possible in the decision-making process if they wish to remain viable.

As business, industry, education, and governments move into the global arena on an ever-increasing basis, the need for the particular talents of the anthropologist are being recognized. As the world struggles with global problems, integration, and ever-increasing dependence and contact, anthropologists have much more to contribute. John Bennett (1987) recommends that anthropologists synthesize their local studies at the micro level with studies of global dimensions, the macro level. This would help in the identification of trends that now militate against international cooperation, and it would help us to understand human existence in the developing global village. Anthropologists can help assess causes of such phenomena as the greenhouse effect by looking at land-use choices and the impacts of economic activities. Anthropology can assist in the development of polices on agriculture, biotechnology, pollution, and population growth by providing information on the linkages between local practices and global processes. Anthropologists can help document local responses to global economic, political, and religious trends, record dislocations caused by global processes and the various ways people attempt to cope with them. They can help clarify some of the consequences of ethnic, political, or religious change. Because all these things require cross-cultural understanding, this may be the most important contribution of anthropological research today and in the future.

Anthropology can help assess global issues with its holistic approach. The Committee on Global Change (1980) called for more interdisciplinary science for understanding global change. Steve Rayner (1989) suggests that anthropology can serve as the model for such a science because of its holism and interdisciplinary nature. But I would suggest that before it could serve as such a model, it must first gets its own house in order. Anthropology must reverse the growing trend toward fragmentation and divisiveness that threatens to break up the discipline. Anthropologists must move from their parochial cultural research interests, develop more global interests, and become much more willing to engage in international activities. The micro-level studies, upon which anthropology has depended for so long, can easily be related to problems and questions at the macro level, for many of the problems of those local settings have now moved into the global context. The lessons learned from such studies for well over 125 years should now be brought to bear on issues that threaten to destroy the very settings the anthropologists have favored for so long. Anthropologists do not have the solutions to the world's problems, but they have valuable contributions to make in finding those solutions if they are willing to work as part of integrated study teams.

CULTURE AND CHANGE

Culture in the future will be no different than it seemingly always has been, an integrated set of beliefs and behaviors that humans learn and share. Some types of cultures will decrease in number, while others will increase. The use of culture to identify a nation-state will be limited to culture on the level of ideas and values that constituent, interest, and scene culture groups may share with others at some level of social and political integration. The shift will be to the shared, but limited culture that today characterizes the pluralistic societies. A global culture will never evolve, for as the world's complexity increases, the diversity of groups sharing beliefs and behaviors will actually increase and the world will become more diverse. Political systems will attempt to orchestrate this diversity, but in the attempt will produce those very resistance patterns experienced by nation-states. The greater the pressure to conform, the greater the tendency to resist and maintain identity. The more distant the source of such pressure, the stronger the resistance.

Becoming involved in the directed culture change that will clearly dominate human responses to problems now and in the future, is not for the fainthearted or those whose personal gratification, identity or legitimacy is tied to "successful programs." The chances for predictable outcomes increase as one obtains the knowledge and understanding of all that can be involved in such a process. But what individual could control such a massive body of information? Chances of successful outcomes can be increased if people come to know themselves, their own motivations, personality traits and skills, and those of others with whom they will interact. But who will truly know themselves, let alone all those others with whom they will interact in their lifetime? Surely, better results can come with the development of skills that transcend limited disciplinary training. But even if these things are acquired, the control being sought will remain elusive because of forces no one seems able to control. Directed culture change will never evolve into a step-by-step process that can be applied by anyone, anywhere, at any time. While all this may sound cynical, it is realistic and suggests, as this entire volume has suggested, that if you want to change something, start with where it is, not where you want it to be.

SUGGESTED READINGS

These readings focus on providing more in-depth treatment of such issues as global trends, development, projections on the future of the world, and the role of anthropology in that world.

Barnet, Richard J., & Ronald E. Muller. 1974. *Global Reach: The Power of the Multinational Corporations.* This is a work on the growth of the multinational corporations, development of their power and influence, perhaps creating an organizational means of globalizing the planet. As such corporation snow function as significant powers in the world economy, the author discusses the good and bad sides of recent development.

Barney, Gerald O. (ed.). 1980. *The Global Report to the President of the United States.* 3 vols. This three-volume report of a study of significant world trends commissioned by the president of the United States contains the predictions of the study group for the year 2000.

Bennett, John. 1987. "Anthropology and the emerging world order: The paradigm of culture in an age of interdependence." In *Waymarks: The Notre Dame Inaugural Lectures in Anthropology.* Kenneth Moore (ed). This work ponders the role of anthropologists in the future in identifying trends that militate against international cooperation and helping to understand human existence in the developing global village. The author also discusses the role of anthropologists in helping to solve global social problems such as AIDS, disasters, the homeless, family violence and abuse, crime, and war.

Bodley, John H. 1985. *Anthropology and Contemporary Human Problems. 2nd ed.*
———. 1988. *Tribal Peoples and Development Issues: A Global Overview.*
———. 1990. *Victims of Progress.* 3rd ed. All of these volumes examine the impacts of development on tribal peoples, some of the most serious global problems affecting such cultural groups, the policies and motives for the interaction between indigenous peoples and members of the global culture.

Davis, Shelton H. 1982. *Victims of the Miracle.* The volume presents a critical review of the efforts and motivations for developing the Amazon region of Brazil. Special attention is paid to the role of the multinational corporations.

Eddy, E. M., & W. Partridge (eds.). 1987. *Applied Anthropology in America.* 2nd ed. This collection of essays focus on the relevance of applied anthropology in American society and presents an overview on how it has contributed and can contribute to policy issues.

Podolefsky, A., & P. J. Brown (eds.). 1989. *Applying Anthropology.* This is an introductory reader on the practical applications of the four major subfields of anthropology and contains articles that present a view of anthropology not readily available in other readers.

Van Willigen, J., B. Rylko-Bauer, & A. McElroy. 1989. *Making Our Research Useful: Case Studies in the Utilization of Anthropological Knowledge.* This work describes projects wherein anthropology has been used, and provides some suggestions as to how anthropology can make use of the knowledge gained in applied research projects.

Worsley, Peter. 1984. *The Three Worlds: Culture and World Development.* In this volume, global economic and political trends are examined, as is the persistent ethnicity around the world.

BIBLIOGRAPHY

Aceves, Joseph B. (ed.). 1972. *Aspects of Cultural change*. Southern Anthropological Society Proceedings, no. 6. Athens: University of Georgia Press.

Angrosino, Michael V. (ed.). 1976. *Do Applied Anthropologists Apply Anthropology*. Southern Anthropological Society Proceedings, no. 10. Athens: University of Georgia Press.

Appell, George N. 1988. "Casting Social Change." In: *The Real and Imagined Role of Culture in Development: Case Studies from Indonesia*. Edited by M. R. Dove. Boulder, CO: Westview Press

Arensberg, Conrad M., & Arthur H. Niehoff. 1971. *Introducing Social Change: A Manual for Community Development*. 2nd ed. Chicago: Aldine.

Arnold, Robert D. 1976. *Alaska Native Land Claims*. Anchorage: Alaska Native Foundation.

Barlett, Peggy F. (ed.). 1980. *Agricultural Decision Making: Anthropological Contributions to Rural Development*. New York: Academic Press.

Barnet, Richard J., & Ronald E. Muller. 1974. *Global Reach: The Power of the Multinational Corporations*. New York: Simon & Schuster.

Barnett, Homer G. 1942. "Invention and culture change." *American Anthropologist* 44, 14–30.

——. 1953. *Innovation: The Basis of Culture Change*. New York: McGraw-Hill.

——. 1956. *Anthropology in Administration*. Evanston, Illinois: Row, Peterson.

Barnett, H. G., B. J. Siegel, & J. Watson. 1954. "Acculturation: an exploratory formulation." *American Anthropologist* 22, 973–1002.

Barrett, Richard A. 1984. *Culture and Conduct*. 2nd ed. Belmont, CA: Wadsworth.

Barth, Frederick. 1981. *Process and Form in Social Life*. London: Routledge & Kegan Paul.

Bates, Daniel G., & Fred Plog. 1991. *Human Adaptive Strategies*. New York: McGraw-Hill.

Batten, T. R. 1969. *The Non-Directive Approach in Group and Community Work*. London: Oxford University Press.

Bee, Robert L. 1974. *Patterns and Process: An Introduction to Anthropological Strategies for the Study of Sociocultural Change*. New York: Free Press.

Benedict, Ruth. 1934. *Patterns of Culture*. Boston: Houghton Mifflin.

Bennett, John. 1987. "Anthropology and the emerging world order: The paradigm of culture in an age of interdependence." In *Waymarks: The Notre Dame Inaugural Lectures in Anthropology*. Edited by Kenneth Moore. Notre Dame University of Notre Dame Press.

Bennis, Warren G. 1966. "A typology of change processes." In *The Planning of Change*. Edited by W. G. Bennis, K. D. Benne, & R. Chin. New York: Holt, Rinehart & Winston.

Bernard, H. Russell, & Pertti Pelto (eds.). 1987. *Technology and Social Change*. 2nd ed. Prospect Heights, IL: Waveland Press.

Bodley, John H. 1982. *Victims of Progress*. 2nd ed. Palo Alto, CA: Mayfield.

————. 1985. *Anthropology and Contemporary Human Problems*. 2nd ed. Mountain View, CA: Mayfield.

————. 1988. *Tribal Peoples and Development Issues: A Global Overview*. Mountain View, CA: Mayfield.

————. 1990. *Victims of Progress*. 3rd ed. Mountain View, CA: Mayfield.

————. 1994. *Cultural Anthropology: Tribes, States, and the Global System*. Mountain View, CA: Mayfield.

Bohannan, Paul, & Mark Glazer (eds.). 1988. *High Points in Anthropology*. 2nd ed. New York: Alfred A. Knopf.

Boyd, Robert, & Peter J. Richerson. 1985. *Culture and the Evolutionary Process*. Chicago: University of Chicago Press.

Brady, Ivan A. I., & Barry L. Isaac. 1975. *A Reader in Culture Change*. 2 vols. New York: Wiley & Sons.

Carbarino, Merwyn. 1976. *Native American Heritage*. Boston: Little, Brown.

Cancian, Frank. 1980. "Risk and uncertainty in agricultural decision making." In *Agricultural Decision-making: Anthropological Contributions to Rural Development*. Edited by Peggy Barlett. New York: Academic Press.

Carneiro, Robert L. 1970. "A theory of the origin of the state." *Science,* 733–738 (August 21).

Chambers, Erve. 1985. *Applied Anthropology*. Englewood Cliffs, NJ: Prentice-Hall.

Choldin, Harvey M. 1968. "Urban co-operatives at Comilla, Pakistan." *Economic Development and Culture Change 16* (2), 189-218.

Clay, Jason W. 1990. "What's a nation?" *Mother Jones 15* (7), 28–30.

Clifton, James A. (ed). 1970. *Applied Anthropology: Readings in the Using of the Science of Man.* Boston: Houghton Mifflin.

Cole, Johnnetta B. 1982. *Anthropology for the Eighties*. New York: Free Press.

Dalton, George. 1971. *Economic Development and Social Change: The Modernization of Village Communities*. Garden City, NY: Natural History Press.

Davis, Shelton H. 1982. *Victims of the Miracle*. Cambridge: Cambridge University Press.

Devos, George A. (ed.). 1976. *Responses to Change*. New York: Van Nostrand.

de Waal Malefijt, Annemarie. 1974. *Images of Man: A History of Anthropological Thought*. New York: Alfred A. Knopf.

DeWalt, Billie R. 1988. "The cultural ecology of development: Ten precepts for survival." *Agriculture and Human Values 5* (1, 2), 112–123.

Dove, M. R. (ed.). 1988. *The Real and Imagined Role of Culture in Development: Case Studies from Indonesia*. Boulder, CO: Westview Press.

Downs, James F. 1975. *Cultures in Crisis*. 2nd ed. Beverly Hills,CA: Glencoe Press.

Eddy, E.M., & W. Partridge (eds.). 1987. *Applied Anthropology in America. 2nd ed.* New York: Columbia University Press.

Ember, Carol R., & Melvin Ember. 1993. *Cultural Anthropology.* 7th ed. Englewood Cliffs, NJ: Prentice-Hall.

Faggan, Brian. 1984. *Clash of Cultures.* New York: Freeman.

Firth, Raymond. 1951. "Contemporary British social anthropology." *American Anthropologist 53*, 474–490.

Forbes, Jack D. 1964. *The Indian in America's Past.* New York: Prentice-Hall.

Foster, George M. 1962. *Traditional Cultures: And the Impact of Technological Change.* New York: Harper & Row.

———. 1969. *Applied Anthropology.* Boston: Little, Brown.

———. 1973. *Traditional Societies and Technological Change.* 2nd ed. New York: Harper & Row.

Frazer, James. 1911. *The Golden Bough.* London: Macmillan. (Originally published 1890).

Freilich, M. (ed.). 1972. *The Meaning of Culture.* Lexington, MA: Xerox.

Fried, Morton H. 1972. *The Study of Anthropology.* New York: Thomas Crowell.

Fuchs, Estelle, & Robert J. Havighurst. 1972. *To Live on This Earth: American Indian Education.* Garden City, NY: Doubleday.

Gamst, F.C., & Edward Norbeck. 1976. *Ideas of Culture: Sources and Uses.* New York: Holt, Rinehart & Winston.

Garbarino, M. S. 1977. *Sociocultural Theory in Anthropology: A Short History.* New York: Holt, Rinehart & Winston.

Gearing, Fred, R. McNetting, & L. R. Peattie (eds.). 1960. *Documentary History of the Fox Project.* Chicago: University of Chicago Press.

Goldstone, J. A. 1982. "The comparative and historical study of revolutions." *Annual Review of Sociology 8*, 187-207.

Grillo, R., & A. Rew (eds.). 1985. *Social Anthropology and Development Policy.* New York: Tavistock.

Hackenberg, Robert A. 1988. "Scientists or survivors: The future of applied anthropology under maximum uncertainty." In *Anthropology for Tomorrow: Creative Practitioner-Oriented Applied Anthropology Programs.* Edited by Robert T. Trotter II. Washington, DC: American Anthropological Association.

Harris, Marvin. 1968. *The Rise of Anthropological Theory.* New York: Thomas Y. Crowell.

Hatch, Elvin. 1983. *Culture and Morality: The Relativity of Values in Anthropology.* New York: Columbia University Press.

Haviland, William A. 1994. *Anthropology.* 7th ed. Ft. Worth, TX: Harcourt Brace College Publishers.

Henry, Jules. 1965. *Culture Against Man.* New York: Vintage Books.

———. 1966. "A theory for an anthropological analysis of American culture." *Anthropological Quarterly 39*, 90-109.

Hersey, Paul, Kenneth H. Blanchard, & Walter E. Natemeyer. 1987. *Situational Leadership, Perception, and the Impact of Power.* San Diego, CA: University Associates.

Herskovits, M. J. 1936. "Applied anthropology and the American anthropologist." *Science 83*, 215–222.

———. 1958. *Acculturation: The Study of Culture Contact.* Gloucester, MA: Peter Smith.

Hogbin, Ian. 1939. *Experiments in Civilization.* London: Oxford University Press.

———. 1970. *Social Change.* 2nd ed. Carlton, Victoria: Melbourne University Press.

Holmberg, Allan R. 1955. "Participant intervention in the field." *Human Organization 14* (1), 23–26.

———. 1958. "The research and development approach to the study of change." *Human Organization 17*, 12–16.

————.1960. "Changing community attitudes and values in the context of national development." *American Behavioral Scientist 8* (7), 3–8.

Homans, G. 1950. *The Human Group.* New York: Harcourt, Brace.

Honigmann, J. J. 1976. *The Development of Anthropological Ideas.* New York: Dorsey Press.

Hsu, Francis L. K. 1972. "American core values and national character." In *Psychological Anthropology.* Edited by F. Hsu. Cambridge, MA: Schenkman.

Kennedy, J. G. 1977. *Struggle for Change in a Nubian Community.* Palo Alto, CA: Mayfield.

Kessing, F. 1928. *Changing Maori.* New Zealand: New Plymouth.

————. 1952. *Culture Change: An Analysis and Bibliography of Anthropology Sources to 1952.* Stanford Anthropological Series, no. 1. Stanford: Stanford University Press.

Kroeber, Alfred L. 1940. "Stimulus diffusion." *American Anthropologist 42,* 1–20.

————. 1963. *Anthropology: Culture Processes and Patterns.* New York: Harcourt Brace.

Kroeber, Alfred, & Clyde Kluckhohn. 1952. *Culture: A Critical Review of Concepts and Definitions.* Papers of the Peabody Museum of American Archaeology and Ethnology, vol. 1. Cambridge, MA: Harvard University Press.

Kushner, Gilbert. 1991. "Applied anthropology." In *Career Explorations in Human Services.* Edited by William G. Emener & Margaret Darrow. Springfield, IL: Charles C. Thomas.

Lane-Fox Pitt-Rivers, A. 1916. *The Evolution of Culture and Other Essays.* London: Oxford University Press.

Lang, Gottfried O. 1973. "Conditions for development in Asmat." *Irian: Bulletin for West Irian Development 2* (1), 38–61.

Lang, Gottfried O., Warren J. Roth, and Martha B. Lang. 1969. "Sukumaland co-operatives as mechanisms of change." In *The Anthropology of Development in Sub-Saharan Africa.* Monograph no. 10. Edited by David Brokensha & Marian Pearsoll. Washington, DC: Society of Applied Anthropology:48-63.

Lange, Charles H. 1968. *Cochiti: A New Mexico Pueblo, Past and Present.* Carbondale, IL: Southern Illinois University Press.

Leach, E. R. 1954. *Political Systems of Highland Burma.* Boston: Beacon Press.

Leighton, Alexander. 1945. *The Governing of Men.* Princeton: Princeton University Press.

Linton, Ralph. 1936. *The Study of Man.* New York: Appleton-Century-Crofts.

————. 1940. *Acculturation in Several American Indian Tribes.* New York: Appleton-Century-Crofts.

Lowie, Robert H. 1937. *The History of Ethnological Theory.* New York: Holt, Rinehart & Winston.

Magnarella, Paul J. 1974. *Tradition and Change in a Turkish Town.* New York: Wiley & Sons.

Mair, Lucy. 1934. *African People in the Twentieth Century.* London: Oxford University Press.

————. 1984. *Anthropology and Development.* London: Macmillan.

Malinowski, Bronislaw. 1922. *Argonauts of the Western Pacific.* New York: Dutton.

————. 1929. "Practical anthropology." *Africa 2,* 23–38.

————. 1939. "The Group and the individual in functional analysis." *American Journal of Sociology 44,* 938–964.

————. 1944. *A Scientific Theory of Culture and Other Essays.* Chapel Hill: University of North Carolina Press.

Manners, R. A., & Kaplan, D. (eds). 1968. *Theory in Anthropology: A Sourcebook.* Chicago: Aldine.

Maybury-Lewis, David (ed.). 1984. *The Prospects for Plural Societies*. Proceedings of the American Ethnological Society. Washington, DC: American Ethnological Society.

McNeill, W.H. 1976. *Plagues and People*. New York: Doubleday Anchor.

Mead, Margaret. 1932. *Changing Culture of an American Indian Tribe*. New York: Columbia University Press.

———. 1955. *Cultural Patterns and Technical Change*. New York: Mentor.

———. 1956. *New Lives for Old*. New York: Mentor.

———. 1978. "The evolving ethics of applied anthropology." In *Applied Anthropology in America*. Edited by Elizabeth M. Eddy & William L. Partridge. New York: Columbia University Press.

Moore, Kenneth (ed.). 1987. *Waymarks: The Notre Dame Inaugural Lectures in Anthropology*. Notre Dame, In: University of Notre Dame Press.

Morgan, Lewis H. 1964. *Ancient Society*. Cambridge, MA: Belknap Press. (Originally published in 1877).

Naylor, Larry L. 1973a. "Applied anthropology: Approaches to using anthropology." *Human Organization 32* (4), 363–369.

———. 1973b. *Culture Change and Development in the Balim: Final Report on Central Highlands Research. FUNDWI/8, November 1971–March 1973*. Carbondale, IL: Southern Illinois University.

———. 1974. *Culture Change and Development in the Balim Valley, Irian Jaya, Indonesia*. Ann Arbor, MI: University Microfilms.

———. 1976. Forum for the Unplanned Consequences of Planned Culture change: Final Report for the Alaska Humanities Forum. Fairbanks, AK: Tanana Chiefs Conference.

Niehoff, Arthur H. 1966. *A Casebook of Social Change*. Chicago: Aldine.

Nietschmann, Bernard. 1987. "The third world war." *Cultural Survival Quarterly 11* (3), 1, 3–16.

Noble, David. 1984. *The Forces of Production*. New York: Knopf.

Operasi Koteka. 1973. Government Operations Plan, West Irian 1971–1973. Jakarta: Indonesian Government.

Partridge, William (ed.). 1984. *Training Manual in Development Anthropology*. Special Publication no. 17. Washington, DC: American Anthropology Association & Society for Applied Anthropology.

Podolefsky, A., & P. J. Brown. 1989. *Applying Anthropology*. Mountain View, CA: Mayfield.

Radcliffe-Brown, A. R. 1922. *Adaman Islanders*. London: Cambridge University Press.

———. 1952. *Structure and Function in Primitive Society*. London: Cohen & West.

Rathje, William L., & Cheryl Ritenbaugh. 1984. "Household refuse analysis: Theory, method and applications in social science." *American Behavioral Scientist 28* (1), 5–153.

Rayner, Steve. 1989. "Fiddling while the globe warms." *Anthropology Today 5* (6), 1–2.

Redfield, Robert. 1953. *The Primitive World and its Transformations*. Ithaca, NY: Cornell University Press.

Redfield, Robert, R. Linton, & M. Herskovits. 1936. "Memorandum on the study of acculturation." *American Anthropologist 38*, 149–152.

Rogers, Everett M. 1983. *Diffusion of Innovation*. 3rd ed. New York: Free Press.

Roseberry, William. 1988. "Political economy." *Annual Review of Anthropology 17*, 161–259.

Rosman, Abraham, & Paula G. Rubel. 1989. *The Tapestry of Culture: An Introduction to Cultural Anthropology*. 3rd ed. New York: Random House.

Sahlins, Marshall D., & Elman R. Service. 1960. *Evolution and Culture*. Ann Arbor: University of Michigan Press.

Schapera, I. 1934. *Eastern Civilization and the Natives of South Africa*. London: Julian Simon.

Scupin, Raymond, & Christopher R. DeCorse. 1992. *Anthropology: A Global Perspective*. Englewood Cliffs, NJ: Prentice-Hall.

Service, E. R. 1971. *Cultural Evolutionism: Theory in Practice*. New York: Holt, Rinehart & Winston.

Shankman, Paul. 1975. "A forestry scheme in Samoa." *Natural History 84* (8), 60–69.

Simon, Julian. 1981. The Ultimate Resource. Princeton, NJ: Princeton University Press.

Singh, Rudra Datt. 1952. "An introduction of green manuring in rural India." In *Human Problems*. Edited by H. Spicer. New York: Russell Sage Foundation.

Smith, A., & J. Fischer. 1970. *Anthropology*. Englewood Cliffs, NJ: Prentice-Hall.

Society of Applied Anthropology. 1975. "Statement on professional and ethnical responsibilities." *Human Organization 34* (2), 108.

Spicer, Edward H. 1961. *Perspectives in American Indian Culture*. Chicago: University of Chicago Press.

Spindler, Louise. 1977. *Culture Change and Modernization*. New York: Holt, Rinehart & Winston.

Spradley, J. P., & David McCurdy. 1972. *The Cultural Experience*. Prospect Heights, IL: Waveland.

———. 1974. *Conformity and Conflict*. Boston: Little, Brown.

Steward, Julian. 1955. *Theory of Culture Change*. Urbana: University of Illinois Press.

Tylor, E. B. 1958. *Primitive Culture*. New York: Harper Torchbooks. (Originally published in 1871).

U.S. Committee on Global Change. 1988. *Toward an Understanding of Global Change*. Washington, DC: National Academy Press.

Van Willigen, J. 1986. *Applied Anthropology: An Introduction*. South Hadley, MA: Bergin & Garvey.

Van Willigen, J. B. Rylko-Bauer, & A. McElroy. 1989. *Making Our Research Useful: Case Studies in the Utilization of Anthropological Knowledge*. Boulder, CO: Westview.

Walker, D. 1972. *The Emergent Native Americans*. Boston: Little, Brown.

White, Leslie. 1949. *The Science of Culture*. New York: Farrar, Straus & Cudahy.

———. 1959. "The concept of evolution in cultural anthropology." In *Evolution and Anthropology*. Washington, DC: Anthropological Society of Washington.

Whittfogel, Karl A. 1957. *Oriental Despotism: A Comparative Study of Total Power*. New Haven: Yale University Press.

Wilson, Godfrey, & Monica Wilson. 1945. *The Analysis of Social Change*. Boston: Cambridge University Press.

Wolfe, Alvin W. 1977. "The supranational organization of production: An evolutionary perspective." *Current Anthropology 18*, 615–635.

———. 1986. "The multinational corporation as a form of sociocultural integration above the level of the state." In *Anthropology and International Business*. Edited by Hendrick Serrie. Williamsberg, VA: Studies in Third World Societies, no. 28.

Woods, Clyde M. 1975. *Culture Change*. Dubuque, IA: Wm. C. Brown.

Worsley, Peter. 1984. *The Three Worlds: Culture and World Development*. Chicago: Illinois: University of Chicago Press.

Zaltman, Gerald, & Robert Dugan. 1977. *Strategies for Planned Change*. New York: Wiley & Sons.

INDEX

Accidental change, 42, 56
Accomplishing change, 166–197
  addressing barriers/stimulants, 191
  basic principles of change, 196
  chances of success, 173
  changing aspects of culture, 189
  changing culture, 179
  changing ideas or behaviors, 195
  changing whole culture, 184
  conflict, 169
  considerations, 168
  context, 170
  generating ideas, 189
  interactions, 169
  key, 169
  knowing about change, 182
  model for, 170, 171
  model of directed culture, 169
  multicultural setting, 169
  selection of strategy, 193
  unplanned consequences, 175
  voluntary change, 168
Acculturation
  assimilation, 41
  borrowing, 66–67
  change, 53–55
  change process, 39, 53–57
  external change, 50
  differentiating change, 48

  diffusion, 54
  directed, 53
  forced, 53–54
  historically, 41–42
  kinds of, 54
  model, 54
  nonvoluntary change, 53–55
  patterned, 54
  studies, 12
  superficial, 54
  syncretism, 54
  technical change, 54
Acculturation and change, 53-55
Action/reaction, 55, 153
Adaptation, 14–15, 38–39, 43–48, 61
Addressing barriers and stimulants,
    191–193. *See also* Changing culture
American culture
  beliefs, values, practices, 99
  change agents, 95
  change and, 147,
  conformity, 93
  cooperation, 142
  core values, 96
  diversity, 93
  education system, 99, 101
  ethnocentrism, 101
  external change, 163
  Henry, Jules, 95–96, 111, 132

American culture (continued)
　　Hsu, Francis, 96, 111, 132
　　idea of change, 4
　　individuality, 207
　　innovation and, 50, 57
　　internal change, 63
　　majority group, 94
　　minority groups, 99
　　motivation for change, 154–155
　　multiculturalism, 63, 79, 93–94
　　problems, 101
　　relocation and, 187–188
　　role characteristics, 101
　　stereotype, 99
　　unplanned consequences, 177–178
　　value perceptions, 131–132
　　values and traditions, 144–145
Ancient Society, 7
Anthropology
　　applied, 12–13, 208
　　as consultants, 209
　　assessing change benefit/cost, 209
　　change, 7–12, 38–39, 200, 209
　　code of conduct, 209
　　culture definition, 16–17
　　culture of, 42
　　devising problem solutions, 209
　　ethical issues, 209–211
　　future focus, 208
　　future of applied, 212–213
　　future problems, 209
　　future roles, 208–209
　　global change and, 200
　　global role, 208–212
　　health care, 209
　　holistic approach, 200
　　international development and, 209
　　monitoring change, 209
　　origins and definition, 5
　　Practical, 12
　　social-impact studies, 209
　　theory, 7
Anthropology and change, 7–12
Appell, George N., 132, 137, 205
Applied anthropology, 12–13, 208
　　future of applied, 212–213
Arensberg, Conrad. *See* Niehoff, A.
Aristotle, 6, 7

Arnold, Robert D., 177, 197
Asian-American, 93
Assimilation, 41, 53–54

Bacon, Francis, 6
Barnet, Richard J., 204, 214
Barnett, Homer G., 12, 49, 50, 60
Barney, Gerald O., 214
Barrett, Richard A., 16, 35
Barriers and stimulants, 191–193.
　　See also Changing culture
　　additive changes, 192
　　attitudes and perceptions, 70
　　barriers, 56, 70–72, 191–193
　　cultural, 72
　　culture values, 70
　　fit, 192
　　motivation, 192
　　psychological, 72
　　replacement change, 193
　　social, 70–72
　　steps, 193
　　stimulants, 191
　　timing, 192
Barth, Frederick, 87
Basic principles for changing culture,
　　196–197
Batten, T. R., 137, 194, 197
Bennett, John, 212, 214
Bennis, Warren G., 118, 137
Bernard, H. Russell, 203
Boas, Franz, 8
Bodley, John H., 3, 197, 203, 208, 214
Bohannon, Paul, 6, 13
Borrowing, 8, 51, 55–56, 62, 66
Brady, Ivan A., 12, 87

Carbarino, Merwyn, 187
Chambers, Erve, 209
Chances of success, 173–179
Change agencies, 67, 204–205
Change agents, 67–86, 88–105
Changing aspects of culture, 189
Changing culture, 179–197. *See also*
　　Accomplishing change
　　aspects of, 189, 242
　　barriers and stimulants, 191–193
　　changing ideas/behaviors, 195–196

Changing culture (continued)
  generating ideas, 189–191
  integrated nature, 178
  knowing change, 182
  knowing context, 179–182
  limited change, 189
  principles of, 196
  selection of strategy, 193
  whole culture, 184–188
Changing ideas or behaviors, 195–196
Changing whole culture, 184–189
Choice variation, 50
Choldin, Harvey M., 125
Civilization, 3, 4, 15, 39–40
Clay, Jason, 24–25
Clifton, James A., 10
Coercion, 51, 89
Collaborators. See Focal groups
Communication, 74–75, 77, 80–81,
  159–160
Community development strategy,
  123–124
Competition, 141–142
Components of directed change
  change agencies, 172
  change agents, 68, 172
  emphasis, 172
  focal group, 68
  focal groups, 172
  idea, 68
  innovating agencies, 68
  innovator, 68
  interaction, 68
  interactional context, 68–69, 77, 171
  interactional model, 77, 170–173
  model, 171
  participant characteristics, 77
  participant interactions, 69
  plan, 80
Conditions for change, 63, 67
Conservatism, 140–141
Constituent culture, 16, 25–26, 30,
  33–35, 37–38, 97–98
Cooperation, 142
Core systems of culture, 19–21, 64–66.
  See also Culture
Cultural adaptation, 54, 61
Cultural characteristics, focal, 105–111
Cultural conflict/opposition, 153

Cultural ecology, 44
Cultural forces of change, 140–141
Cultural relativism, 5, 6, 8–9
Cultural scenes, 26–27, 50, 90, 94
Cultural values and traditions, 144–146
Culturation, 18
Culture
  abstraction, 16
  agency, 39
  alternatives, 19
  baggage, 148
  basis of action/reaction, 78
  behavior, 19
  behavioral, 17
  characteristics as forces of change,
    139–142
  characteristics of, 139
  complexes, 19
  complex society, 30
  components, 39
  components of, 58
  conceptualizations of, 17–18
  construct, 33, 38
  contact, 39, 63, 66, 126, 129
  context, 15, 72, 179
  contradictions of, 20
  core systems, 19–21, 64–66
  creation, 14, 24
  culture characteristics, 140
  definition, 16–19
  economic system, 19
  elements, 19
  evolution of, 45
  functions, 20
  human adaptation, 63
  idea, 19
  ideal, 32, 38
  institutions, 19
  integrated systems, 8, 18–21, 45
  nature of, 58
  organizational systems, 145–146
  political system, 20
  problem solving solutions, 45, 46,
    37–38, 45
  process, 39
  products, 19
  psychological systems, 147–151
  real, 31, 32

Cuture (continued)
    social system, 20
    structural systems, 147
    transmission and acquisition, 18, 37
    truth as, 22
    types of definition, 17
    uniqueness of, 14
    values and traditions, 144–146
    world, 206
    worldview, 20
Culture change. *See also* Directed
        culture change
    acceptance, 58
    accidental, 1, 42
    adaptation, 39
    agent characteristics, 82–83
    agents in, 102
    barriers and stimulants, 58, 139
    basic elements, 89
    basic principles, 196
    borrowing, 57
    broad level, 38–41
    chances for success, 179
    change regularities, 183
    civilization, 39
    completion, 57, 63
    complexity, 179
    concepts and terms, 39
    conditions for, 67
    conflict, 89
    contact, 54, 62, 88
    context, 48–50, 66, 72–73, 101
    core systems, 64
    defined, 10, 43
    development, 39
    diffusion, 57
    directed, 2, 12, 53, 55
    discovery, 57
    dynamics, 12, 52
    enforced, 42, 53
    essential considerations, 58
    evolution, 37
    external, 66
    external forces of, 50, 60
    felt need, 58
    fit, 58
    focal groups, 102
    forces of, 196

    future, 213–214
    general model, 38, 59
    history, 6, 38
    innovation, 60
    integrated, 64
    interaction and, 57–58, 184
    internal process, 50–51, 59, 66,
        89–91
    invention, 57
    kinds of, 68
    levels of, 6
    mini-models, 41
    model, 58
    modernization, 39
    motivations, 99
    multicultural settings, 91–94
    nativistic movements, 183
    nondirected, 50
    nonvoluntary change, 53
    origins, 47–49, 57
    outcomes, 182
    patterned, 179
    planned, 2
    planning for, 112–117
    pressures for, 48
    process(es), 37, 41, 58, 61, 88, 179,
        182
    progress, 39
    rejection, 50
    role characteristics, 101
    role of the individual, 52
    setting, 88–89
    specific, 39
    strategies, 12, 111–135
    subprocesses, 42
    timing, 58
    urbanization, 39
    voluntary, 42, 55, 58, 62, 89
Culture change agents
    attributes, 82
    coercion and, 89
    constituent characteristics, 79,
        97–99
    constituent culture, 95–99
    contact settings and, 62
    cultural baggage, 95
    cultural characteristics, 70–71,
        78–79, 82, 95

Culture change agents (continued)
   cultural scene characteristics, 79,
      99–100
   culture shock, 102
   culture knowledge, 90
   cultures of agents, 82
   culture shock, 102
   directed change, 78
   discipline symbols, 100
   distinct cultures, 95
   individual gratification, 100
   interaction, 62, 92
   internal change and, 90
   key to change, 102
   living habits, 83
   major participants in the process, 68
   motives, 92
   multicultural settings, 62, 92–94
   nation-state, 95
   national characteristics, 94–96
   nondirected change and, 50, 62
   participant of change, 72
   personal perceptions, 102
   personal style, 82, 128–130
   plan or strategy of, 68
   practices, 103–105
   problems, 74
   reactions to, 74
   role characteristics, 74, 82–83, 88,
      100–103
   scene characteristics, 95, 99–100
   sentiments, 74
   specialists as, 82
   symbols of competence, 100
   voluntary change and, 91
Culture change concepts, 39–42
   accidental change, 42
   acculturation, 39
   decree, 42
   development, 40
   diffusion, 39
   directed, 39
   fiat, 42
   forced draft, 42
   innovation, 39
   modernization, 40
   nondirected, 39
   nonvoluntary, 39

   progress, 40
   surface, 42
   syncretism, 42
   voluntary, 39, 42
Culture change context, 14–35
   179–185
Culture change forces, 140
Culture change model, general, 37–60
   acculturation, 53–55
   diffusion, 55–56
   evolution, 43–46
   historical, 38
   innovation, 49–53
   interaction, 38, 41, 47–49
   invention, 38–41
   major components, 38
   model, 56–60
   ongoing process, 39–40
   process, 38
Culture change models, 39, 41,
    54, 57–60
   directed change model, 67–70
   ecological, 44
   ethnocentric, 41
   evolutionary model, 44
   Foster model, 70–72
   grand models, 37–60
   interactional, 77–86
   Leighton model, 72–74
   Niehoff model, 74–77
   unilineal models, 44
Culture change pressures, 48
Culture change process, 37, 40, 47–48,
    50–52, 54, 57–58, 61, 65, 88–99
   basic processes, 57–58
   broad level, 40
   contacts, 57
   definition, 47
   directed, 57
   directed change, 61
   first step, 51
   human interaction, 61
   infant stage, 65
   innovation, 51, 58
   innovator, 58
   internal process, 49
   originates, 61
   voluntarily accepted, 57–61

Culture change rejection, 50, 58
Culture change responses, 73
Culture change settings, 88–90, 141
Culture change strategies, 112–136
    focal group, 130–135
    general strategy, 117–125
    implementation, 125–130
    responsive, 135–136
Culture contact
    change agencies, 113–116
    conflict, 79–80, 132–133
    direct/indirect, 60
    innovation and, 50, 58
    scene cultures, 90
    truth, stress, conflict, 80, 133
    voluntary change and, 63
    voluntary interaction, 66
Culture forms, 16, 29–35, 37–38
Culture groupings
    community, 21
    constituent, 4, 37
    construct, 37
    cultural scene, 37
    definition, 21
    ethnic, 2, 25–26, 93, 99
    general, 37
    kinds of, 21–28
    membership, 21, 27
    multiculturalism, 29
    reasons for, 35
    sense of belonging, 21
    societies, 21
    special interest, 27
    specific, 37
    structure, 21
Culture scenes, 4, 26–28, 99–100
Culture shock, 102
Culture substitution. See also
    Replacement
Culture types, 16, 63
Culture values and traditions, 145–146

Dalton, George, 125
Dani, 151–158, 177, 178, 115
Darwin, Charles, 7
Davis, Shelton H., 215
de Waal Malefijt, Annemarie, 6, 13
Decree, change by, 42

Democritus, 6
Descartes, René, 6
Development, 4, 39–40, 105, 204–206
Development trends, 205–206
Devos, George A., 12
DeWalt, Billie, 205
Diffusion, 55–56, 60–70
    accidental change, 56
    acculturation, 42
    barriers and stimulants, 56
    borrowing, 66
    change process, 50, 55–57, 67–70
    components, 56
    contact, 55
    definition, 56
    directed/nondirected, 57
    forced, 56–57
    forms, 56
    innovation, 41, 56
    interaction, 56
    mechanism, 55
    models, 56
    nonvoluntary, 57
    planned or directed settings, 55
    reciprocal borrowing, 55
    regularities, 55
    reinterpretation, 55
    selectivity, 55
    spread of traits, 41
    superficial change, 56
    syncretism, 55, 56
    technology, 39
    terminology, 41
    voluntary, 56–57
Diffusion and change, 56–57
Directed change model, 170–173
Directed culture change
    acceleration, 67
    accidents of history, 70
    accomplishing, 68
    action/reaction setting, 67–69, 77
    barriers and stimulants, 74
    change agents, 68, 74, 80
    coercion, 66–67, 69, 74, 77
    communication, 75
    component characteristics, 80–81
    components, 67, 77
    conditions, 67

Directed culture change (continued)
consequences, 67
contact, 67, 69, 88
context, 68, 77, 89
diffusion, 91
dynamics, 66
external process, 67
focal groups, 74
forced, 66–67
formal/informal, 69
Foster, George M., model of, 70–73
future, 213
history, 38–42
implementation, 67
influences on, 75
innovator, 68
intended, 62
interactional, 77–81
interactional model, 77–86
interactions, 68, 80
internal, 68, 51–53, 68
Leighton, Alexander, 72–74
mechanism of change, 58
models, 67–86
Niehoff, Arthur, 74–77
organizational interventions, 67
outcomes, 69, 71, 78
outside forces, 70
participants, 69, 74, 78, 80
plan, 67–68, 74, 80
postulates and principles, 72
process, 58, 70, 72, 88, 138, 214
recipe approach (school solutions),
24, 71
requirement, 74
settings, 68
steps, 68
stress, 77
unplanned consequences, 69
variables, 75
Directive approaches, 118
Discovery, 41, 50–51
Dove, M. R., 206
Downs, James F., 5, 22, 193
Dugan, Robert, 120
Dynamics of change, 138–166
Dysfunction, 11
Dysnomia, 10

Economic trends, 203–205
Eddy, E.M., 215
Education, 18, 99, 101
Elements of directed change, 67
Ember, Carol, and Ember, Melvin, 3,
207
Enculturation, 18, 140–141
Engineering strategy, 121–123
Environment, 47–49
adaptation, 14, 47–48
change, 64
change source, 57
interaction, 47–49
limitations, 44
natural, 38, 43–45, 47, 63–64
physical, 1, 3
sociocultural environment, 1, 3,
24, 38, 43, 47, 64
Environmental trends, 202–203
Eradication, 185–186
Ethical issues for anthropology,
209–212
Ethnic groupings
African-Americans, 2, 25
Anglo-Americans, 25
Asian-American, 93
Euro-Americans, 2, 93, 99
Hispanic-Americans, 25–26, 93
Native-Americans, 26, 93
Ethnicity, 25
Ethnocentrism, 5, 22, 33, 41, 93,
101, 131, 141
Evolution, 37–60
adaptation, 43–49
change, 37–60
definition, 43
evolutionary process, 43
historically, 38–42
physical terms, 43
prime movers, 45
process, 43
thinking, 37–42
Evolutionary trends, 200–201
External change, 57, 79, 139
External forces, 162–166

Facilitative assistance strategy,
125–130

Factionalism, 4
Felt need, 67, 72. *See also* Motivation
Fiat, change by, 42, 53, 67
Firth, Raymond, 11
Fisher, J., 5
Fit, 58, 70–72, 89–90, 157–158
Focal group
    context, 83
    cultural characteristics, 69, 75,
        78–79, 83–84, 106–109
    dealing with outsiders, 84
    definition, 68–69
    directed change, 106–107,
    history, 84
    interactive model, 77–86
    motivations, 134
    multicultural setting, 79
    Niehoff, Arthur, 74–77
    participants in directed change, 72
    partners, 69
    passive receptors, 69
    primary culture, 83
    real and ideal culture, 83
    strategies, 84, 130–135
    truth and, 83
Focal group strategies, 130–135,
    109–111
Forbes, Jack D., 187
Forced change, 42, 53
Forces of change, 140–145, 164
Foster, George, M.
    barriers and stimulants, 70–72
    change agents characteristics,
        70–72, 101, 111, 126
    communication, 158–159
    directed change, 70–73
    dynamic aspects of change, 70, 72
    elements of success, 71
    fit, 70
    focal group characteristics, 70–71
    forces of change, 140–146
    interactional settings, 72
    issues and aspects of change, 12
    model, 70, 71, 77
    motivation, 70, 154, 156
    participants, directed change, 71
    problems, 71
    recipe approach, 71

    stimulants, 70, 72
    technical experts, 89
Foundations for change, 6–7
Frazer, James, 7
Freilich, M., 16, 35
Fuchs, Estelle. *See* Havighurst, Robert
Functionalism. *See* Theory
Fund for the Development of West
    Irian, 165
Future culture and change, 213–214

Gamst, F. C., 16, 36
Garbarino, Merwyn S., 13
Gearing, Fred, 125
General change plans and strategies,
    112–125
    approaches, 118
    change agency, 118
    community development, 118–119
    directive/directive, 119
    distinguishing approaches, 118
    distinguishing characteristics, 119
    engineering strategy, 118
    facilitative assistance, 118
    interactions, 118
    paternalistic strategy, 118–119
    power strategies, 118
    resources, 118
General model of directed culture
    change, 67–70
Generating ideas for change, 189–190
Genocide. *See* Eradication
Glazer, Mark, 6, 13
Global change, 199–213
    change, 200, 213
    culture, 199, 213
    interdependence, 199
    development, 205–206
    economic trends, 203–205
    environmental trends, 202–203
    ethnocentrism, 200
    evolution, 199
    evolutionary trends, 200–201
    integration, 200
    one world culture, 206–208
    political trends, 206
    problems, 201
    role of anthropology, 208–213
    tendencies, 208
    threats, 200

Global change (continued)
    trends, 199–206
Global culture, 199
Global forces, 164–166
Global trends, 200–206
The Golden Bough, 7
Goldstone, J. A., 187
Graebner, Fritz, 8

Hackenberg, 208
Harris, Marvin, 6, 7, 13
Hatch, Elvin, 211–212
Haviland, William A., 2
Henry, Jules, 95, 96, 111, 132
Hersey, Paul, 118
Herskovits, Melville, 12
Historical particularists. *See* Theory
Hogbin, Ian, 6, 11, 13, 60, 167
Holism, 5, 180–182, 200, 213
Holmberg, Alan R., 125
Homans, George, 10
Honigmann, J. J., 6
Hsu, Francis, 96, 111, 132
Human culture, 23
Human rights, 211

Ideas and change, 50, 61, 69, 75,
    77–80
Ideal culture, 30–32, 37–38, 91
Implementation strategies, 125–130
    accommodation style, 130
    adapting the change, 130
    agent action, 126
    assertive, 129
    assertive persuasion, 126–127
    avoidance style, 130
    challenges, 127
    change agents, 126–128
    change agents and focal groups,
        126–127
    communication, 127–130
    competitive, 129
    compromise management styles, 130
    considerations, 130
    contacts, 126, 129
    cooperative, 129
    developing connections, 127
    establishing climate, 127
    functional/pragmatic, 126
    interactional, 126

local participation, 129
logic/reason, 127
personal agent styles, 128
reward and punishment strategies,
    127
use of intermediaries, 126
Initiating change, 68
Innovation
    in acculturation, 51, 53–55
    borrowing, 60
    choice variation, 50
    contact situations, 51
    as culture change, 41, 49–53
    diffusion and, 55–56
    discovery, 41, 60
    first step to change, 50–51
        invention, 41, 50, 60
    model, 52
    nondirected, 41
    nondirected change, 55
    primary/secondary, 41
    terminology, 39
    timing, 71
Innovation and change, 49–54
Innovator
    as change agent, 89
    change and, 50–53, 58, 68
    directed change and, 68
    generate ideas, 51, 61–62, 74, 76
    not at change agents, 51
    voluntary change and, 66
Integration, 54
Interaction, 46–48
    action/reaction, 86, 153
    adaptation, 47–48
    agent motivation, 86
    associational, 88, 153
    characteristics, 85–86
    communication, 85, 157–159
    conflict, 153
    contact, 88
    context, 69, 77, 171
    demonstration, 58
    designed campaign, 58
    diffusion, 55–56
    directed change, 78–80, 85–86
    environment, 57, 82
    evolution, 38, 44
    factors, 80

Interaction (continued)
  focal group, 86
  forces, 151–162
  implementation, 86
  innovation, 53–55
  issues, 10
  motivations, 154
  outcome, 80
  outside influences, 86
  participants, 69
  power of its own, 86
  settings, 80–86, 157–159
  strategies, 80, 86
  timing and fit, 157
  type/quality, 88
  voluntary, 63, 65, 88
Interactional forces, 152–162
  barriers/stimulants, 152
  coercion, 152
  communication, 158–160
  conflict, 152
  context, 152
  culture development, 152
  directed change, 85–86
  interactions, 152
  motivations, 154–157
  multicultural settings, 152–153
  strategy, 160–162
  timing and fit, 157–158
Interactional model, 77–86
  actions and reactions, 80, 86
  change agents characteristics, 78–84
  characteristics of interaction, 80
  communication, 77, 85–86
  component characteristics, 77,
    80–81
  contact and conflict, 77–80
  context, 78
  an external process, 78–79
  flexibility, 86
  focal group, 77–78, 83–84
  ideas for change, 77–78
  innovators, 76
  interaction, 78–79, 85
  model, 78
  motivation, 85
  outcomes, 78, 80
  outside influences, 86
  participant characteristics, 77–84

  plan, 83–85
  plan characteristics, 84–85
  resources, technology, and expertise,
    84
  settings, 77, 79, 82, 85–86
  strategies, 79
  timing, fit, and strategy, 84–85
  utilization of local culture, 86
Internal change, 60, 79, 88–92
Internal change agent, 68, 90–92
International Red Cross, 2
Intervention, 42, 66
Invention, 50, 51
Isaac, Barry L., 12, 87

Keesing, Felix M., 10
Kennedy, J. G., 176
Kinds of change, 68
Klemm, Gustav, 7
Kluckhohn, Clyde, 17
Kroeber, Alfred, 8, 17, 51

Lang, Gottfried O., 118, 125, 137
Lang, Martha B. See Lang, Gottfried
Lange, Charles H., 90
Language, 20, 24
Leach, Edmond, 11
Leacock, Eleanor, 9
Leighton, Alexander
  change agents, 72–73
  communication, 74
  contact, 72–73
  contexts, 73
  directed change model, 73
  education, 74
  emotion, 73, 77–78
  essential tools, 74
  fit, 74
  focal groups, 73
  interaction, 72–73
  legacy, 73
  participant characteristics, 74
  postulates and principles, 72
  problems of change, 74
  result, 74
  role, 74
  sentiment and behavior, 73, 156
  settings, 72–73
  social elements, 74

Leighton, Alexander (continued)
  stress, 72–74
Levels of culture groupings, 22–23
Linton, Ralph, 12, 60
Lowie, Robert, 6–7

Macro-culture, 26
Magnarella, Paul J., 60
Mair, Lucy, 10, 197
Malinowski, Bronislaw, 8, 10, 11
McCurdy, David, 16, 27, 36
McElroy, A., 215
McNetting, Robert. See Gearing, Fred
Mead, Margaret, 10-12
Micro-culture, 26
Mini-models of change, 41
Mintz, Sidney, 9
Model for Culture change, 56–58
Modernization, 3, 4, 39, 40, 54, 205
Montaigne, Michel de, 6
Morgan, Lewis Henry, 7
Motivation
  Arensberg, Conrad and Niehoff,
    Arthur, 154
  change agents, 154
  comfort, 65
  competition, 65, 77, 155
  directed culture change, 156
  economics, 65
  efficiency, 65
  felt need, 63, 65, 72, 77, 154
  focal group, 154, 133–134
  Foster, George M., 154
  industrial world, 65
  Leighton, Alexander, 156
  novelty, 65, 77
  opportunity, 63
  practical benefit, 77
  presence of motivation, 155
  prestige, 65
  punishment/reward, 77
  security, 65
  status, 65
Muller, Ronald E. See Barnet, Richard
Multiculturalism, 28–29, 90
Multicultural settings, 63, 88, 92–94,
  139

Nation, 24

Nation-state, 4, 24–26, 63, 95–97
Native Land Claims Settlement Act,
  177
Naylor, 13, 116, 151, 158, 177, 198,
  209
Niehoff, Arthur A.
  advisers, 74
  barriers or stimulants, 74
  change agents, 74–75, 101, 126
  change process, 75
  coercion, 70
  communication, 75, 159
  directed change, 74–77
  directed change model, 74–77
  dynamics of change, 12
  felt need, 77
  forces of action and reaction, 70, 74,
    77
  idea for change, 74
  ideas and plans, 70
  influences on directed change, 76
  integration, 74
  legacy, 75
  motivation, 154
  motivations, 77
  personality, 77
  recipe approach, 75
  recipient groups, 74–75
  sociocultural components, 74
  success and failure, 75
  technical competence, 77
  use of local language, 77
Nietschmann, Bernard, 185
Noble, David, 203
Nondirected change, 39, 49, 55, 67
Nondirective approach, 118
Nonvoluntary change, 39, 53
Norbeck, Edward, 16, 36

Operasi Koteka, 116–117
Oppositions, 11
Organizational culture, 67
Organizational sytems as forces
  146–147

Participants, directed change, 72,
  77–78
Partridge, William, 209, 215

Paternalistic Approach, 119–121
Pelto, Pertti. *See* Russell, Bernard, H.
Perry, William J., 8
Peattie, L. R. *See* Gearing, Fred
Philosophy, 18
Plan, directed change, 84–85, 113–114
Planned change. *See* Directed change
Planning for culture change, 113–118
Podolefsky, A, 215
Political trends, 206
Practices of focal groups, 110
Practicing anthropology. *See* Applied
    anthropology
Predictability, 38
Primitive Culture, 7
Principles of change, 196
Processes of culture change, 61–86,
    138–139
Progress, 3, 4, 39, 40
Prospects for change, 199–214
Psychological forces of change,
    149–151, 147–148
Psychological systems of culture,
    147–151

Radcliffe-Brown, A. R., 8, 10
Rathje,William L., 13
Ratzel, Fredrich, 8
Rayner, Steve, 213
Reactive behavior, 73
Real culture, 16, 31–33, 37–38, 91
Recipient group. *See* Focal group
Redfield, Robert, 11, 12, 53
Relativism, 5, 211
Relocation, 187–188
Replacement, 186–187
Response strategies, 135–136
Ritenbaugh, Cheryl, 13
Rivers, W. H. R., 8
Rogers, Everett, 55, 60
Role characteristics of agents, 101–105
Role characteristics of focal groups,
    109–110
Role of anthropology, 208–209
Roseberry, William, 9
Rosman, Abraham, 16, 36
Roth, Warren. *See* Lang, Gottfried O.
Rousseau, Jean Jacques, 6, 7

Rubel, Paula G., 36
Rylko-Bauer, B., 215

Sahlins, Marshall D., 9, 60
Schapera, I., 10
Schmidt, Wilhelm, 8
Selection of strategy, 193–194
Service, Elman R., 9, 60
Shankman, Paul, 164
Simon, Julian, 203
Singh, Rudra Datt, 124
Smith, A., 5
Smith, G. Elliot, 8
Social structure, 20
Socialization, 18
Societies, types, 16
    agricultural, 4
    industrial, 4, 46, 199
    nation-states, 4
    prestate, 4, 40
    small-scale, 4, 63, 79
Society for Applied Anthropology, 209
Sociocultural environment, 64
Sources of change, 64
Specific cultures, 23–25
Specific forces of change, 142–152
    organizational systems, 146–147
    psychological aspects, 147–151
    structural systems, 147
    values and traditions, 144–145
Spencer, Herbert, 7
Spicer, Edward H., 121
Spindler, Louise, 38, 41, 42, 60
Spradley, J. P., 16, 27, 36
State, 24, 25
Steward, Julian, 9
Stimulants for change, 70
Strategy as change force, 160–161
Strategy characteristics, 84–85
Structural systems as forces, 147
Subculture, 25, 26
Subsistence, 45
Surface change, 42
Survival, 65
Syncretism, 42

Target group. *See* Focal group
Technological change, 40

Theory, 7–10, 42, 55
Timing, 70, 72, 157–158
Tylor, E. B., 7

United Nations, 2, 24, 67, 165, 205,
   211
United Nations Educational, Scientific
   and Cultural Organization, 3, 165
United States Agency for International
   Development, 165
United States Committee on Global
   Change, 200
United States Peace Corps, 166
Unplanned consequences of planned
   culture change, 58, 74, 175–179
Urbanization, 41, 54

Van Willigen, John B., 13, 215
Variables of directed change, 75
Voluntary change
   acceptance, 42
   association, 66
   borrowing, 41, 56, 66
   change spread, 66
   communication, 91
   contact, 66
   definition, 61–63
   dynamics, 66
   felt need, 58, 66
   idea, 66
   informal, 66
   innovators, 66
   interaction, 65–67, 88–89
   necessary conditions, 63, 66
   nondirected, 61, 66
   process, 58, 138
Voluntary interaction, 65–67
Walker, D., 187
Wallace, Alfred Russel, 7
Western culture, 3, 6, 7, 10, 39, 53, 67
White, Leslie, 9
Wilson, Godfrey, and Wilson, Monica,
   11
Wissler, Clark, 8
Wolf, Eric, 9
Wolfe, Alvin, 164, 204
Woods, Clyde M., 38, 60
World Bank, 2, 3, 67, 165, 204
World Culture, 27–28, 206–207

World Health Organization, 3, 67, 165,
   205
Worsley, Peter, 203, 215

Zaltman, Gerald and Dugan, Robert,
   118, 126

About the Author

LARRY L. NAYLOR is Associate Professor and Director of the Cultural Sensitivity Training and Research Center, Institute of Anthropology, at the University of North Texas. He is coauthor of *Eskimos, Reindeer, and Land* (1981) and has extensive fieldwork and consulting experience in New Guinea amd Alaska.

ISBN 0-89789-464-2

90000>

EAN

9 780897 894647

HARDCOVER BAR CODE

1708029